THE AFRICAN CHARTER ON THE RIGHTS AND WELFARE OF THE CHILD

VIRGINIA PAOLA LALLI

Traslated by Sara Pasetto

authorHOUSE®

AuthorHouse™
1663 Liberty Drive
Bloomington, IN 47403
www.authorhouse.com
Phone: 1 (800) 839-8640

Published by AuthorHouse 11/15/2018

ISBN: 978-1-5462-6838-3 (sc)
ISBN: 978-1-5462-6839-0 (e)

Library of Congress Control Number: 2018913538

Print information available on the last page.

Any people depicted in stock imagery provided by Getty Images are models, and such images are being used for illustrative purposes only.
Certain stock imagery © Getty Images.

This book is printed on acid-free paper.

Because of the dynamic nature of the Internet, any web addresses or links contained in this book may have changed since publication and may no longer be valid. The views expressed in this work are solely those of the author and do not necessarily reflect the views of the publisher, and the publisher hereby disclaims any responsibility for them.

From a tale recorded in the early 20th century in Benaland, Tanganyika (currently in the United Republic of Tanzania) by Rev. Julius Oelke, of the Berlin Mission Church

'That night, the headman declared a great feast to reward the children for what they had done. "You are the only ones who hear truly and whose eyes are clear," he said. "You are the eyes and the ears of our tribe."'

Nelson Mandela, *Nelson Mandela's Favorite African Folktales*

In publishing my Ph.D. thesis on the International Legal Order and Protection of Human Rights, I wish to express my deepest gratitude to the Department of Comparative Public Law of "La Sapienza" University of Rome for the professionalism and competence experiences and peaceful discussions held.

CONTENTS

ACRONYMS

ACERWC	African Committee of Experts on the Rights and Welfare of the Child
ACRWC	African Charter on the Rights and Welfare of the Child
ACHPR	African Charter on Human and Peoples' Rights
AU	African Union
CESR	Commission on Economic, Social and Cultural Rights
FGM	Female Genital Mutilation
HTP	Harmful Traditional Practice(s)
IAC	Inter-African Committee on Traditional Practices
ICC	International Criminal Court
IDP	internationally displaced person(s)
GIZ	*Deutsche Gesellschaft für International Zusammenarbeit*
MOU	Memorandum of Understanding
NAPTIP	National Agency for Prohibition of Traffic in Persons and Other Related Matters
SCSL	Special Court for Sierra Leone
TFV	Trust Fund for Victims
UN	United Nations
UNGA	United Nations General Assembly
UNICRI	United Nations Interregional Crime and Justice Research Institute

PREFACE

The protection of the fundamental rights and freedoms that pertain to human beings from birth to death extends to all persons, regardless of nationality or religion.

On the basis of values such as dignity, equity, equality, respect and autonomy, human rights activists and advocates strive to promote fundamental rights, especially of persons who suffer oppression and abuse.

In the context of Africa, children and minors are a category of persons who suffer oppression or abuse. In addition to other sources of malaise, they are oppressed as a result of adverse sociocultural practices and wars, against which they must instead be protected.

Thus, several efforts have been made to date to save children and minors from the dangers that they must constantly face due to adverse sociocultural practices, endless wars and the consequences thereof. One of these efforts is the ratification of the African Charter on the Rights and Welfare of the Child (ACRWC), which is making significant contributions to the promotion and protection of the fundamental rights of children in Africa, with a view to their overall development.

This work seeks to contribute to the promotion of the rights of children in Africa. It traces the history of the ACRWC, starting from the United Nations Convention on the Rights of the Child (CRC), while also taking into consideration other African sources of law that have been invoked from time to time to promote the rights and welfare of children. This work does not merely describe the ACRWC, but also explores the innovations it brings to the debate on children's rights. From the ACRWC, a specific body of law may be drawn to protect and promote the rights and welfare of African children. The book discusses how the ACRWC promotes and protects the best interest of the child, emphasizing that African children remain members of a wider family: the broader African family. As such, the rights of the child are established with the main aim of helping African children to become integrated citizens and responsible members of the broader African family.

Among the innovations introduced by the ACRWC into the debate on the promotion of children and of children's rights, the author examines the responsibilities of the parents and the duties of the child in the context of the ACRWC's application, exploring also the issues raised by the ACRWC in its application *vis-à-vis* local customs.

Often, African children do not enjoy protection from certain social and cultural practices, which results in their suffering inhuman treatment. This book is particularly interesting because the author identifies the gaps in the ACRWC's application with reference to specific situations of the African context. These gaps are illustrated within the ACRWC and beyond, thus making this work an important point of reference for those who work for the promotion of the rights and welfare of children in Africa. The book examines certain rights of children that should receive particular protection in the African setting and highlights the efforts made to date to implement them, on part of the Committee and the Member States, to promote and protect the rights of children and minors.

The ratification of the ACRWC does not remove the other sources of law previously invoked to protect and promote the rights and welfare of children and minors.

Because of its originality, the incisiveness of its critical analysis and its depth, this book is an important source of information on the approach that might be adopted by human rights activists, advocates or judges in addressing disputes on the protection and promotion of the rights of children, in various situations in Africa.

Father Kambere Kasai Florent *crm*

INTRODUCTION

The African Charter on the Rights and Welfare of the Child (ACRWC) is a treaty concluded by African States. Its objective is to protect the rights of African minors while taking into consideration the specificities of the African continent.

The Preamble to the ACRWC reiterates loyalty to the principles of the rights and welfare of minors enshrined in United Nations (UN) declarations and the Convention on the Rights of the Child (CRC), as well as in other legal instruments of the UN and the African Union (AU). Indeed, the ACRWC grants minors rights that are essentially analogous to those enshrined in the CRC. However, it lays down children's rights in light of the African context and of the specific situations that, in Africa, particularly require protection, addressing general topics such as harmful traditional practices (HTP), among which female genital mutilation (FGM) and forced marriage, as well as the protection of certain categories of children, such as child soldiers, refugee children, displaced children or children who are exploited for vagrancy or child trafficking.

The specific nature of the protection afforded by the ACRWC also emerges, in a more general sense, in relation to the role of the cultural heritage, history and values of African civilization, which should inspire and distinguish the protection of the rights and welfare of children. African cultural and traditional heritage is a source of inspiration for the African Committee of Experts on the Rights and Welfare of the Child (ACERWC), as established in Article 46 ACRWC.

Therefore, the first part of this work will focus on illustrating the specificities of the African system, compared to the universal system, for the protection of rights, and on examining the particular situations that require regulation adapted to the African context.

The cultural peculiarities and local customs entrenched in the continent may, at times, prevent the effective protection of the rights of African minors. Indeed, the ACRWC requires States Parties to take all appropriate measures to eliminate harmful social and cultural practices that are incompatible with the ACRWC, such as FGM and forced marriage. The ACERWC, which is tasked with interpreting and monitoring the implementation of the ACRWC, has dealt with a number of particular cases that shed light on the specific needs for protection that exist on the African continent. The second part of the work will, therefore, analyse the ACRWC's effectiveness and the issues currently surrounding it, the progress made, its concrete application, and the gaps that remain despite the ACRWC's entry into force.

Finally, the work of the ACERWC will be considered, to ascertain how, in both general and specific circumstances, the ACRWC's norms succeed in guaranteeing the protection of the rights of African children, and how they modulate such protection on the basis of the particular context of their application.

CHAPTER

THE ORIGINS AND EVOLUTION OF THE RIGHTS OF THE CHILD: FROM THE CONVENTION ON THE RIGHTS OF THE CHILD TO THE AFRICAN CHARTER

I.1 The origins and evolution of the rights of the child

In the early 1900s, children began to receive a great deal of attention, because a new cultural approach took shape to seek to define their rights.

In this respect, one may recall "Century of the child", the book published in 1906 by the pedagogue Ellen Key, in which she proposed dedicating the new century to the welfare of children[1]. The book was enormously successful and was highly influential in Europe. It proposed a new conception of the child, positing that it was necessary to build an environment tailor-made to the child and that the child should become the focus of social policies.

In 1908, the English Liberal Party obtained the approval of the Children Act, better known as the "Children's Charter". The law established the first national court for minors, introduced a registry of parents willing to foster children, prohibited the employment of children in dangerous work and raised the minimum age for the death penalty to 16 years of age. In time, local authorities would also establish social services and orphanages.

At the international level, a number of milestones were reached in the development of legislation on children's rights. After the devastating consequences of World War I, in 1924, the League of Nations drafted the Declaration on the Rights of the Child[2]. However, this document considered the child as a passive recipient of rights and did not impose duties upon the States Parties, rather addressing humanity in general.

After World War II, in 1946, the Economic and Social Council of the United Nations (ECOSOC) began discussing the need for a new declaration on the rights of children. In addition, within the

---

[1] Becchi, "Il nostro secolo", in J. Becchi (ed.) *Storia dell'infanzia 2. Dal Settecento a oggi*, Bari, Laterza, 1996, p. 555.

[2] Scarpati. *I diritti dei bambini*. Modena, Infinito, 2012, p. 35.

victorious countries, a working group had already formed to commence drafting the Universal Declaration of Human Rights (UDHR).

On 11 December 1946, with Resolution No. 57, the UN General Assembly (UNGA) established the United Nations Children Fund (UNICEF). On 10 December 1948, the UNGA approved the Universal Declaration of Human Rights (UDHR), which, in turn, established a number of important principles on the protection of children, whether born within or out of wedlock[3].

In March 1949, a document in favour of the approval of a declaration on children's rights, signed by the representatives of 21 states, was submitted to then-Secretary General of the United Nations Trygve Lie. A first draft circulated among the various UN commissions for approximately a decade, as there was little will to promote its adoption. UNICEF's pressures were not taken into consideration[4].

In 1957, finally, the Commission for Human Rights discussed and prepared a document on children's rights, which was submitted to the ECOSOC in 1959. The document was then discussed during the works of the UNGA's Third Committee on Social, Humanitarian and Cultural Issues, and was approved unanimously (with two abstentions) during the session of 19 October 1959. The next month, 20 November 1959, the Declaration on the Rights of the Child was submitted to the General Assembly, which adopted it unanimously[5].

The 1959 Declaration contains a Preamble and ten Principles. Although it is more systematic and thorough than its 1924 counterpart, it was also not binding upon States, constituting rather a mere declaration of principles which committed States exclusively in a moral sense.

Nevertheless, the ten principles enshrined in the 1959 Declaration were fundamental, because they covered all areas of a child's family and social life. It also contained new principles and considerations – such as those on handicapped children – that were not included in the UDHR[6] and introduced the notion that the child could hold rights.

However, the 1959 Declaration did not establish the maximum age after which individuals were no longer to be considered children, thus in fact leaving this important issue to national laws.

One of the most important aspects of the Declaration is that it introduced the concept of the best interest of the child. It states that children are to "enjoy special protection, and shall be given opportunities and facilities, by law and by other means, to enable [them] to develop physically, mentally, morally, spiritually and socially in a healthy and normal manner and in conditions of

---

[3] Article 25(2) states that "[m]otherhood and childhood are entitled to special care and assistance. All children, whether born in or out of wedlock, shall enjoy the same social protection."

[4] *I diritti dei bambini, op. cit.*, p. 38.

[5] *Ibidem*, p. 39.

[6] Principle 5 of the 1959 Declaration on the Rights of the Child states that "[t]he child who is physically, mentally or socially handicapped shall be given the special treatment, education and care required by his particular condition."

freedom and dignity. In the enactment of laws for this purpose, the best interest of the child shall be the paramount consideration."[7]

A draft Convention on the Rights of the Child was proposed on 7 February 1978 by the Representative of the Polish Government, and was discussed during the 34th Session of the United Nations Commission on Human Rights[8]. This proposal was made during a time when the international debate on children and their rights was becoming more urgent. A couple of years earlier, specifically on 21 December 1976, with Resolution 269 (XXXI), the UNGA declared 1979 as the International Year of the Child, to appropriately commemorate the 20th anniversary of the 1959 Declaration.

The drafting of the Convention was no easy task, and was completed only several years later. For ten years, many experts from around the world – some independent, others appointed by the governments of UN Member States – met in a special Working Group established within the UN Human Rights Commission. Throughout the world, independent technical bodies were established upon the initiative of civil society to study the drafts and amendments proposed over the years, suggesting amendments themselves and enhancing the dialogue between experts and scholars at all levels.

However, the true innovation consisted in the fact that the directly interested parties were consulted – children, who were gathered in (local and national) assemblies for the specific purpose of explaining to them, in appropriate terms, the initiative developing in the United Nations, and to ensure their effective participation in the elaboration of the Convention. In this process, Unicef and a number of the most important international NGOs played a core part in the initiatives unfurling all over the world. Children's participation was not merely formal, but important and necessary, because the Convention was bringing about the recognition of new rights-bearing subjects. Therefore, it was necessary to change the attitude, previously prevailing in all fields, of providing important solutions for children without even attempting to hear the opinions of the directly interested parties[9].

On 20 November 1989, precisely thirty years after the Declaration on the Rights of the Child was adopted, in New York, with a unanimous vote of the UNGA, Resolution 44/25 containing the text of the Convention on the Rights of the Child (CRC) was adopted.

The CRC rapidly entered into force: as soon as August 1990, the 20 instruments of ratification required had been deposited with the Secretary General of the United Nations. The CFRC thus entered into force on 2 September 1990, 30 days after the twentieth instrument of ratification was deposited. To date, the CRC has been ratified by 195 countries[10]; it therefore remains the UN convention with the highest number of ratifications.

---

[7] Principle 2 of the 1959 Declaration on the Rights of the Child.
[8] The draft was proposed as an annex to a Resolution to be voted upon by the ECOSOC, and that recommended that the United Nations adopt a Convention on children's rights based on the principles of the 1959 Declaration.
[9] Scarpati. *I diritti dei bambini. Op. cit.* p. 61.
[10] Except for the United States of America, as the CRC prohibits imposition of capital punishment upon persons below eighteen years of age (Article 37(a)).

Another important innovation thus brought about by international law with regard to children is the fact that children have acquired legal title to rights, distinct from those enjoyed by adults. These guarantees are expressed in the CRC's final version, in which 41 articles (out of the total number of 54) recognize specific rights and liberties to children.

However, few States have decided to adapt their children and family laws to the CRC, because these areas of law receive scant attention at national level given the important financial commitments that they entail. An important tool to fill these gaps is provided in Article 3 CRC, which establishes that the best interest of the child are to be a primary consideration in all actions concerning children, for the ultimate purpose of affording protection to each and every one of them. In particular, the provision states that "[i]n all actions concerning children, whether undertaken by public or private social welfare institutions, courts of law, administrative authorities or legislative bodies, the best interests of the child shall be a primary consideration."

"The strength of this article lies precisely in the fact that the notion of the best interest of the child is not based on an essentially juridical reasoning. Rather, it is based on a concept of fact, tied to an evaluation of the specific well-being of the child, even if not necessarily with reference to the current situation; to the contrary, said evaluation is often carried out in consideration of the future. […] Precisely because of the great adaptability of this provision, it is absolutely impossible to indicate, once and for all and for all addressees, what constitutes these interests, because there are far too many parameters that the interpreters are to consider each time"[11].

However, this principle also affords a certain margin of discretion to those who are called to apply it. Where such figures are, for example, judges called upon to decide disputes, they are required to provide attentive, thorough and detailed reasons of fact to support their decision; in addition, such decision should in any case be subject to checks and, where possible, to appeal.

It is also worthy to note that the CRC has established a Committee on the Rights of the Child (hereafter, CRC Committee), for the purpose of examining the States' implementation of and progress towards executing their obligations under the CRC. This Committee has noted that the concept of the best interest of the child should not be interpreted as an abstract principle, devoid of any link to the principles enshrined in other articles of the CRC. Rather, it should be considered together with those articles that make children bearers of rights, recognizing to them those political and civil freedoms that, for all purposes, make them persons[12].

---

[11] Scarpati, *I diritti dei bambini*, *op. cit.*, p. 109 (author's translation).

[12] Committee on the Rights of the Child, "Concluding Observations of the Committee on the Rights of the Child, United Kingdom of Great Britain and Northern Ireland", 15 February 1995. UN CRC/C/15/Add 34, http://www1.umn.edu/humanrts/crc/UK8.htm. Consulted on 22 March 2016. In particular, the document states that "[w]ith regard to the implementation of article 4 of the Convention, the Committee would like to suggest that the general principles of the Convention, particularly the provisions of its article 3, relating to the best interests of the child, should guide the determination of policy-making at both the central and local levels of government…" (para. 24).

In this connection, UNICEF recommended that each State Party to the CRC incorporate within their legal systems not only the new freedoms established by the CRC, but the very concept of best interest of the child: "[p]rinciples relating the best interest of the child and prohibition of discrimination on relation to children should be incorporated into law, and it should be possible to invoke them before the Courts"[13].

Making provision for the concept of the best interest of the child within national legal orders, and applying it to actual cases, allows judges to effectively intervene and bring about the interests of every child[14].

The importance of this principle has also been underscored by regional international courts[15] and national judges themselves[16].

However, it is necessary to note a shortcoming in the CRC: it does not provide protection from those violations of human rights that may be committed in specific areas of the African continent, with regard to certain categories of African children. Hence, the need to intervene with an ad hoc juridical instrument: the ACRWC.

I.2   From the CRC to the ACRWC

In Africa, the season of human rights developed somewhat later than in Europe and America. The history (even recent) of many African states is marked by several conflicts: ethnic rivalries; cruel dictatorships; religious clashes (such as in Nigeria, where the Christian population has been suffering violent attacks by Islamic militia since 2009); secessionist struggles (consider the region of Katanga in Democratic Republic of the Congo, Casamance in Senegal, and South Sudan, which recently gained independence); inter-state border conflicts (such as those between Eritrea and Ethiopia, Benin and Nigeria, Egypt and Sudan, Mozambique and Malawi); and various types of regional conflicts. All this certainly contributed to the continent's "drift" away from seeking awareness of human rights, which at the same time was spreading in most of the rest of the world or, at any rate, most of the Western world.

In 1963, the Organisation of African Unity (or OAU; today, African Union) was established to unite the voices of the common needs of the African peoples and states. The first commitment

---

[13] "General measures of implementation of the Convention on the Rights of the Child" (articles 4, 42 and 44, para. 6). 27 November 2003. http://unicef.bg/en/article/General-Comments-of-the-UN-Committee-on-the-Rights-of-the-Child/825. Consulted on 6 June 2016.

[14] Scarpati, *I diritti dei bambini, op. cit.*, p. 114.

[15] See, for example, European Court of Human Rights, *Zaunegger v. Germany*, App. No. 22028/2004, 3 December 2009. http://hudoc.echr.coe.int/eng-press#{"display":["1"],"dmdocnumber":["859050"],"itemid":["003-2953286-3250185"]}. Consulted on 31 March 2016.

[16] As for the case law of the Italian Constitutional Court, see especially Judgments No. 44 of 1990 (http://www.giurcost.org/decisioni/1990/0044s-90.html); 148 of 1992 (http://www.giurcost. org/decisioni/1992/0148s-92.html; 303 of 1996 (http://www.giurcost.org/decisioni/1996/0303s-96.htm); and 349 of 1998 (http://juriswiki.it/provvedimenti/sentenza-corte-costituzionale-349-1998-it). All websites were consulted on 29 March 2016.

of its Member States' representatives was surely not that of creating a continent-wide system of human rights. The new states emerging from the thirty-year process of decolonizing the continent focused first on consolidating their fragile national sovereignty and applying the principle of self-determination to all African territories, also within the context of the OAU. As a consequence, the OAU's early overall and lawmaking activities concerned primarily decolonization policies, the resolution of the many conflicts between its Member States, economic cooperation between such States and between them and third countries, and guidelines for the continent's economic development. In addition, the history of many of the states created following decolonization was far from peaceful, but rather scarred by bloody conflicts between internal factions and ancient ethnic conflicts, never resolved and exacerbated by the creation of national borders that did not reflect the needs of the local populations (as in the Berlin Conference of 1884-1885).

Before adopting the ACRWC, during the 16th Ordinary Session of the Assembly of Heads of State and Government of the OAU (Monrovia, 17–20 July 1979), the Member States drafted the Declaration on the Rights and Welfare of the African Child, which was based on the model of the Declaration of the Rights of the Child that had been unanimously adopted by the UNGA in 1959[17]. Indeed, when the latter instrument had been adopted, most African states were still under colonial rule. The principles set out in the UN Declaration were not drafted for the benefit of children living in colonial territories, regardless of its universalistic tone.

Furthermore, the 1979 Declaration on the Rights and Welfare of the African Child stated that "[e]fforts should be made to preserve and develop African arts, languages and culture and to stimulate the interest and appreciation of African children in the cultural heritage of their own countries and of Africa as a whole"[18]. The protection of African culture and traditions enhances the protection of the rights of African children, provided that they do not contrast with the rights enshrined in the ACRWC.

In this context, it is to be emphasized that the socio-economic causes of violations of human rights, such as poverty and war, bear a disproportionate impact on African children compared to the children of other continents. In addition, harmful cultural practices clearly conflict with the rights of African children.

The 1979 Declaration had little influence on the legal systems of the region's states: a few months prior to its adoption, the ECOSOC had commenced works to draft the CRC. The provisions of the latter made those of the African 1979 Declaration, which were in any case generic and non-binding, obsolete. When the CRC was adopted by the UNGA in 1989, the African states began to work on a regional Charter on children to update and adapt the 1979 Declaration.

---

[17] Declaration of the Rights and Welfare of the African Child. www.chr.up.ac.za/chr_old/hr_docs/african/docs/.../ahsg36.doc. Consulted on 6 June 2016.
[18] Article 10.

The ACRWC was adopted in Addis Ababa on 11 July 1990, and entered into force on 29 November 1999. It has been ratified by 47 African states[19], while 7 have yet to adhere: the Central African Republic, the Democratic Republic of Congo, São Tome, Sarawi, Somalia, South Sudan and Tunisia. The Democratic Republic of Congo, São Tome and Tunisia have signed the Charter, but have not ratified it. Somalia is the most recent state to ratify the Charter (in 2015).

The ACRWC is the second international charter, after the CRC, and the first regional juridical instrument, to recognize the child as bearer of positive rights, which concern both the private-familial and the public-administrative spheres.

Overall, the ACRWC guarantees the same rights and protections enshrined in the CRC, but paying attention to the African context and the specific issues concerning Africa[20]. The ACRWC was drafted by a working group including African experts on the rights and welfare of children precisely to address certainly typically African problems. Indeed, the CRC does not account for some peculiarities of the African socio-economic context. Therefore, the African states have sought to strengthen children's rights by means of an instrument that would take "into consideration the virtues of their cultural heritage, historical background and the values of African civilization"[21]. Thus, the ACRWC is notable as an attempt to address, on the legal level, the many problems that suppress youth on the continent.

In particular, in addition to the rights that are also protected by the CRC, the ACRWC includes some rights whose protection is a sign of progress, in the African context. As the CRC is unable to provide adequate protection in specific situations faced by African children, the African community has sought to close this gap.

The ACRWC surely draws inspiration from the CRC. The two instruments share a number of fundamental, universally recognized principles, such as the principle of nondiscrimination (Article 2 CRC, Article 3 ACRWC), respect for the best interest of the child (Article 3 CRC, Article 4 ACRWC), children's right to participate in community life (Article 15 CRC, Article 8 ACRWC), survival and development (Article 6 CRC, Article 6 ACRWC), accommodating the development of children's mental faculties (Article 5 CRC, Article 9 ACRWC). These principles inspire the set of political and civil rights, economic, social and cultural rights, and some specific rights to protection, enjoyed by children. Some special rights to protection include the right to life (Article 6 CRC, Article 5 ACRWC), the prohibition on sentencing children to death (Article 37 CRC, Article 4 ACRWC), the right to a name and to registration from birth (Article 7 CRC, Article 6 ACRWC), the right to a nationality (Article 7 CRC, Article 6 ACRWC), the right to

---

[19] The states that have ratified the ACRWC are: Algeria, Angola, Benin, Botswana, Burkina Faso, Burundi, Cameroon, Cabo Verde, Chad, Côte d'Ivoire, Djibouti, Congo, Comoros, Egypt, Equatorial Guinea, Eritrea, Ethiopia, Gabon, Gambia, Ghana, Guinea Bissau, Guinea, Kenya, Libya, Lesotho, Liberia, Madagascar, Mali, Malawi, Mozambique, Mauritania, Mauritius, Namibia, Nigeria, Niger, Rwanda, South Africa, Senegal, Seychelles, Sierra Leone, Sudan, the United Republic of Tanzania, Togo, Uganda, Zambia and Zimbabwe.
[20] Chirwa, "The merits and demerits of the African Charter on the Rights and Welfare of the Child" *The International Journal of Children's Rights*, 2002, p. 157.
[21] Preamble to the ACRWC.

freedom of expression (Article 13 CRC, Article 7 ACRWC), of association (Article 15 CRC, Article 8 ACRWC), thought, conscience and religion (Article 14 CRC, Article 9 ACRWC) and the right to the protection of one's privacy (Article 16 CRC, Article 10 ACRWC). Likewise, protection is afforded to the right to an education (Articles 28–29 CRC, Article 11 ACRWC), to leisure, recreation and cultural activities (Article 31 CRC, Article 12 ACRWC), the protection of handicapped children (Article 23 CRC, Article 13 ACRWC) and to the right to health and health services (Article 24 CRC, Article 14 ACRWC).

As for the more specific rights established by the ACRWC, we may recall those provided for the protection of refugee children. Indeed, compared to Article 22 CRC, Article 23 ACRWC affords broader protection, because it also refers to internally displaced children through natural disasters, internal armed conflicts, civil strife, breakdown of economic and social order and any other reason; in addition, it applies Deng's principles[22] to children. In fact, in Africa, millions of people are currently internally displaced because of violence, persecution, natural disasters or armed conflict. People leave their place of residence for reasons similar to those spurring refugees, but unlike these, internally displaced people have not crossed any national borders. They too are a vulnerable group, but cannot avail themselves of the protection of international conventions, such as that on refugees. The international community refers to them as "internally displaced persons" (IDPs)[23].

Article 23 ACRWC provides protection for internally displaced children – other than because of natural disaster, internal conflict, civil unrest, or a collapse in economic and social order – "howsoever caused". This term includes war or land expropriations (for example, to build dams).

As for children who have been separated from their parents (Article 20 CRC, Article 25 ACRWC), unlike the CRC, the ACRWC provides that states shall take all necessary measures to trace and re-unite children with parents or relatives where separation is caused by internal and external displacement arising from armed conflicts or natural disasters. Thus, while the CRC considers generic problems relating to the child's family, when the best interest of the child require that he

---

[22] United Nations, "The Guiding Principles on Internal Displacement", UN doc. E/CN.4/1998/53/Add.2 (http://www.ohchr.org/EN/Issues/IDPersons/Pages/Standards.aspx, accessed on 16 May 2016). The guiding principles are not binding on States, as they have not been enshrined in a treaty and governments have neither signed nor ratified them. The elaboration of a definition of internally displaced person (IDP) that could be used by the international community, was the first step taken by the Special Representative for IDPs, when it began to address the plight of such populations; Deng defined the displaced as those people who, while still in their own country, had been forced to flee in large numbers from their homes, immediately or unexpectedly, because of armed conflict, subversion, systematic violation of human rights, or natural or man-made disasters. Beccaro, *Il regime internazionale di protezione e assistenza degli sfollati all'interno dei confini statali*, graduation thesis, Università degli studi di Bologna, a.a. 2004/2005, p. 38.

[23] For example, in March 2015, the Internal Displacement Monitoring Center estimated, on the basis of data published by the UN and the High Commissioner for Refugees (UNHCR), that there were 436 300 IDPs in the Central African Republic. In 2003, the Democratic Republic of the Congo hosted more than 1 million IDPs. Sudan has 6 million IDPs. Beccaro. *Il regime internazionale di protezione e assistenza degli sfollati all'interno dei confini statali* op cit, p. 33.

or she no longer be allowed to remain in that environment, the ACRWC refers to situations that reflect the African context more closely.

Another more specific provision is that concerning the sale, trafficking and abduction of children (Article 35 CRC, Article 29 ACRWC): unlike the CRC, the ACRWC requires States Parties to adopt appropriate measures to prevent the use of children in all forms of begging.

On the other hand, the ACRWC does present some gaps compared to the protection enshrined by the CRC. Both provide that children should be protected from economic exploitation (Article 39 CRC, Article 27 ACRWC), from all forms of abuse and maltreatment (Article 19 CRC, Article 27 ACRWC) and sexual exploitation (Article 34 CRC, Article 27 ACRWC). However, at Article 19, the CRC also envisages the "establishment of social programmes to provide necessary support for the child and for those who have the care of the child", as well as procedures "for judicial involvement". In addition, Article 39 CRC states that the "States Parties shall take all appropriate measures to promote physical and psychological recovery and social reintegration of a child victim of: any form of neglect, exploitation, or abuse; torture or any other form of cruel, inhuman or degrading treatment or punishment; or armed conflicts". The ACRWC does not provide for such forms of rehabilitation.

Likewise, Article 25 CRC recognizes "the right of a child who has been placed by the competent authorities for the purposes of care, protection or treatment of his or her physical or mental health, to a periodic review of the treatment provided to the child and all other circumstances relevant to his or her placement." Such a provision is not envisaged by the ACRWC. Indeed, the national legal systems of African states rarely contain measures for the psychological and social rehabilitation of children suffering due to armed conflict, although the ACRWC may be considered to imply that their adoption is necessary.

Furthermore, Article 4 CRC provides that "States Parties shall undertake all appropriate legislative, administrative, and other measures for the implementation" of economic, social and cultural rights "to the maximum extent of their available resources". The ACRWC, on the other hand, does not impose any such duty upon its States Parties to allocate resources to ensure that children's rights are implemented.

The CRC establishes a right to ethnic identity: according to Article 30, "[i]n those States in which ethnic, religious or linguistic minorities […] exist, a child belonging to such a minority or who is indigenous shall not be denied the right […] to enjoy his or her own culture [and] to profess and practice his or her own religion". The ACRWC does not contain an analogous provision, although the various African regions are often home to several different indigenous and minority groups[24].

---

[24] Agbobli, Somda, Akonumbo, Vohito, Joof-Conteh, Kweku Appiah, Cissè, Amadou, Abotsi, Odewale, Wilson, Atchadam, "In the best interest of the child: Harmonising Laws on Children in West and Central Africa", *The African Child Policy forum*, Addis Ababa, 2011, p. 4, (http://resourcecentre.savethechildren.se/sites/default/files/documents/6325.pdf, accessed on 18 March 2016).

While Article 17 CRC ensures children's access to the mass media to obtain information and "material from a diversity of national and international sources" to contribute to his or her information and well-being, there is no such measure in the ACRWC, probably also because a vast number of African children are unable to access mass media.

The same can be said of the publicization of the legal instruments. Article 42 CRC affirms that the "States Parties undertake to make the [...] [CRC] widely known [...] to adults and children alike", while the ACRWC contains no such provision. However, every year, the Day of the African Child is celebrated, to promote the ACRWC and specific topics concerning African children. Each year, the ACERWC selects the theme of the occasion.

However, the ACRWC contains several provisions confirming its nature as a specific document, tailored to African society, to protect the rights of children in Africa. The ACRWC makes express reference to the customs, traditions, and cultural and religious practices that are incompatible with the rights, duties and obligations under the ACRWC; and realistically provides that the States Parties are required to discourage adoption of such practices. Indeed, these are deeply entrenched and a gradual process – including on the cultural level – is required to eradicate them[25].

Article 29 CRC establishes that the education of children should develop their respect for human rights and fundamental freedoms, as well as respect for their own parents and their cultural and national values, for the purpose of preparing them for responsible life as an adult. The ACRWC, instead, sets out immediate and onerous responsibilities upon the child: Article 31 ACRWC imposes the duty not only to respect one's parents but also one's "superiors and elders at all times and to assist them in case of need".

Unlike the CRC, the ACRWC endows children with a political role, providing that they should serve their national communities, preserve and strengthen the independence and integrity of their countries and, finally, contribute to the best of their abilities to promote and achieve African Unity. These provisions are more appropriately established towards adult subjects; also, the ACRWC does not specify what form compliance with such duties could take.

On one hand, individual rights do not make sense without corresponding duties on the part of the individual. On the other hand, it must be recalled that the African concept of the person does not consider the individual as an abstract and isolated entity, but only as a member of a group inspired

---

[25] The ACERWC's recommendations and observations to the Government of Senegal in relation to its 2011 Report states that "The Committee encourages campaigns to sensitize, train and promote the rights of men and children and in particular of the child; the awareness and involvement of priests and other religious and traditional guides, in promoting the rights of the minor of both sexes with special attention to rape and FGM, early marriages and encourages the inclusion of a module on the Rights of the Child in the training programs of personnel in charge of child-related issues (magistrates, police forces, military and specialized educators or social workers) for a better management of this problem." ACERWC, *Recommandations et observations adressées au gouvernement du Senegal par le Comité african d'experts sur les droits et le bien etre de l'enfant sur le rapport initial de la mise en oeuvre de la Charte africaine des droits et du bien etre de l'enfant*, 30 April 2012, https://acerwc.africa/wp-content/uploads/2018/14/CO_Senegal_French.pdf

by a spirit of solidarity[26]. It is in line with this concept that the ACRWC imposes, upon children, duties towards their families, societies and States[27]. In traditional African communities, rights and duties go hand in hand, and individuals must be prepared to take on their social responsibilities. Therefore, it is no coincidence that, as well as recognizing protections to minors, the ACRWC also introduces corresponding duties.

However, it remains that such duties should be commensurate with the children's age and abilities, and with the limitations established by Article 31 ACRWC. In balancing duties and rights, these limitations serve to ensure proportionality between the children's age and abilities, to avoid the duties placed upon them from turning into abuse and, therefore, violations of their rights[28]. Confirming this observation, the Preamble to the ACRWC states that "the promotion and protection of the rights and welfare of the child also implies the performance of duties on the part of everyone". Thus, the duties must be *balanced* between adults and children.

In addition, the CRC and the ACRWC contain different provisions regarding the child's duty to obey their parents' supervision. In the CRC, such supervision means the direction and guidance imparted to the child, consistently with his or her evolving skills. Indeed, according to Article 5 CRC, the parents or legal guardians of the child provide him or her, "in a manner consistent with the evolving capacities of the child, appropriate direction and guidance in the exercise by the child of the rights recognized in the [...] Convention"[29].

On the other hand, Article 31 ACRWC establishes that children have the duty to respect their parents, superiors and elders "at all times". Parents have the duty of ensuring that parental discipline be administered humanely and with respect for the dignity of the child. This implies that parents have the right to punish the child, including through corporal means[30].

The ACRWC lacks a specific and express provision on corporal punishment, although Article 16 ACRWC protects against child abuse and torture. The issue of corporal punishment is a sociocultural problem in many parts of Africa. Corporal discipline and other forms of humiliating and degrading punishment of children are widely practiced, for example in the Republic of

---

[26] Matua, "The Banjul Charter and the African Cultural Fingerprint: An Evaluation of the Language of Duties", *Review of the African Commission on Human and Peoples 's Rights*, (1996-7), p. 32

[27] Njungwe. "International protection of children's rights: an analysis of African attributes in the African charter on the rights and welfare of the child", *Cameroon Journal on Democracy and Human Rights*, 2009, p. 22.

[28] See Sloth-Nielsen (ed.), *Children's Rights in Africa. A Legal Perspective*, Burlington USA, Ashgate, 2010, p. 64; Odongo, "The domestication of international standard on the rights of the child: a critical and comparative evaluation of the Kenyan example", *The International Journal of Children's Rights*, 2004, p. 424.

[29] Van der Vyver, "Children's Rights, Family Values, and Federal Constraints", *Journal of Markets and Morality*, 2012, p. 121.

[30] Boezaart, "Building bridges: African customary family law and children's rights", *International Journal of Private Law*, 2013, p.6. the African Child Policy Forum and the Global Initiative, in collaboration with the ACERWC, held a Strategic Consultation in Ouagadougou (Burkina Faso) from 28 February to 1 March 2011, to review the status of corporal punishment in Africa and progress towards its prohibition and eradication.

South Africa[31]. Several countries, such as South Africa, Burkina Faso, Ethiopia, Namibia, Zambia, Kenya and Egypt, have taken measures to prohibit the use of corporal punishment in children's public lives (such as in schools, detention centres and children care facilities)[32]. Significant efforts has been made to prohibit this form of violence against children, and national judges have begun to state that it is unacceptable[33]. It may be recalled that South Sudan is the first country in Africa to ban corporal punishment, and that the Interim Constitution of 2005 includes a provision that prohibits parents from meting out corporal punishment: "every child has a right to be free from corporal punishment and cruel and inhuman treatment from any person including parents, school administrations and other institutions" (Article 21(f))[34]. Another relevant example is provided by Kenyan case law, according to which children must be protected from torture, maltreatment and punishment by their parents[35]. The case is important because the High Court stated that private parties, including a child's parents, may be found responsible of committing torture, cruelties and inhuman and degrading treatment under the pretext of imposing discipline; this confirms the power of Kenya's courts to subject the matter of corporal punishment to detailed judicial scrutiny.

The ACRWC enhanced the standard of protection afforded to children's rights, because it appropriately took into consideration the specific circumstances of the African continent and omitted certain non-relevant aspects of the CRC, such as the relationship between children and mass media, leaving it, where applicable, to secondary protection under the CRC. Thus, the question is whether the ACRWC has succeeded in effectively protecting children, balancing traditional heritage with children's internationally guaranteed rights.

---

[31] A study conducted in 2005 by the NGO Save the Children found that corporal punishment is widespread in South Africa. See Dawes, De Sas kropiwinicki, Zuhayrkafaar e Richter (Save the children - Sweden), "Corporal Punishment of children: a South African National Survey", 2005, p. 3 (https://www.researchgate.net/publication/237520045_CORPORAL_PUNISHMENT_OF_CHILDREN_A_SOUTH_AFRICAN_NATIONAL_SURVEY, Accessed 4 February 2016).

[32] Kassan, "The protection of children from all forms of violence-African Experiences", in Sloth-Nielsen (ed.), *Children's Rights in Africa. A legal perspective*, Burlington Usa, Ashgate, 2010, p. 175.

[33] *Ibidem*, p. 174.

[34] South Sudan's Interim Constitution and Article 21.1(f) are available at http://www.refworld.org/pdfid/4ba74c4a2.pdf (accessed on 18 March 2016).

[35] High Court of Kenya, *Isaac Mwangi Wachira v. Republic*, Criminal Appeal n. 185/2004 (http://kenyalaw.org /caselaw/cases/view/13058, accessed 15 July 2015). The appellant was sentenced to 3 years in prison for committing acts of torture contrary to Section 20 of the Children's Act no. 8 of 2001. The appellant voluntarily subjected her three-year-old daughter to torture by pinching her face, ears, back, thighs with her nails to punish her.

I.3 The cultural and traditional heritage of Africa as a source of law, and the child's right to his or her best interest

In Africa, positive law is to be found alongside customary law, which consists of those local customs through which African peoples, to this day, regulate certain relationships[36]. For centuries, the term customary law has always evoked the idea of primitive, traditional or immutable norms that from an outsider and positivist's point of view do not even qualify to be called 'law'"[37].

For example, in customs dating back to the precolonial era, the system of *lobolo* (the wife's dowry) required the groom's family to give the bride's family a certain number of heads of livestock. This gift symbolized the formation of a valid marriage. However, when the colonial powers took control, young men left the rural areas and moved towards the cities, seeking work. Thus, it became common to provide cash instead of livestock, for the *lobolo*. Gradually, the African state's legal orders recognized the application of local customs, albeit with conditions and limitations. For example, in South Africa, case law recognized the applicability of local customs; however, they were to be considered subordinate to common law.

The Preamble to the ACRWC acknowledges local customs: "[t]aking into consideration the virtues of their cultural heritage, historical background and the values of the African civilization which should inspire and characterize their reflection on the concept of the rights and welfare of the child". Precillar maintains that local customs regulate community life as they reflect the common traditions and cultures, alongside official law[38]. However, this poses the problem of compatibility with the rights enshrined by the ACRWC.

Several African states do not have a particularly organized welfare system. In such a context, the extended family, or the clan, maintains a crucial role in dealing with personal crises, such as illness and death[39]. Typical African families extend vertically (incorporating generations of relatives in the

---

[36] According to Hamnett, customary law is "a set of norms which actors in a social situation abstract from practice and which they invest with binding authority". Hamnett. *Chieftainship and Legitimacy: an anthropological study of executive law in Lesotho*, Routledge and Kegan, Londra, 1975, p. 14.

[37] See Ahrèn, "Indigenous peoples culture, customs, and traditions and customary law - The Saami people's perspective", *Arizona Journal of International & Comparative Law*, 2004, p. 1: "Thus, customary law does not gain its authority from formal acts such as a vote from an assembly but derives its existence and content from social acceptance. Intrinsically connected to the culture of the people whose conduct it is supposed to govern, it is subject to constant change and modification".

[38] Precillar. "The relevance of culture and religion to the understanding of children's rights in South Africa", Postgraduate thesis, Faculty of Law, University of Cape Town, 2014, p. 22 (http://core.ac.uk/display/29053102. Accessed on 27 December 2015): "It has arguably lost its characteristic flexibility that made it responsive to the ever-changing needs of the communities its serves. This is not to say that with the formalization of customary law, its actors or participants ceased regulating their lives in accordance with culturally binding norms. Rather, customary law continues to operate today alongside the legislated and judicial customary law. It is from this mix that we get the terms 'living' and 'official' customary law. Today, the disjunction between official and living customary law remains one of the most contentious issues in South African jurisprudence".

[39] Kurankye, "The Ghanaian (African) Extended Family (system)", 4 April 2009 (www.ghanaweb.com. Accessed on 15 July 2015).

ascending line and descendants) as well as horizontally (through polygamous unions). Therefore, a family may comprise of one man, his wives and their children, unmarried brothers and sisters, parents and all other persons who choose to stay with them. This unit meets all material and social needs of its individual members. Such a society emphasizes duties more than rights[40]. In Africa, individualism does not have the same standing as in the West. Therefore, a person may expect his or her interests to be compromised for the benefit of a wider circle of persons. Supporting the individual rights of a single person would be deemed "anti-social". Therefore, the principal rights are those enjoyed by the family or the group[41].

This trait is particularly relevant to the well-being of the child. In the African tradition, the rights of the child are a social issue, with broader social implications; a child is welcome when it is possible to provide him or her with food, shelter and support. However, the protection of the child is remitted entirely to the mutual solidarity due between the family members, such that the interests of the child are to be placed within the context of the family's right to claim the child as its member. It is the group to constitute a legal entity – not the individual[42]. African custom is based on a concept of human dignity that does not necessarily derive from the quest for individual freedom, but that is based essentially on membership of a group. This particularity is emphasized by several scholars[43].

The best interest of the child are encompassed in the concept of membership; therefore, according to local custom, the well-being of the child is inseparable from that of his or her family. Thus, duties of children are often recognized – such as the duty to guard the family's flock or to help with ploughing the field – in line with the general concept of communitarian responsibility[44]. The best interest of the individual child is fundamental, and while traditional African values are to be considered with sensitivity, the importance of the principle cannot be voided or diminished[45]. The principle of the best interest of the child must extend to all aspects of his or her life: nutrition, health, education, culture, religion... When local custom, traditional values and religion conflict with the

---

[40] Gluckman, *The Ideas in Barotse jurisprudence*, Manchester, Manchester University Press, 1972, p. 8

[41] Holleman, *Issues in African Law*, Mouton, The Hague, 1974, pp. 2-6.

[42] Boezaart, "Building bridges: African customary family law and children's rights", *International Journal of Private Law*, 2013, p. 398.

[43] South African law commission, "Issue paper n. 13", *Review of the Child Care Act, First Issue Paper 18 April 1998*, p. 113 (http://www.justice.gov.za/salrc/ipapers/ip13_prj110_1998.pdf, accessed on 28 March 2016). See Nhlapo, "The African family and women's rights: Friends or foes?", *Acta Juridica*, 1991, p. 135; Nhlapo, "South African family law at the crossroads: From Parliamentary supremacy to constitutionalism", *International Survey of Family Law*, 1994, p. 419; Kerr, "Customary law, fundamental rights and the Constitution", *South African Law Journal*, 1994, p. 720; Kerr, *The Bill of Rights in the new Constitution and customary law*, South African Law Journal, 1997, p. 346.

[44] Van Bueren, "The African Charter on the Rights and Welfare of the Child: A New Children's Treaty", *International Children's Rights Monitor*, 1991, p. 22; Karin, "The international protection of children's rights in Africa: The 1990 OAU Charter on the Rights and Welfare of the Child", *African Journal of International & Comparative Law*, 1992, pp. 144-145 and 153-154; Boezaart, "Building bridges: African customary family law and children's rights", *International Journal of Private Law*, 2013, p. 4.

[45] South African Law Commission Report, "Customary Law affecting children", University of Cape Town, p. 285 (http://www.ci.org.za/depts/ci/plr/pdf/salrc_dis/24-dp103-ch21.pdf, accessed on 10 April 2016).

child's best interest, the latter should take precedence. The duties established by international law commit States Parties to pursue the standard of the best interest, whenever children are involved.

However, what constitutes the best interest of the child depends on the facts of each individual case. For this reason, the criterion of the best interest of the child has been criticized as excessively vague and indeterminate[46]. On the other hand, however, this general principle allows national judges to exercise the necessary discretion to evaluate different cultural norms in different situations. This is surely an advantage[47]. The well-being of the child is indivisible from that of their families, and, therefore, some degree of sacrifice is required to protect the common good of the family[48].

The Preamble to the ACRWC and its Article 46 expressly recognizes positive African traditions, without however giving way to them. According to the Preamble, positive tradition "should inspire and characterize […] reflection on the concept of the rights and welfare of the child"; therefore, they are not considered in themselves. This means that positive traditions are subordinate to the norms – that is, the rights – established by the ACRWC to protect children and, more broadly, to the principle of the best interest of the child. Positive African traditions may foster their effectiveness, contributing to their greater sharing. However, where these traditions trespass upon the rights of the child, they are deemed incompatible and not functional to the affirmation and possession of rights on the part of children.

I.4 Customary law and the extended family: parental responsibilities and the duties of the child according to Articles 20 and 31 ACRWC

Article 20 ACRWC concerns the responsibilities of parents and other persons responsible for the child in terms of his or her education, securing the living conditions necessary for his or her development, and administering domestic discipline. On the other hand, Article 20 ACRWC, titled "Parental responsibilities", parents or other persons responsible for the child have the primary responsibility of the upbringing and development of the child and are required to ensure that the best interest of the child are their basic concern at all times, as well as to secure the conditions of living necessary to his or her development.

Unlike the CRC, the ACRWC contains a provision on the duties of the child: Article 31. The provision is detailed and enshrines the responsibilities of the child not only towards his or her

---

[46] See Heaton, "Some General Remarks on the Concept "Best Interests of the Child", *Tydskrif vir Hedensdaagse Romeins-Hollandse Reg*, 1990, p. 95; Parker, "The Best Interests of the Child–Principles and Problems", *International journal of law policy and the family*, 1994, p. 30; Alston (ed.), The Best Interests of the Child–Reconciling Culture and Human Rights, *International Journal of Law, Policy and family*, 1994, pp. 26 and 29; Boezaart, "Building Bridges: African Customary Family Law and Children's Rights", *International Journal of Private Law*, 2013, p. 401.

[47] Alston, "The best interest principle", *International Journal of Law and the Family*, 1994, p. 1; Rwezaura, "The Concept of the Child's Best Interests in the Changing Economic and Social Context of Sub-Sahara Africa", *International Journal of Law and the Family*, 1994, p. 82.

[48] Bennett, "Customary Law in South Africa", *Journal of African Law*, 2004, p. 295.

family, but also towards society, the State and other legally recognized communities, and, finally, towards the international community as a whole. In particular, Article 31 ACRWC provides that the child must, at all times, respect and assist his or her family; preserve and strengthen African cultural values and contribute to the moral well-being of society; preserve and strengthen the national independence and integrity of his or her country; contribute to promote and achieve African Unity. In the ACRWC, the set of duties imposed upon the child is greater than the responsibilities set out for parents.

The question that bears analysis is when, in light of the ACRWC, the application of local customs regarding the traditional extended family achieves the best interest of the child. Indeed, according to local customs, the child's individual rights give way to the rights enjoyed by the family.

The concept of the extended family is relevant to several rights of the child that are protected by the ACRWC, and may influence the very recognition of such rights. To avoid this, it is necessary to verify whether it is possible to balance the child's duties towards the family and the child's rights.

For example, the South African *Children Act* acknowledges that the extended family plays a part in protecting these rights, including the individual members of the extended family – grandparents, siblings, uncles, aunts and cousins are all encompassed in the term "family member"[49] (of the child). The significance of the extended family should be seen primarily as an effective social welfare network, in the context of poor rural communities where people live close to one another and children are often left in the care of adult members of the extended family. Some sociologists have found that the extended family "benefits children by protecting them from rape and helps rape victims to recover more easily through relying on the support provided by the family"[50].

However, it is also noted that the family or the group may disadvantage the child. This may happen with the child's individual needs are ignored, giving way to those of the family or of the relevant group. Members of the extended family may abuse the children in their care, subjecting them to grave ill-treatment or exploiting them to secure low-cost labour. Nhlapo argues that the African family, conceived of as a clan, masks inequalities between men and women resulting from local customs, in so far as women and children are disadvantaged because they have a secondary role in the articulation of the group[51]. Armstrong maintains that "the community and state solutions

---

[49] Article 1(1) defines the family member as "(a) a parent of the child; (b) any other person who has parental responsibilities and rights in respect of the child; (c) a grandparent, brother, sister, uncle, aunt or cousin of the child; or any other person with whom the child has developed a significant relationship, based on psychological or emotional attachment, which resembles a family relationship". The South African Children Act establishes that it is in the best interests of children to remain in the care of their parents and of their extended family, in accordance with their culture and traditions. The "best interests of the child" standard is defined as "the need for the child: (i) to remain in the care of his or her parent, family and extended family; and (ii) to maintain a connection with his or her family, extended family, culture or tradition" (http://www.justice.gov.za/ legislation/ acts/2005-038%20childrensact.pdf, last accessed on 9 June 2016).

[50] Armstrong, "A Consent and Compensation: The Sexual Abuse of Girls in Zimbabwe", in Ncube (ed.), *Law, Culture, Tradition and Children's Rights in Eastern and Southern Africa*, Darmouth – England, Ashgate, 1998, p. 141.

[51] Nhlapo, "The African family and women's rights: friends or foes?", *Acta Juridica*, 1991, p. 137.

are not necessarily mutually exclusive. There is a role for involving the family and community in the state system"[52]. The solution, therefore, would be to "work with both the individual and the community, which support individual rights and autonomy but at the same time support the family and belonging"[53]. The author admits that conventions enshrining children's rights that include the extended family in the rights to protection may allow for a balancing between the rights of groups, on one hand, and the individual rights and autonomy of children on the other[54].

Closely linked to the concept of extended family is the value of the common ethic. This is a concept that is better explained with reference to another crucial value, that of *Ubuntu*, which describes group relations inspired by solidarity and mutual assistance. An attempt to define *Ubuntu* was made by the Constitutional Court of South Africa in *State v Makwanyane*, which abolished the death penalty[55]. The Court defined *Ubuntu*[56] in the following terms: "An outstanding feature of ubuntu in a community sense is the value it puts on life and human dignity. The dominant theme of the culture is that the life of another person is at least as valuable as one's own. Respect for the dignity of every person is integral to this concept". In *DPP v Pete*, the Court of Appeal of the United Republic of Tanzania considered the "African communal ethic" to be "(the) co-existence of the individual and society, and also the reality of co-existence of rights and duties of the individual on the one hand, and the collective of communitarian rights and duties of society on the other, which in effect means that the rights and duties of the individual are limited by rights and duties of society, and vice versa"[57]. In its consideration of the practical effects of *Ubuntu*, there is a close link between the concept of the extended family and *Ubuntu*. As a result, societies based on *Ubuntu* greatly emphasize family duties. Family members are obliged to help one another. The concept of extended family may fall within the positive strengths of the cultural heritage and values of African civilizations, which should be inherent in any reflections on the rights and well-being of children, in accordance with the Preamble to the ACRWC.

Raising children is a responsibility, which concerns their parents and the community in which the children live. This affirmation goes hand in hand with the idea, accepted by the community, that adults' behaviour towards children should be controlled. For example, a parent may be stopped by a member of the community for abusing of his or her children, or for disciplining them too harshly. All members of the community that witness abuse against children may intervene to protect them. Such intervention may include criminal reports or resort to the relevant local networks or

---

[52] Achilihu, *Do African Children Have Rights? A Comparative and legal Analysis of the United Nations Convention on the Rights of the Child*, Universal Publishers, Boca Raton - USA, 2010, p. 184.

[53] *Ibidem*, p. 184.

[54] Armstrong, "A Consent and Compensation: The Sexual Abuse of Girls in Zimbabwe", *op. cit.*, p. 148.

[55] Constitutional Court of South Africa, *State v. Makwanyane*, Case no. CCT/3/94, 6 June 1995, para. 317: "[w]hich authorises the death penalty under these unnecessarily inhuman and degrading circumstances is inconsistent with the right to life and human dignity embodied in Sections 9 and 10 of the Constitution, respectively, and is in direct conflict with the values that Section 35 aims to promote in the interpretation of these sections".

[56] Constitutional Court of South Africa, *State v. Makwanyane*, Case no. CCT/3/94, 6 June 1995, para. 24 (http://www.saflii.org/za/cases/ZACC/1995/3.html, accessed 22 July 2015).

[57] Court of Appeal of Tanzania, 16 May 1990. http://www.saflii.org/tz/cases/TZCA/1991/1.html.

authorities. The concept that "a child belongs to everyone" intersects with the rights of children protecting them from abuse and exploitation, as provided for in the Preamble to the ACRWC, which imposes general duties to ensure respect for the rights of children enshrined in the ACRWC itself. Indeed, the members of the extended family have the duty to protect its children.

However, the concepts of the family and the clan may be exasperated, giving rise to an ideological vision in which the family and its internal rules constitute the primary value, such that in their name, the rights of the child may be arbitrarily and uncontrolledly denied.

Article 16(1) of the ACRWC requires "States Parties to the present Charter shall take specific legislative, administrative, social and educational measures to protect the child from all forms of torture, inhuman or degrading treatment and especially physical or mental injury or abuse, neglect or maltreatment including sexual abuse, while in the care of the child." Subsection (2) of the article provides that "[p]rotective measures under this Article shall include effective procedures for the establishment of special monitoring units to provide necessary support for the child and for those who have the care of the child, as well as other forms of prevention and for identification, reporting referral investigation, treatment, and follow-up of instances of child abuse and neglect." According to Viljoen[58], the duty to "always" respect the parents must be interpreted to take into consideration the peculiarities of the African context. According to Article 31 of the ACRWC, children's duties toward their family, society and State are subordinated to the "age and ability" of the children, and are subject to other limitations established by the ACRWC. Indeed, for example, the duty to obey must be balanced with the child's freedom of expression (Article) and the protection of his or her privacy (Article 10), while the parents' duty is to always assure the best interest of the child.

Odongo notes that adults are not given as many duties and responsibilities towards children; however, the value of reciprocity is impressed in the common ethic and in the concept of *Ubuntu*. For this reason, it was not necessary to expressly impose such responsibilities and duties upon adults[59]. For example, the Constitution of Eritrea expressly establishes the reciprocity of rights and duties; Article 22 states that "[p]arents have the right and duty to bring up their children with due care and affection; and, in turn, children shall have the right and the duty to respect their parents and to sustain them in their old age".

The ACRWC recognizes the existence of children's duties. However, these duties are subject to two forms of attenuation, commensurate with the age and the abilities that denote the limitations of those same duties. This should also enable consideration of the peculiar African notion of family, increasingly within observance of the rights enshrined in the ACRWC.

---

[58] Viljoen, *International Human Rights Law in Africa*, Oxford, Oxford University Press, 2012, p. 394.

[59] Odongo, "Harmonization of National and International Laws to Protect Children's Rights: The Kenya Case Study", paper presented at the *African Child policy Forum Conference on harmonization of laws in eastern and southern Africa*, Nairobi, Kenya, 25-27 October 2006, p. 12.

I.4.1   The application of the ACRWC: the duties of the child

This section examines the application of Article 31 ACRWC in practice, by analysing the reports submitted by States to the ACERWC, entrusted, *inter alia*, with monitoring the implementation of the ACRWC. The section will explore how the duties imposed on children and the limits that, in practice, have arisen in the performance of such duties as set out in the ACRWC, have been interpreted.

Article 31 ACRWC states that every child has responsibilities towards his or her family, society, state and the international community. However, this article, which appears to burden children with an excessive degree of responsibility, also refers to attenuations to the duties of children. These attenuations relate to the age and abilities of the child,a s well as to other limitations contained in the ACRWC.

In the report submitted by Burkina Faso[60], Article 508 states that "the child, at any age, owes honour and respect to his father and mother and other ascendants, as well as to his uncles, aunts, and brothers and sisters who are of age or are emancipated". The limits on the duties are established in Article 10 ACRWC, on the protection of privacy. Parents exercise a degree of control over the conduct of their children; however, the latter cannot be subjected to arbitrary interference in their private life nor to attacks on their honour and reputation.

Article 39 of the Education Orientation Law (Law N. 13/96) deals with the rights and duties of the child within the educational system. Under this article, pupils and students must perform the tasks related to their studies; they must respect the rules governing the functioning of the collective life of the scholastic establishments and must ensure that the exercise of the freedom of expression recognized to them does not endanger teaching activities. The responsibilities of the child are a value to be nurtured.

According to the report submitted by Cameroon[61], the child has the duty to obey and respect his or her parents and family. The child must behave in an exemplary manner, without any deviancy, respect the African tradition and be proud of his community. Order N. 81/02 of 29 June 1981, on the registration of the civil status of natural persons and the effects of the registration of births, marriages and deaths, as well as the Civil Code of Cameroon, all reaffirm these duties. The child also has duties towards his or her supervisors, such as teachers and religious ministers. The child must be obedient and submit to any punishment that may be meted out, provided that such punishments correspond to the violation of rules and do not damage the child's integrity.

---

[60] Burkina Faso Initial Report on the Implementation of the ACRWC, p. 139, http://acerwc.org/?wpdmdl=8780 (accessed on 27 December 2015).

[61] Cameroon Initial Report on the Implementation of the ACRWC, p. 76, http://acerwc.org/?wpdmdl=8781 (accessed on 27 December 2015).

The Gabon report[62] refers to Articles 493 and 494 of the Civil Code, according to which the child must respect and honour his or her father and mother and other ascendants, and must serve the national community according to his or her physical and intellectual abilities. The youth of Gabon, organized in associations, often lead large-scale cleanup operations (weeding, cleaning of neighbourhood and village drain canals), with a great deal of enthusiasm. These activities are usually justified by the need to clear waterways, which may cause flooding during the rainy season. Children may also be required to perform a sort of neighbourhood watch, when threats to security arise. However, this activities must comply with appropriate age limits, as established by Article 31, and avoid any risk of economic exploitation or harm to the child's health.

As for the duty to preserve and enhance solidarity within society and between nations, the Government established the yearly festivity of National Youth Day. The event draws the participation of several NGOs and is an opportunity to promote the organization of sports activities, conferences and debates. Pupils also take part in cleaning their schools and colleges. Meetings with education professionals are set up, to promote attitudes that can foster a life devoid of armed or other forms of conflict. On 25 February 2013, the Director General of the Gabonese Red Cross presented a project against AIDS, in which 1,620 youth participated as volunteers. "Our youth plays an essential role in our country's march towards competitiveness, growth, development and solidarity," declared the representative of the Gabonese Red Cross to the president of national youth policies.

According to the Ghana report[63], every child belongs to a hearth; the family provides for the child's fundamental needs, such as education, health, growth, nourishment, love and other needs relating to the child's growth and development. The child also owes duties to his or her family, which include: respect for the parents, helping with household chores, protecting younger or weaker siblings, protect the family's assets, showing respect to the elderly in the community, and help community members in case of need. The scholastic authorities have the duty to educate and instruct children, as well as protect them from dangers. In the school context too, children have responsibilities. These include: respecting the school regulations, respecting the school authorities, respecting classmates, performing the tasks assigned within the school, protecting younger or weaker classmates and protecting the school's assets.

However, these duties also involve States: indeed, according to Article 16 ACRWC, the States Parties commit to protect children from abuse by means of appropriate legislative, administrative, social and educational measures.

In the Lesotho report[64], section 21 of the Law on the Protection and Well-being of Children establishes the duties incumbent upon the child and the responsibility to respect parents, tutors,

---

[62] Gabon Initial Report on the implementation of the ACRWC, p. 178, http://acerwc.org/?wpdmdl=8773 (accessed on 27 December 2015).
[63] Ghana Initial Report on the implementation of the ACRWC, p. 121, http://acerwc.org/?wpdmdl=8775 (accessed on 27 December 2015).
[64] Lesotho Initial Report on the implementation of the ACRWC, p. 82, http://acerwc.org/?wpdmdl=8774 (accessed on 27 December 2015).

uncles and aunts and to assist them in case of need. More broadly, the report confirms the principles enshrined in Article 31: children have the duty to contribute to serving their community, preserve and strengthen national and social solidarity and the positive values of society.

The limitation upon such duties may be found in Article 11 ACRWC, according to which education must foster respect for human rights and fundamental freedoms; the same article prescribes that education must also be directed at preserving and strengthening the positive moral values of the traditions and cultures of Africa.

The Mali report[65] refers to Article 1, subsections (e) and (f) of the Child Protection Code of 5 June 2002, according to which one of the objectives set by said Code is to instill a sense of morality into children, a sense of respect for their parents, family and social entourage; ensure that children learn the virtue of labour, the value of personal efforts, and a sense of responsibility towards their own parents. Another objective established by the Code is to raise children with a sense of national identity and citizenship, loyalty to Mali, its history, and a sense of belonging to national humanistic and scientific values.

Article 31(d), on the other hand, affirms the preparation of children for a responsible life in a free society, in a spirit of understanding, tolerance, dialogue, mutual respect and goodwill among all peoples and tribal and religious groups.

Mozambique's report states that Article 8 of the Law on the Promotion and Protection of the Rights of Children establishes duties upon children in compliance with the provisions of the ACRWC:

Without prejudice to the provision of the other legislation, the child, according to his/her age and maturity, has the duty to:

a) Respect his/her parents, family members, teachers, educators, the elderly, people with disabilities and, if necessary, assist them;
b) Participate in the family and community life in the development of the country and in the preservation of the environment, by putting their physical and intellectual skills towards the service of the Nation;
c) Contribute for the preservation and strengthening of the family, cultural values and national unity in the spirit of peace, tolerance, dialogue and solidarity".

With regard to these duties, it is emphasized that, according to Article 13 ACRWC, States Parties commit to support handicapped children. In addition, according to Article 11 on education, children have the right to develop their individual personalities, talents and physical and mental abilities, not only to serve their nations.

---

[65] Mali Initial Report on the implementation of the ACRWC, p. 121, http://acerwc.org/?wpdmdl=8782 (accessed on 27 December 2015).

The duties of children are usually publicized by means of awareness sessions, debates and programs, within which children are encouraged to perform activities to promote solidarity. In this context, the Parliament of Children, student councils, the Girls' Club and Community-Based Child Protection Committees are all spaces within which children may reflect upon their obligations.

In the Concluding Observations of Mozambique's report[66], the ACERWC expressed appreciation for the fact that the State Party had devoted a specific provision to the responsibilities of children in the Law on the Promotion and Protection of Children's Rights, as it was considered to encourage children to undertake solidarity activities through the the Parliament of Children, student councils, the Girls' Club and Community-Based Child Protection Committees. The ACERWC invited the State Party to continue in its efforts to promote the responsibilities of children, by establishing a participatory forum for children, which would enable the latter to be involved in matters that may affect their interests[67].

Togo's Report[68] recalls the Children's Code, Articles 428 and 429 of which establish the duties of children towards their parents: children are to respect their parents, superiors and elders in all circumstances and assist them in case of need; respect other children; respect their own identity, language, and cultural and national values; respect and protect their natural environment; respect the rights, reputation and honour of others; work to foster family cohesion and the well-being of the national and international community, placing their physical and intellectual capabilities at their service; and work to safeguard public order, health and morals.

The Commission welcomed Rwanda's recognition of the provisions of the ACRWC that define children's responsibilities towards the elderly, the local and national community and Africa overall. In addition, the Commission noted that Rwanda's Government endorses the principles of respect for parents and the elderly, and that obedience extends to schoolteachers.

Rwanda's Report[69] envisages a program of civic life education, which promotes values such as national unity, social solidarity, patriotism, integration and mutual tolerance.

However, in light of the events that overwhelmed Rwanda in 1994, the duty of complete obedience for one's parents, the elderly and educators showed its limits. Indeed, according to the information received by the Commission, a large number of children were required to take part in massacres during the genocide. The absence of norms to allow children to refuse executing orders of parents, elders or educators, there where required by their moral conscience, is certainly a flaw in the application of the overall principle. The Commission recommended that the Government

---

[66] Mozambique Initial Report on the implementation of the ACRWC, p. 74, http://acerwc.org/?wpdmdl=8650 (accessed on 27 December 2015).

[67] Concluding Observations and Recommendations of the ACERWC on the Mozambique Report, p. 9, www.acerwc.org/?wpdmdl=8749 (accessed 27 December 2015).

[68] Togo Initial Report on the implementation of the ACRWC, p. 9, http://acerwc.org/?wpdmdl=8789 (accessed on 27 December 2015).

[69] Rwanda Initial Report on the implementation of the ACRWC, p. 55, http://acerwc.org/?wpdmdl=8653 (accessed on 27 December 2015).

review the drafting of these texts, to acknowledge that obedience is a positive trait for children while also emphasizing its limitations; children, within the limits of their capacity for discernment and their age, may evaluate the need to disobey in light of the responsibilities assigned to them by the ACRWC and the values of peace and non-discrimination. Therefore, the Commission encouraged the Rwandan Government to enhance its efforts to raise awareness among youth on their responsibilities concerning the future of their family, nation and continent[70].

In its Concluding Observations on South Africa's Report, the Commission appreciated the fact that the country encouraged children to engage in activities fostering solidarity through the Children's Parliament. The Commission invited South Africa to continue its efforts to promote children's responsibilities, such as their participation in forums allowing them to have a say in issues engaging their rights. In addition, the Commission recommended that the State Party ensure that the responsibilities incumbent upon adults remain in line with those required of children[71].

The duties imposed upon children towards adults by Article 31 ACRWC remain in force as long as adults advance the values endorsed by the ACRWC, and within the bounds of the best interest of the child. If obedience is exploited – as in the case of the Rwandan child soldiers – to employ children in adversarial combat on battlefields, then children's duties turn into abuse on the part of adults.

The duties provided at Article 31 risk becoming instrumentalized by adults. Therefore, the limitation upon the ACRWC's norms established in the same provision refers to other articles, such as Article 4, on the best interest of the child, the right to express opinions on any topic and the right to be heard (Article 7), freedom of thought, conscience and religion (Article 9), leisure, recreation and cultural activities (Article 12), protection against abuse and torture (Article 16), and protection from exploitation in formal and informal labour (Article 15). Thus, it is necessary to progress the implementation of children's rights, to ensure the best possible performance of their duties.

1.5   The role of local customs in disputes regarding children

The administration of justice can also be delegated to local bodies which follow and apply local customs, traditions and cultural practices. Article 1(3) ACRWC, however, admits that this can take place only if such norms are compatible with the rights enshrined in the ACRWC itself. The risk is that delegating disputes concerning children to traditional bodies, without any guidelines nor duty to apply the ACRWC, may lead to the enforcement of norms that are contrary to the ACRWC's provisions. In this case, the ACRWC would simply give way to traditional practices.

---

[70] Concluding Observations and Recommendations of the ACERWC on the Rwanda Report, p. 89, http://www.acerwc.org/?wpdmdl=8753 (accessed 27 December 2015).

[71] Concluding Observations and Recommendations of the ACERWC on the South Africa Report, p. 8, http://www.acerwc.org/?wpdmdl=8754 (accessed 27 December 2015).

In modern legal systems, including African ones, national judges are the primary agents to apply rights. However, courts may be notoriously difficult, if not impossible, to access especially for rural African communities, where for many children, life is governed by customary law and disputes are resolved by traditional bodies.

The ACRWC deals with the topic of juvenile penal justice (Article 17), requiring that "special treatment" be accorded to minors who have been accused or found guilty of infringing penal law. Article 17(2) establishes that children's rights shall be ensured by the States Parties and that the matters concerning them are to be determined as speedily as possible by an impartial court. Article 17 also requires States Parties to provide a number of specific guarantees: to ensure that children who are detained are not subjected to torture or inhuman or degrading treatment or punishment; that children are separated from adults in their place of detention or imprisonment; that children accused of infringing the penal law be presumed innocent until duly recognized guilty, be informed promptly in a language he or she understands of the charge against him, be afforded legal and other appropriate assistance, have the matter determined as quickly as possible by an impartial tribunal and, if found guilty, be entitled to appeal, as well as to prohibit the press and the public from trial.

Local customs also influence judgments concerning children's rights. South African legislation on children confers a role upon traditional leaders in court cases regarding children's rights. In particular, children's rights should be remanded to a "lay forum, including a traditional authority, in an attempt to settle the matter by way of mediation out of court" (Child care Act of 1983 Section 71. Mediation buy a lay – forum or traditional authority). Traditional authorities may, within the terms of local customs, manage the affairs of each group of indigenous persons residing in the area under its control[72].

The South African Initial Report[73] considers this to be a positive practice: the country's *Child Justice Act* established a system based on Ubuntu, restorative justice and the resolution of disputes within the community's forums, to deal with children involved in conflicts with the law.

South Africa's *Children's Act* and *Child Justice Act* thus institutionalize traditional mediation, as well as traditional leaders' oversight and relational role towards vulnerable children. In addition, the *Council of Traditional Leaders Act* (of 1997) and the *Traditional Leadership and Governance Framework Act* (2003) require traditional leaders to develop customary law compatibly with the Bill of Rights.

Therefore, traditional justice must be carried out, and customary law be applied, in conformity with children's fundamental rights.

---

[72] Section 1(1) of the South African *Children's Act* defines traditional leaders as "any authority which in terms of indigenous law or any other law administers the affairs of any group of indigenous people or any other persons resident within an area under the control of a traditional leader".

[73] South Africa Initial Report on the implementation of the ACRWC, p. 18 (http://acerwc.org/?wpdmdl=8787, last accessed on 27 December 2015).

Similarly, Uganda's Children Act and Lesotho's draft law on children's welfare and protection provide that dispute resolution should be entrusted to the alternative instrument of restorative justice, that is, mediation between the wrongdoer and the victim done by family groups, parents or other suitable adults[74]. The underlying value to this mechanism lies in its reconciliation of the disputing parties[75]. The advantage is that the members of the community are not alienated from one another because of a judgment that results in a victory or a loss, as such decisions require[76].

However, a problem is that, when dispute resolution is delegated, the legislator usually refrains from specifying the applicable law. Involving traditional leaders in the resolution of disputes regarding children entails the risk that traditional values and practices contrary to children's rights are applied, and made to prevail over the rights enshrined in the ACRWC.

A possible solution could be to limit the powers of traditional authorities. For example, in South Africa, traditional authorities cannot decide upon child abuse or sexual abuse[77].

Otherwise, when applying the ACRWC, traditional judges could consider the positive force of the cultural heritage and values of African civilization, to reach an equitable decision that conforms to the ACRWC's provisions. The Preamble to the ACRWC refers to a positive notion of the cultural heritage and values of African civilization, which should inspire and distinguish the judges' reflections on the notion of the rights and welfare of the child. Indeed, with regard

---

[74] Article 130(1) of Lesotho's *Child Care and Protection Bill* provides that "[r]eferral to restorative justice process may be made by the: (a) child or his/her parent, guardian or any appropriate adult; (3) A child or children who persist(s) in engaging in anti - social behaviour that render him/her a child at risk of offending may be referred to any restorative justice process by: (a) his/her parent(s), guardian(s) or any appropriate adult, (b) any chief who is concerned with anti-social behaviour of any child residing in his/her village, the parents of whom are considered unable to control." Article 147(2) describes the alternative dispute resolution mechanisms available in cases regarding children, stating that "[i]f, at any time before conviction, or after conviction and before sentence, the Children's Court is of the opinion that substantial grounds exist that an alternative dispute resolution mechanism may be appropriate to the resolution of the matter before the court, the court may stop the proceedings and order that the matter be referred to a victim-offender mediation, a family group conference or other restorative dispute resolution or make any other order as it may deem necessary to resolve the matter" (http://www.aclr.info/images/stories/uploader/Publication_files/Bills/Lesotho_ childrens_protection_bill_2004.pdf, last accessed on 9 June 2016).

[75] Himonga, "African Customary Law and Children's Rights: Intersections and Domains in a New Era", in Sloth-Nielsen (ed.), *Children's Rights in Africa. A legal perspective*, Burlington USA, Ashgate, 2010, p. 85.

[76] Scharf, *The other Law: non – State ordering in South Africa*, University of Michigan, Juta, 2001, p. 47.

[77] Article 71(2) of Law No. 38 of 2005 states that "(1) The children's court may, where circumstances permit, refer a matter brought on referred to a children's court to any appropriate lay-forum, including a traditional authority, in an attempt to settle the matter by way of mediation out of court. (2) Lay-forums may not be held in the event of a matter involving the alleged abuse or sexual abuse of a child." (http://www.justice.gov.za/legislation/acts/2005-038%20childrensact.pdf, last accessed on 17 May 2016). Article 17 of the ACRWC deals with juvenile criminal justice, referring to "special treatment" to be accorded to children who have been accused or held responsible of a violation of criminal law. However, subsection 2 of the provision establishes that children's rights are to guaranteed by the States Parties, and that the case against the child should be dealt with as quickly as possible by an impartial court.

to the activities of the ACRWC Commission, Africa's culture and traditions may, in its positive aspects (as established by Article 46 ACRWC) become a source of inspiration, alongside other instruments of international law. Besides, on the subject of conflicts between customary law, official law and children's rights, Article 1(3) ACRWC clearly states that "Any custom, tradition, cultural or religious practice that is inconsistent with the rights, duties and obligations contained in the present Charter shall to the extent of such inconsistency be discouraged." Customary law has been a part of Africa's post-colonial legal systems, and the application of local customs can lead to an internal conflict of legal orders.

Various approaches have been attempted to resolve this issue. The first approach assumes that local customs apply only to certain specific subjects, such as inheritance, marriage and land or to certain types of dispute. For example, Zambia's Subordinate Courts Act considers the application of African customary law: (Article 16. "[S]uch African customary law not being [...] incompatible [...] with any written law for the time being in force in Zambia [...] shall be deemed applicable [...] in civil causes and matters relating to marriage [...] and to the tenure and transfer of real and personal property, and to inheritance and testamentary dispositions, and also in civil causes and matters between Africans and non-Africans"[78].

According to the second approach, local customs are to be applied to particular groups, such as the members of traditional communities or tribes. Indeed, some constitutions recognize the application of local customs, and simply use them without addressing the conflict between local customs and human rights provisions[79].

Customary law is constitutionally recognized in Botswana. Article 15 of the Constitution refers to local customs, with the exception of discrimination. The Customary Law Act regulates customary law as being applicable "in relation to any particular tribe or tribal community, the customary law of that tribe or community so far as it is not incompatible with the provisions of any written law or contrary to morality, humanity or natural justice." The Act envisages the application of customary law in some civil law cases, or when an agreement to the effect is reached, and in matters concerning child custody, places the welfare of the child as a fundamental consideration. In succession matters, the law provides that "customary law shall be applicable in determining the intestate heirs of a tribesman and the nature and extent of their inheritances." In addition, local customs cannot be "contrary to morality, humanity or natural justice."[80]

The third approach concerns the application of local customs in function of the parties' claims[81]. This approach demands the decision of when local customs should be applied to the judge's

[78] See Zambia's *Subordinate Courts (Amendment) Act* dello Zambia, ch. 28, of 1 April 1934 (http://www.zamlii. org/zm/legislation/consolidated-act/28 (accessed on 8 February 2016).
[79] Ndulo, "African Customary Law, Customs, and Women's Rights", *Cornell Law Faculty Publications*, 2011, p. 89 (http://scholarship.law.cornell.edu/facpub/187 (accessed on 8 February 2016).
[80] Koboyankwe. "Legal Pluralism and discriminatory application of progressive laws to women subject to customary law in Botswana". Graduation thesis, Loyola University, Chicago School of Law, 2013–2014, p. 18.
[81] Bennett, "Law as expression of culture", in Steyn & Motshabi (eds), *Cultural Synergy in South Africa*, Knowledge Resources, Johannesburg, 1996, p. 51.

discretion. If the dispute can be decided on grounds of either customary or official law, the parties are free to decide which system to adopt. If they cannot reach agreement, the decision will be made by the court.

However, while customary law must conform to the Constitution, the South African Law Commission began to examine customary law too, to recommend changes and ensure its compatibility with the Constitution, especially to avoid discrimination (for example, in the context of marriage or succession). The Law Commission published a draft law entitled *Application of Customary Law Bill: Conflict of Personal Laws.* The proposal suggests endowing courts with the discretion to choose when to apply local customs or civil law, and recommends that in so doing, judges take into consideration elements such as:

a. The law chosen by the parties to the case;
b. The type of dispute or legal action;
c. The location of the dispute or legal action;
d. The lifestyle of the parties involved; and
e. Their understanding of customary and common law[82].

According to some scholars[83], the advantages of the traditional justice system are superior compared to its disadvantages. Among the advantages are their: accessibility in geographical and social terms; availability (considering the low transport costs, the minimal "fees" required for their use and the absence of any need to appoint expensive professionals); application of local customs that are familiar to traditional leaders and claimants alike; application of simple and informal procedures; and use of a familiar local language. The disadvantages include the exclusion of legal professionals (which may be relevant when enforcing constitutional protections) and of women as officials and witnesses, as well as the fact that the deciding figure often lacks legal training.

In any case, it must be recalled that according to the ACRWC, the application of customary law must be guided by the principle of the best interest of the child, which is but one of the fundamental rights of children in international law. As in the constitutional law of many legal systems, solutions to legal problems in this sphere are directed by this very concept. Such an approach requires that in matters concerning children, courts choose the legal system that best meets their best interest.

In *Hlophe v Mahlalela*, decided by the High Court of South Africa, after his wife's death, the claimant sought custody of their son. The claimant and his wife had been married in civil law. According to local custom, however, the claimant was required to pay the *lobolo* (livestock dowry) in full to the family of the bride, pending which the child would be obliged to live with his maternal grandmother. The High Court stated that in matters concerning child custody, the

---

[82] South Africa Law Reform Commission Report. 2002, p. 8 (http://www.section27.org.za/wp-content/uploads/2010/04/09Manual.pdf (accessed on 8 February 2016).

[83] Souh African Law Commission. "Discussion Paper 82 on The Harmonisation of the Common Law and Indigenous Law: Traditional Courts and the Judicial Function of Traditional Leaders". May 1999, http://www.justice.gov.za /salrc/dpapers/dp82_prj90_tradl_1999.pdf (accessed on 6 June 2016).

interests of the child are a pre-eminent consideration. Parties who have contracted a civil law marriage are to be recognized remedies regulated by civil law[84]. This principle does not exclude the applicability of local customs; rather, it provides direction as to which body of law should be applied, which may be, equally, either civil law or local custom. As this principle now forms part of international law, as enshrined in the CRC and the ACRWC, it should guide the choice of law in all countries that have ratified them, and therefore in matters concerning children. The principle of the "best interest of the child", established by the CRC and the ACRWC, should thus enable the resolution of the main conflicts in terms of choice of law.

According to the ACRWC, which safeguards positive local customs, nothing prevents from juvenile justice from being administered by traditional leaders. However, as per the ACRWC, the criteria applied in deciding must conform to its own provisions. Therefore, traditions leaders must make a commitment to that effect, because otherwise, the application of local customs would bring about a deterioration of the protection standards established by the ACRWC.

1.6 Local customs in South African case law

The ACRWC envisages the use of local customs, which often entails the existence, within African legal orders, of two parallel systems: local customs and common law. Local customs are customs that are well-entrenched in local culture, regulate daily life and are considered binding. Common law, on the other hand, is a normative system composed of legislative acts and judicial precedent.

With regard to the criteria to be followed when deciding whether to apply local customs or positive law, this section will examine three judgments issued in South Africa. The judgments all concern the succession of minors; however, each reached different conclusions.

In the first decision, the South African judge chose local customs on the rights of the clan over the rights of the child; in the other two, official law recognized the children's rights on the basis of the positive law in force.

In particular, the following paragraphs will examine the interpretative criteria that lead to the choice of local customs or positive law, both of which are envisaged by the ACRWC.

---

[84] Court Transvaal Provincial Division, *Hlophe vs Mahlalela and another*, [24 June 1997] 1998, Case no. 13084/95 (http://learning.ufs.ac.za/RPL224_OFF/Resources/1%20RESOURCES/3.Additional%20material%20and%20 court%20cases/16.%20%20HLOPHE%20V%20MAHLALELA%20AND%20ANOTHER%201998%20 910%20SA%20449/HLOPHE%20V%20MAHLALELA%20AND%20ANOTHER%201998%20910%20SA%20 449.pdf, accessed on 22 March 2016): "What was clear was (1) that in custody matters the interests of the child had to take precedence; (2) that where parties concluded a marriage by civil rights after a customary marriage it imposed on the spouses a new personal status governed by the common law, with the result that the parent-child relationship was governed by the common law; ...(At 458E/F--459C.) Though counsel for applicant had during the course of the trial tendered the outstanding *lobolo* to respondent it was plain that issues relating to the custody of a minor child could not be determined by the mere delivery or non-delivery of a certain number of cattle".

Judges are required to apply one criterion or the other, on the basis of the best interest of the child. As mentioned above, this is the main principle that must guide the judges' work.

In *Mthembu v Letsela and another*[85], the mother of Thembi, a seven-year-old girl who was born out of wedlock, sought to enforce her right to succeed upon the death of the child's father. African local custom upholds the system of male primogeniture prevails, such that property may be passed only to a male descendant heir, parent or grandparent. The heir must be male, because in traditional society, only a man may be the head of the family. In succession cases, local custom establishes that when the dies, her surviving spouse manages the family property; when the husband dies, the heir gains control of the family property and succeeds to the legal position of the deceased. The heir is the first male son of the (monogamous) marriage, and is charged with taking care of the family property and protecting its members, including the widow[86]. The surviving wife has no personal rights over the family property, although she is entitled to use it[87]. Such rules perpetuate male predominance and pursue the goals of family unity and economic stability[88].

According to local customs, the death of the husband does not end the marriage. The wife (who is not to be termed a widow) remains such, and a member of his family. In other words, the wife and the deceased are still legally married. The duty to support applies only to the legitimate widow and son.

Therefore, the case was decided on the basis of the fact that Thembi was the deceased's illegitimate child, and as such could not qualify as the heir to the deceased's property. In this case, the system of male primogeniture leads to discrimination, not only towards women and children, but also against children born out of wedlock. The duty to support the widow and her children should necessarily correspond to the system of male primogeniture[89]. In the case at hand, the deceased promised that he would pay the *lobolo* in full; however, at the time he died, he had paid 45 percent of the established amount. This circumstance should be taken into consideration when referring to the notion of the best interest of the child, and constitute a valid reason to hold that the conditions for a valid marriage had been met, such that Thembi was, therefore, a legitimate child[90].

---

[85] First case to question the constitutionality of succession carried out according to customary law.

[86] Supreme Court of Appeal, *Mthembu v Letsela*, 30 May 2000, (71/98), para. 8 (http://www.saflii. org/za/ cases/ZASCA/2000/181.html, accessed on 1 February 2016): "When the head of the family dies his heir takes his position as head of the family and becomes owner of all the deceased's property, movable and immovable; he becomes liable for the debts of the deceased and assumes the deceased's position as guardian of the women and minor sons in the family. He is obliged to support and maintain them, if necessary from his own resources, and not to expel them from his home".

[87] *Ibidem*, para. 2.

[88] As noted by the Law Reform Commission of the United Republic of Tanzania, the widow is "kicked out from the matrimonial home by relatives of the deceased under the pretext of safeguarding clan interests". See Ezer, "Inheritance law in Tanzania: the impoverishment of widows and daughters", *The Georgetown Journal of gender and the law*, 2006, p. 623.

[89] *Ibidem*, para. 11.

[90] Van Rensburg, "Mthembu v Letsela: the non-decision", 2001, p. 10, (accessed on 06 June 2016, http://www. nwu.ac.za /files/images/2001x1xjvr_art.pdf).

The best interest of both parties, and especially of the child, could be better pursued if the marriage were considered valid from the very beginning, overlooking that the full amount of the *lobolo* had never been paid because of the husband's premature death. This conclusion is based on the fact that, on the contrary, it is not necessary to pay the *lobolo* in full for the marriage to be deemed valid, and that the best interest of the child must always be pursued.

The judgment applied local customs, without taking into consideration the ACRWC and the principle of the best interest of the child. Article 21 ACRWC establishes that social and cultural customs that adversely impact the life of the child and that lead to discrimination against some children for gender and other reasons should be disapplied.

The Court should have followed the second approach outlined above, and held that the claimant, as putative spouse of the deceased, was able to inherit on the basis of the common law on succession, in particular Article 1(1)(c) of the law on succession[91].

However, the approach adopted by South African courts radically changed a few years later. In *Bhe and Others v Magistrate Khayelitsha*[92], the Constitutional Court of South Africa declared that the system of male primogeniture was incompatible with the Constitution[93]. The facts are similar to those of the first case. The mother of two female children born out of wedlock sought to enforce the daughters' right to succession to the property of their deceased father. However, unlike the judgment in *Mthembu*, the Constitutional Court expressly recognized that local customs on succession discriminate on grounds of sex, age and birth, and violate the children's constitutional rights. The Constitutional Court of South Africa held that to assign different rights to children depending on whether they were born within a marriage or out of wedlock is discrimination on grounds of birth[94]. The majority of the judges considered that a fair and equitable remedy on the devolution of their father's estate could be regulated by Article 81 of the 1987 Intestate Succession Act.

Scholarship has noted that comparatively, *Bhe* was a better judgment to *Mthembu*, [although] both judgments manifest similar flaws. The main criticisms against these decisions rests on two aspects:

---

[91] *Ibidem*, p. 13.

[92] Constitutional Court of South Africa, *Bhe and Others v Magistrate Khayelitsha*. 15 October 2004, (para. 47). P. 28. http://www.saflii.org/za/cases/ZACC/2004/17.html, accessed on 20 December 2016.

[93] Section 23 of the *Black Administration Act* on the application of male primogeniture were held unconstitutional under Articles 9 (equality) and 10 (dignity) of the Constitution.

[94] "The Court went on to examine the relevant provisions of the African Children's Charter, noting that Article 3 of the African Charter on the Rights and Welfare of the Child provides that children are entitled to enjoy the rights and freedoms recognised and guaranteed in the Charter 'irrespective of the child's or his/her parents' or legal guardians' race, ethnic group, colour, sex, birth or other status'. The Court found that unfair discrimination on the ground of 'birth' should be interpreted to include a prohibition of differentiation between children on the grounds of whether the children's parents were married at the time of conception or birth. The differentiation was thus found to be unfair discrimination. The wording of article 3 appears to have played a significant role in the Court's decision". Skelton. "The development of a fledgling child rights jurisprudence in Eastern and Southern Africa based on international and regional instruments". *African Human Rights Law Journal*. Vol.2. 2009, pp. 482-500.

the manner in which they both apply customary law and their failure/reluctance to develop it, and the manner in which they dismally neglect the best interest principle which is a fundamental principle of both customary and constitutional law[95].

More recently, *Maneli vs Maneli* concerned a dispute between two spouses who had married in 1992 according to local custom. In 1997, they legally adopted a child as per the requirements of local Xhosa custom[96]. The parties separated in 2004 and the child remained in the care of the mother, the claimant. Although the respondent supported the child and provided for his education and medical needs while the couple lived together, he argued that after the separation, he was no longer obliged to continue such support. His reasoning was based on the fact that he was not the biological father of the child and had not adopted him legally, as established by the Children Act of 2005. The Court held that the respondent was legally obliged to support the child as per Article 10(9) of the Maintenance Act 99 of 1998[97]. The Court clarified that local customs and common law must both be compatible with the best interest of the child.

The broader question is that of the conformity, in Africa, of local customs to international human rights standards. To this end, it is necessary to evaluate what should be retained and what, instead, discarded of African culture and tradition such as to guarantee the protection of the rights of children. The ACRWC's approach is to foster the cultural practices that constitute an advance in the promotion of children's rights and to disapply those deemed harmful to the protection of children's rights.

The Constitution of South Africa invites all courts to lean towards interpretations that conform to international law[98], including the ACRWC. Indeed, the child's best interest is one of the basic principles of international law regarding children. Decisions regarding children must aim to enhance their growth and development. Another fundamental rule is that children's participation is compulsory and the voices of children are to be heard in all cultural practices in which they

---

[95] Precillar, "The relevance of culture and religion to the understanding of children's rights in South Africa", *op. cit.*, p. 43.

[96] Chapter 4 of the Child Care Act, no. 74 of 1983, today Chapter of the Children's Act, no. 38 of 2005.

[97] South Gauteng High Court, *Maneli vs Maneli*, [19 April 2010], Case no. 14/3/2-234/05 (http://www.saflii.org /za/cases/ZAGPJHC/2010/22.html, accessed on 18 March 2016). The Court examined several provisions of the Constitution. Article 28(2) of the Constitution states that "[a] child's best interests are of paramount importance in every matter concerning the child". Article 211(3) affirms that: "[t]he courts must apply customary law when that law is applicable, subject to the Constitution and any legislation that specifically deals with customary law". According to Article 30, "[e]veryone has the right to use the language and to participate in the cultural life of their choice, but no one exercising these rights may do so in a manner inconsistent with any provision of the Bill of Rights."

[98] Article 39 of the Constitution of the Republic of South Africa provides that: "[w]hen interpreting the Bill of Rights, a court, tribunal or forum (a) must promote the values that underlie an open and democratic society based on human dignity, equality and freedom; (b) must consider international law; and (c) may consider foreign law."

participate. Although children do not have specific rights, local customs endow them with the chance to express their needs and opinions[99].

The role of courts should not be underestimated in the balancing of the right to culture and local customs and other constitutionally protected rights. An approach that is sensitive to local customs ensures that judges evaluate the constitutionality of customary law[100].

A fundamental principle is that of equality and tolerance[101]. These values should guide the interpretation of the best interest towards a multicultural approach[102]. Several studies have demonstrated that local customs are verifiable and can evolve, especially those regarding inheritance, which adapt to changes in the family's socio-economic circumstances[103]. Omotola argues that "living customary law" certainly recognizes the best interest of the child in so far as it enables reaching a fair and equitable solution, in accordance with values that assure the continuity and cohesion of the family as a unit.

Nevertheless, it is interesting that no mention is made of the best interest of the child in *Tembi* and *Mthembu*. Himonga noted that "inheritance rights must not be seen merely as a matter of rights that should be protected by laws as such, but also as a way of realising the child's right to life and survival"[104].

In *Bhe,* the court based its decision on the supremacy of common law. however, in a dissenting opinion, Justice Ngcobo stated that where there are minor children it may therefore be in their *best interest,* in certain circumstances, that indigenous law be applied"[105]. Second, the judge recognized that "that it is always in the best interests of the child for the family unit to be protected and kept intact. International, regional and domestic human rights instruments all recognise that the family environment is the best for children"[106].

---

[99] Himonga, "The Right of the Child to Participate in Decision Making: A Perspective from Zambia", in Ncube (ed), *Law, Culture,Tradition and Children's Rights in Eastern and Southern Africa*, Burlington USA, Ashgate, 1998, p.10.

[100] Lehnert, "Role of the Courts in the Conflict between African Customary Law and Human Rights", *South African Journal on Human Rights*, 2005, p. 265.

[101] Pieterse, "Culture and Customary Law in a Society Founded on Non- Racialism", *South African Law Journal*, 2001, p. 403.

[102] Nazeem Goolam, "Constitutional Interpretation of the "Best Interests" Principle in South Africa in Relation to Custody", in Eeckelaar and Nhlapo (ed), *The Changing Family: International Perspectives on the Family and Family Law*, Portland, Hart Publishing, 2008, p. 370.

[103] Precillar, "The relevance of culture and religion to the understanding of children's rights in South Africa", *op. cit.*, p. 47.

[104] Himonga, *Protecting the minor child's inheritance rights. The International Survey of Family Law*, Bristol, Jourdan Publishing, 2001, p. 457.

[105] Precillar, "The relevance of culture and religion to the understanding of children's rights in South Africa", *op cit.*, p. 48.

[106] *Ibidem*, p. 49.

For many scholars, the family is the best institution that can guarantee the welfare of the child. It is important that judges and legislators be aware of this cultural value when making decisions, because on this basis, it is possible to act in the best interest of the child. Therefore, it is noteworthy that the decisions examined above ascertained that the best traditional practices were widespread and pursued in the best interest of the children, and not turned into a pretext for abusing those children[107].

In practice, abuse may still occur in the context of custody, even if local customs are applied. Indeed, there do exist cultural traditions that are adverse to children. In these cases, positive law may legally qualify individual cases, ensuring that reference is made to cultural and traditional principles, but, where the latter are insufficient to protect the child, positive law is capable of identifying legal responsibility.

In *Mthembu v Letsela*, local customs were considered without interpreting them in function of the best interest of the child. On the other hand, in *Bhe v Magistrate Khayelitsha*, according to the Court's interpretation, local customs obviously violated the child's rights and were not, therefore, applied. Finally, in *Maneli v Maneli*, tradition and law were considered together, in a complementary relationship: the marriage had been contracted according to local custom and deemed valid by positive law, while the rights of the children were established by positive law.

Thus, the judgments were compatible with the ACRWC and the criteria it established for balancing rights. The ACRWC was granted effectiveness to pursue the best interest of the child, between local customs and observance of the ACRWC's own provisions.

1.7 Conclusions

The drafters of the ACRWC intended to adapt the standards of child protection established by the CRC to the African child and specific context and, as stated in the Preamble, to the "the unique factors of their socio-economic, cultural, traditional and developmental circumstances, natural disasters, armed conflicts, exploitation and hunger".

The ACRWC has the merit of drawing attention to specific needs of the child, which otherwise would have been excluded from the protection of those rights not enshrined in the CRC, given the particular needs of the African context.

---

[107] Consider the accusations of witchcraft made against children, with the consequent concerted actions undertaken through the child's clan (as per Article 161(2) of Law n. 09/001 of 10 January 2009 on child protection, of the Democratic Republic of the Congo: *"En cas d'accusation de sorcellerie à l'égard d'un enfant, l'auteur est puni de un à trois ans de servitude pénale principale et d'une amende de deux cents mille à un million de francs congolais".*) In Kinshasa, there has been a dramatic and disturbing increase in the number of witchcraft accusations against children (made often by relatives, and even parents: De Boeck, Plissart, *Kinshasa. Tales of the Invisible City*, Leuven, Leuven University Press, 2004, p. 156).

On one hand, the ACRWC recognizes (Article 1) that custom, tradition, cultural and religious practices are to be discouraged in so far as they are inconsistent with the rights, duties and obligations established by the ACRWC itself. On the other, however, it also acknowledges the positive force of the cultural heritage, history and values of African civilization, which, according to the Preamble, should inspire and characterize reflection on the notion of the rights and welfare of the child.

The ACRWC appears to provide for a dual track: one consisting in the validity of local customs (Preamble, Article 11, Article 46) and the rights established in the ACRWC itself. Local customs may be applied when they provide a greater standard of protection than the ACRWC in ensuring the protection of the best interest of the child. A number of legal texts that pursue such a purpose were tested in the application of the ACRWC. However, African states must yet undertake significant efforts to interpret and apply local customs in light of the ACRWC's principle of the best interest of the child and achieve an effective balance between the two systems.

The next chapter will analyse in further detail the ACRWC's provisions on protecting children in typically African contexts, to evaluate its actual application and scope for protection.

CHAPTER

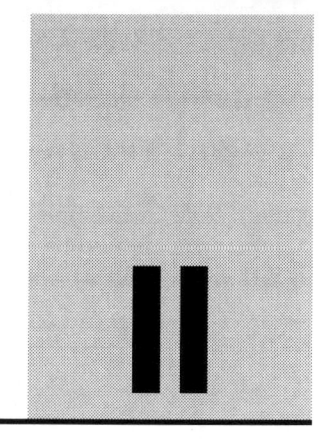

APPLYING THE ACRWC IN THE AFRICAN CONTEXT: EFFECTIVENESS

The Preamble to the ACRWC recognizes the positive force that the cultural heritage, history and values of African civilization may have, which should inspire and characterize the rights and welfare of children. In addition, Article 11(2)(c) on education states that "[t]he education of the child shall be directed to [...] the preservation and strengthening of positive African morals, traditional values and cultures", while Article 46 affirms that "The Committee shall draw inspiration from International Law on Human Rights [...] and from African values and traditions."

On the other hand, the ACRWC takes pains to contrast the efficacy of local customs that are incompatible with the fundamental rights enshrined in the ACRWC. Indeed, Article 1(3) states that "[a]ny custom, tradition, cultural or religious practice that is inconsistent with the rights, duties and obligations contained in the present Charter shall to the extent of such inconsistency be discouraged." However, the provision does not clarify the means through which, nor the parties entrusted with, discouraging such practices. It may be stated that this task pertains, first and foremost, to the States Parties, as per Article 21(1)(a) ACRWC: "States Parties to the present Charter shall take all appropriate measures to eliminate harmful social and cultural practices affecting the welfare, dignity, normal growth and development of the child and in particular [...] those customs and practices prejudicial to the health or life of the child." Article 1(1) ACRWC provides that the States Parties shall "adopt such legislative or other measures as may be necessary to give effect to the provisions of this Charter." Therefore, it is necessary to examine which measures should be adopted by the States Parties to prevent violations of the rights of children, punish those responsible for such violations and assure the rehabilitation and reintegration into society of the victims.

Such an examination is certainly complex, because of the interdependence of human rights and of the fact an adverse practice may violate more than one right at the same time – thus, several provisions of the ACRWC – as well as the fact that violations of human rights may concern several categories of persons, such as handicapped children, refugee children, etc.

This chapter shall examine the main adverse practices that violates fundamental rights protected by the ACRWC and that may be considered "typical" of the African context. In particular, these practices are Female Genital Mutilation (FGM), forced marriages, the rights of handicapped children, refugee children and child soldiers, child trafficking, and displaced children. The ACRWC's effectiveness in protecting these categories will be analysed.

II.1   Protecting against negative social and cultural practices

The ACRWC acknowledges the positive force of the cultural heritage, history and values of African civilization. Article 21 ACRWC protects children from cultural practices deemed "negative", inviting States Parties to abolish those practices that are prejudicial to the dignity, welfare, normal growth and development of the child, and that are discriminatory on grounds of sex or other reasons. In particular, the marriage and engagement of individuals under 18 years of age is prohibited. Article 4 ACRWC, according to which the best interest of the child is to be a primary consideration in all actions undertaken by any person or authority; it flows that actions or events falling under the definition of harmful cultural practices are not in the best interest of the child, regardless of their traditional significance and value to traditional culture.

Indeed, such traditional cultural practices reflect the values and beliefs of the members of a given community, creating common ground among generations. All social groups in the world share specific practices and beliefs, which often have strong cultural bases. These may be legitimate or not, if they contrast with the provisions of the ACRWC. An example is FGM, practiced upon young girls, and the consequent violation of the right to health protected by Article 14 ACRWC. Harmful cultural practices persist because individuals and communities may, at times, hesitate to give up what they consider important, even though they realize its harmfulness.

The practices followed by States Parties in implementing the ACRWC may be usefully examined to more precisely identify the content of the ACRWC's provision. Indeed, the ACRWC is binding upon the states that have ratified it. Therefore, they are required to ensure that their domestic legislation conforms to the ACRWC. Several countries have abolished those traditional practices that are incompatible with human rights[108]. Certain states, such as Uganda[109] or Ghana[110], have established that harmful practices are to be considered illegal. Other states have introduced specific measures to ban those practices deemed "negative". For example, South Africa has

---

[108] For example, Article 14 of Kenya's Children's Act provides that "no person shall subject a child to female circumcision, early marriage or other cultural rites, customs or traditional practices that are likely to negatively affect the child's life, health, social welfare, dignity or physical or psychological development".

[109] See Article 5 of Uganda's Children Statute 1996: "A child has the right to be protected from any social or customary practices that are dangerous to the child's health".

[110] According to Article 26(2) of Ghana's Constitution, "all customary practices which dehumanize or are injurious to the physical and mental well-being of a person are prohibited".

expressly prohibited genital mutilation (Section 12(3) of the Children's Act)[111]. Ethiopia imposes a penalty of three to five years' imprisonment for infibulation (Article 565 of the Criminal Code)[112].

More specifically, Kenya's Prohibition of Female Genital Mutilation Act 2011 bans and punishes FGM. The law criminalizes the aiding and abetting of FGM by procuring persons who perform the excision; the transportation of a person from Kenya to another country (and from another country into Kenya) to perform FGM; the possession of tools or equipment connected with FGM; the failure to report commission of the offence to the authorities; the performance of FGM outside Kenya; and the use of derogatory language against those who have not been subjected to FGM.

The law may also protect children only in part, providing that certain traditional practices shall not be performed on children under a certain age. Article 12(2)(5) of South Africa's Children's Act[113] does not appear to be ACRWC-compliant: the latter protects children under the age of eighteen without exception, because these would contrast with the best interest of children. Therefore, the national standard of protection is lower than that provided by the ACRWC and should be enhanced to match it.

The practice under examination may be useful to understand how the ACRWC's obligation to "discourage" traditional practices incompatible with human rights may be implemented. In this regard, it is necessary to ask whether it is enough to enact legislation banning such practices, or whether states should also adopt other positive actions capable of bearing an impact on the culture of local populations, to bring about real change. Indeed, according to Article 1 ACRWC, States Parties undertake to the "necessary steps" to adopt such legislative or "other" measures as may be necessary. Therefore, the ACRWC envisages the possibility of open interventions, at states' discretion, to implement the ACRWC's provisions. Legal measures are certainly the most appropriate means through which to introduce internal, generally applicable obligations. However, when seeking to ensure that the domestic order is ACRWC-compliant, States Parties should also take all appropriate measures required to abolish customs and practices that have an adverse effect on the health or life of children, as established by Article 21 ACRWC.

According to Eritrea's country report[114], the country's Minister of Health has formulated a national scheme to eliminate FGM and accompanying promotional material, including a documentary

---

[111] The Children's Act prohibits FGM: "Genital mutilation or the circumcision of female children is prohibited" (Article 12(3)).

[112] Ethiopia Initial Report on the implementation of the ACRWC, p. 120, http://acerwc.org/?wpdmdl=8645, accessed on 27 December 2015).

[113] Article 12(2)(5) of the South Africa Children's Act allows for virginity tests from 16 years of age, with the consent of the person to be tested. Therefore, the practice has not been abolished, as Article 3 ACRWC calls for, but rather simply mitigated, requiring that the child give consent and that the established methods be applied: "Virginity testing of children older than 16 may only be performer-
    a)   If the child has given consent to the testing in the prescribed manner;
    b)   After proper counseling of the child; and
    c)   in the manner prescribed."

[114] Eritrea Initial Report on the implementation of the ACRWC, p. 44, http://acerwc.org/?wpdmdl=897, accessed on 27 December 2015.

illustrating the changes in community behaviour. This shows that awareness campaigns involving the media contributes to the fight against FGM.

Should the parties entrusted with "discouraging" such practices be states alone, or would it be desirable – and perhaps more effective – to involve the base? The Preamble to the ACRWC considers "that the promotion and protection of the rights and welfare of the child also implies the performance of duties on the part of everyone". However, it does not define who "everyone" should be. The first parties with the duty to fight harmful traditional practices are not NGOs, but rather governments and African regional organizations. The African Union may encourage governments to pass and enhance legislation against such practices, and even establish measures that control their implementation. However, civil society and NGOs do play an important part in raising awareness regarding harmful practices. While legal reform is a necessary step, it may nevertheless be insufficient if unaccompanied by intervention to change the cultural beliefs behind such practices. Harmful traditional practices, or "HTP are sometimes viewed as a religious issue, in that some are officially promoted by religious leaders, some leaders never speak out against it, and others have banned these practices, but they are still practiced by people in the name of religion […] [R]eligious leaders need to be included in the dialogue on HTP at all times, and […] a Conference should be held with religious leaders under the auspices of the AU on HTP"[115]. It is important that the population living in rural areas be aware of and understand their rights. In this connection, language is a significant obstacle. It must therefore be emphasized that laws and documents should be translated into local languages, such that their addressees may fully understand them. This requirement to translate should also extend to the results of research on the harmfulness of the practices.

According to Article 1 ACRWC, the laws against HTP should be complemented with measures relating to education, health, awareness campaigns among the elders on the current legal framework, the involvement of religious leaders as essential guides to change, and the participation of traditional leaders and civil society. Several African states are engaged in efforts to eliminate HTP by legislative means but also through awareness-raising measures targeting communities. However, despite these initiatives, there remains a vast gap between the aspirations and values embodied in current legislation, on one hand, and reality on the other, where HTP endure.

Together, the AU States have discussed which measures to take to discourage, for example, FGM. The Pan-African Conference on Celebrating Courage and Overcoming Harmful Traditional Practices in Africa (Addis Ababa, Ethiopia, 5-7 October 2011) organized by the AU Commission and the Deutsche Gesellschaft für International Zusammenarbeit (GIZ), a German company supporting the German government in attaining its international cooperation objectives within the context of sustainable development, was attended by 80 representatives of 24 African countries.

---

[115] "Panafrican Conference on celebrating courage and overcoming harmful traditional practices in Africa", Plenary Session, Session I, Human Rights and Legal Protection of Women and Girls with regard to HTP. 5-7 October 2011, Addis Ababa, Ethiopia, p. 7 (http://sa.au.int/en/sites/default/files/English%20Final%20 Report%20HTP%20.pdf, accessed on 13 June 2016).

The purpose of the Conference was to help Africa find African solutions to African problems arising from sociocultural factors.

The Inter-African Committee on Traditional Practices (IAC) deserves a separate mention. The IAC is an African regional protection body in charge of elaborating political programmes and actions to halt HTP such as FGM in the African continent. The IAC was created to materialize the duties imposed upon States Parties by Article 1(3) ACRWC, according to which "[a] ny custom, tradition, cultural or religious practice that is inconsistent with the rights, duties and obligations contained in the present Charter shall to the extent of such inconsistency be discouraged" through the efforts of the States Parties themselves. The IAC was established by the African delegates during a seminar organized by a United Nations Non-Governmental Working Group on Traditional practices headquartered in Geneva, Switzerland, with the support of the United Nations Population Fund (UNFPA), the United Nations Children's Fund (UNICEF), the World Health Organization (WHO) and the Ministry of Health of Senegal. At the time of the IAC's institution[116], FGM was a highly sensitive and controversial topic.

The IAC's mission is, self-proclaimedly, to free Africa from FGM and harmful gender-based practices. Operating within the context of the implementation of the 1979 United Nations Convention on the Elimination of all Forms of Discrimination Against Women (CEDAW), which protects women's human rights in all fields, as established in its Article 1, the IAC was able to contribute crucially to the development, at all levels, of policies on harmful practices, especially FGM. In particular, its work led to the creation of mechanisms to monitor the efforts made by various interested parties (governments, UN organizations, parliaments, legislators, politicians, NGOs) fighting HTP and campaigning for the inclusion of courses on FGM, forced marriage and child marriage in the syllabuses of African schools and universities.

In the 29 African countries where FGM are a traditional practice, the IAC national committees and their affiliated partners have spared no effort to prevent FGM at the local level. In 1998 (Banjul, Gambia), 2001 (Dar Es Salaam, United Republic of Tanzania), 2005 (Egypt and Burkina Faso) and 2007 (Abidjan, Côte d'Ivoire), the IAC organized conferences for religious leaders, creating a network of African religious leaders against FGM and for development. In 2000, the IAC created the Regional Network of Youth for the elimination of female genital mutilation (FGM), composed of young people in its 29 Member States. The second Forum of this Network was held in November 2006, in Addis Ababa, and resulted in the formulation of a program involving young people at national and regional levels.

---

[116] The headquarters of the IAC are in Addis Ababa, Ethiopia, where it is registered as a non-profit organization. It has a liaison office in Geneva. The IAC has national divisions, called national committees, in 29 African countries and is in contact with groups of African citizens who have emigrated through its many affiliates in the world (Belgium, France, United Kingdom, Spain, Germany, Sweden, Norway, Italy, Canada, USA, New Zealand, Japan). The IAC has consultative status at the United Nations (UN/UNESCO) and holds observer status with the AU. It works in collaboration with the UNFPA, the WHO and UNICEF and is a member of the NGO network affiliated to the International Organization of French-speaking countries. The IAC also collaborates with various international organizations active in the field of the protection of the human rights of women and children.

On the basis of the awareness and advocacy work done by the IAC since 1984, sixteen African countries have developed specific legislation[117]. These countries are Benin (2003), Burkina Faso (1995), Côte d'Ivoire (1998), Djibouti (1994), Egypt (2008), Eritrea (2007), Ethiopia (2005), Ghana (2007), Guinea (2000), Kenya (2001), Nigeria (2002), Central African Republic (1995), Senegal (1999), United Republic of Tanzania (1998), Chad (2002) and Togo (1998).

These efforts show how the elimination of cultural traditions and practices inconsistent with the rights enshrined in the ACRWC require, in addition to specific prohibiting legislation, other forms of cultural mediation to eradicate such phenomena in the long term.

II.1.1   The Commission's observations on traditional practices

Country reports are useful to discern the practices that are considered positive, as they describe the measures undertaken and progress made towards the abolition or, at least, discouragement, of HTP inconsistent with the ACRWC.

As emerges from Lesotho's country report[118], positive African practices are, for example, breastfeeding and carrying children on one's back. Burkina Faso's report[119] shows that positive values, traditions and practices for children are also the form of solidarity, persisting in certain communities, which enables the recovery of a child who has lost one or both parents; extended breastfeeding, which occurs especially in rural regions; and carrying children on the back, which fosters the child's affective development.

Negative practices include FGM, forced marriage, child marriage, tattoos and scarification (which entail the risk of infecting and transmitting HIV), the marginalization and rejection of certain more vulnerable categories of children[120], the education of children with principles based on the division of labour according to sex, discrimination against girls, and food-based taboos which endure in certain regions.

The measures to foster positive practices are the creation of the Ministry of Social Action and National Security, and a General Directorate of National Solidarity. The main concern is to strengthen, other than solidarity, the creation of a National Solidarity Fund financed by the state,

---

[117] United Nations Division for the Advancement of Women, United Nations Economic Commission for Africa, "Report of Expert Group Meeting on good practices in legislation to address harmful practices against women", [UN doc.EGM/GPLHP/2009/EP.07], United Nations Conference Centre. Addis Ababa, Ethiopia. 25–28 May 2009 (http://www.un.org/womenwatch/daw/egm/vaw_legislation_2009/Expert%20Paper%20 EGMGPLHP%20_Morissanda%20Kouyate_.pdf accessed on 18 July 2015).

[118] Lesotho Initial Report on the implementation of the ACRWC, p. 10, http://acerwc.org/?wpdmdl=8774, accessed on 27 December 2015.

[119] Burkina Faso Initial Report on the implementation of the ACRWC, p. 10, http://acerwc.org/?wpdmdl=8780, accessed on 27 December 2015.

[120] In Lesotho, according to superstition, such children should be sent away. See Lesotho Initial Report, *op. cit.*, p. 10.

and of the Ministry of Health and the Family, which would operate to promote the health of the child and maternal breastfeeding.

As for the definition of the negative practice of child marriage, according to Article 21 ACRWC, Article 195 of Rwanda's Criminal Code[121] punishes those who participate in the forced marriage of minors. A person who lives or attempts to live with a child as husband and wife receives the same punishment as those who corrupt minors. Those who live together as husband and wife with individuals under 21 years of age are also punished.

In this respect, the protection is greater than that afforded by the ACRWC, according to which the age of adulthood is 18.

On the subject of exclusively legislative action against child marriage in Rwanda, the Commission observed that the practice endures, and recommended that the State Party take all measures required to eradicate all types of cultural practices that could harm the health and good development of children, especially to: raise awareness among the population; involve traditional and religious leaders in the fight against such practices; adopt and implement legal and criminal provisions to punish the perpetrators and their accomplices, as well as to train judges and police forces; and create phone helplines and online services to report child abuse and violence[122].

In Senegal[123], according to Article 18 of the Criminal Code, forced marriage is a violation of personal freedom and, if affecting children under the age of 13, is punished with a term of imprisonment between two to five years, as well as a fine.

In this regard, the Commission encouraged Senegal to hold awareness campaigns, efforts to train on and promote the human rights of children (especially girls), initiatives to raise awareness among and involve *marabouts*, priests and other religious and social leaders on the promotion of the rights of boys and girls, focusing on violence and FGM, child marriage and the inclusion of a module on children's rights in the initial training programmes for staff in charge of issues relating to children: judges, police forces, gendarmes, military forces and specialized educators or social workers[124].

In addition, the Commission[125] invited the South African government to take all measures required to fight the practice of *ukuthwala,* which, as will be seen in further detail later, girls subjected to forced marriage. In addition, the ACERWC recommended the adoption of measures to abolish virginity tests for children.

---

[121] Rwanda Initial Report on the implementation of the ACRWC, p. 47, http://acerwc.org/?wpdmdl=8653, accessed on 27 December 2015.

[122] *Ibidem,* p. 8.

[123] Senegal Initial Report on the implementation of the ACRWC, p. 93, http://acerwc.org/?wpdmdl=8788, accessed on 27 December 2015.

[124] *Ibidem,* p. 8.

[125] Concluding Observations and Recommendations of the ACERWC on the South Africa Report, p. 7, accessed on 27 December 2015.

In Zimbabwe[126], law enforcement is hindered due to the high number of HTP reports. Families and communities collude with one another and cover the HTP that may be pursued, such that it is difficult for the law to fully protect children. In response, the government has formed partnerships to raise awareness of these practices and encourage families and communities to work with the government to protect children.

The ACERWC appreciated the efforts of the Government which, in collaboration with partners such as the UNPFA, has intensified the measures to enhance public awareness of the risks inherent in child marriage. However, the ACERWC noted that the existing law, which allows marriage at 16, increases the rate of child marriages.

The ACERWC noted that 21 percent of girls in Burkina Faso[127] are already married at the age of 15 and 62 percent at the age of 18. The provisions on marriage establish that the legal age for marriage is 17, with the possibility of contracting marriage at 15 for "serious reasons". This too encourages child marriage.

Therefore, the Commission noted that the age of marriage established by law is inconsistent with the provisions of the ACRWC, and recommended that the Government of Burkina Faso proceed to harmonize the age of marriage accordingly.

The Commission recommended that the State Party reinforce its strategies against excision, FGM and HTP to raise awareness among the competent services of the urgent need to apply legal instruments repressing such practices, such as provisions of the Criminal Code concerning excision. The Commission has suggested a collaboration with the Minister of Social Action and National Solidarity, other ministers and NGOs to address these issues[128].

As for the Egypt report, the Commission notes that the age of marriage does not comply with ACRWC requirements and recommends that States Parties undertake legislative reforms to ensure harmonization in this respect[129].

The Commission called for Guinea to undertake a massive awareness-raising campaign about the negative consequences of child marriage and to ensure that all children are enrolled in school until the age of 18[130].

---

[126] Zimbabwe Initial Report on the implementation of the ACRWC, p. 65, http://acerwc.org/?wpdmdl=8778, accessed on 27 December 2015.

[127] Burkina Faso Initial Report on the implementation of the ACRWC, p. 137, http://www.acerwc.org/?wpdmdl=8780, accessed on 27 December 2015.

[128] Concluding Observations and Recommendations of the ACERWC on the Burkina Faso Report, p. 7, http://www.acerwc.org/?wpdmdl=8740, accessed on 19 January 2016.

[129] Concluding Observations and Recommendations of the ACERWC on the Egypt Report, p. 2, http://www.acerwc.org/?wpdmdl=8743, accessed on 19 January 2016.

[130] Concluding Observations and Recommendations of the ACERWC on the Guinea Report, p. 7, http://www.acerwc.org/?wpdmdl=8745, accessed on 2 February 2016.

With regard to the FGM practices that have not been specifically described in the ACRWC as negative practices, it should be noted that the Commission has always qualified the practice of FGM as negative, and one to be abolished.

Mali[131] undertakes information campaigns, education efforts and communication activities regarding harmful practices such as FGM. Significant progress has been made on the physical and psychological rehabilitation and social integration of children, including: the introduction of standards for care institutions; the prohibition of corporal punishment in schools; the creation of new courts for children; an increase in the number of childcare facilities; the launch of data collection activities on categories of children; and information and awareness programs.

The Commission, considering the extent of the practice of FGM in Mali, has strongly recommended that the Government adopt a legal text to prohibit these practices and severely punish offenders[132].

On the traditional practices of Liberia, the Commission noted with concern the fact that the practice of FGM and other HTP are widespread in all four counties of Montserrado, Bomi, Lofa and Grand Cape Mount. The State Party should hold extensive consultations and then adopt a law that prohibits child FGM, and ensure its implementation[133].

In its Concluding Observations on the Mozambique report, the Commission noted that in certain communities, including refugees and migrants, HTP are still performed. In particular, the Commission recommended that the State Party take appropriate legislative and administrative measures, including creating awareness of the effects of such practices which include child marriage and the killing of albino children to use their body parts in traditional rites[134].

The Commission also noted with concern that Sudan's Child Act does not prohibit excision, which remains common in the country. It has also expressed concern on forced and child marriage. The Commission recommended that the Government of the Republic of Sudan legislate to expressly forbid FGM and set the minimum age of marriage at 18, in accordance with the ACRWC[135].

The Commission recognized that in Ethiopia, FGM and child marriage are prevalent in many regions of the country. The Commission considered it urgent that the Government take the necessary measures to combat these practices, recommending the State Party to adopt practical strategies to reduce and eliminate all forms of HTP, especially child marriages and FGM,

---

[131] Mali Initial Report on the implementation of the ACRWC, p. 46, http://acerwc.org/?wpdmdl=8782, accessed on 27 December 2015.

[132] *Ibidem.* p. 7.

[133] Concluding Observations and Recommendations of the ACERWC on the Liberia Report, p. 14, http://www.acerwc.org/?wpdmdl=8747, accessed on 27 December 2015.

[134] Concluding Observations and Recommendations of the ACERWC on the Mozambique Report, p. 8, http://www.acerwc.org/?wpdmdl=8749, accessed on 27 December 2015.

[135] Concluding Observations and Recommendations of the ACERWC on the Sudan Report, p. 7, http://www.acerwc.org/?wpdmdl=8754, accessed on 27 December 2015.

including through the prosecution of perpetrators and sensitization of the community on these issues[136].

The ACERWC noted with great concern that in Guinea, the FGM rate stands at 97 percent. The ACERWC has therefore requested that its elimination become a priority of the Government and recommended that the following measures be taken: reinforcing the law prohibiting FGM; conducting massive awareness campaigns involving traditional media and leaders; assessing impact by collecting results to verify the efficacy of campaigns; investigating thoroughly, prosecuting and convicting perpetrators; placing an obligation on government officials and the public service to report FGM cases; and establishing an alternative income activity for those who practiced FGM. The Commission also asked for detailed indications on the legal and practical measures adopted against the practice to be included in forthcoming reports. The information should report the number of reported cases and the number of convictions, the number of campaigns and the actions to verify the impact of the measures taken[137].

Finally, the Commission hoped that South Africa would address the issue of the death and mutilation of girls due to poorly executed FGM[138].

Because the prevalence of FGM is extremely high, especially in the Somali community (where 90 percent of girls have been subjected to it) and 53 percent of Kenyan girls are victims of forced marriage, the Commission has recommended that States Parties also develop awareness plans and information programs for the population, to change the prevailing mentality. This is envisaged to lead to a behavioural change that should lead to the abandonment of FGM and forced marriage; the development of mechanisms for reporting the perpetrators of these acts; the training of magistrates and judicial police for the effective application of the right to be free from these practices[139].

From the Commission's recommendations, it may be inferred that the most urgent measure that African states should adopt is to adapt their internal laws to the ACRWC's prohibitions. However, to effectively prevent harmful practices such as child marriage and FGM, institutional measures, effective collaboration between State authorities and measures seeking to change the behaviour of the population (such as awareness-raising campaigns on HTP and their effects) are also necessary. Finally, monitoring the progress of these reforms and campaigns are essential to check the results achieved, or consider whether other, more persuasive ways, may be required.

---

[136] Concluding Observations and Recommendations of the ACERWC on the Ethiopia Report, p. 10, http://www.acerwc.org/?wpdmdl=8744, accessed on 27 December 2015.

[137] Concluding Observations and Recommendations of the ACERWC on the Guinea Report, p. 7, http://www.acerwc.org/?wpdmdl=8745, accessed on 2 February 2016.

[138] Concluding Observations and Recommendations of the ACERWC on the South Africa Report, p. 7, http://www.acerwc.org/?wpdmdl=8754, accessed on 27 December 2015.

[139] *Ibidem*, p. 6.

II.1.2   Female Genital Mutilation (FGM)

Figures for 2014 report that 130 million girls have suffered FGM in 29 African countries[140]. According to UNICEF, "Africa is by far the continent where the phenomenon of FGM is most widespread, with 91.5 million girls over the age of 9 being victims of this practice and approximately 3 million other girls being added to the total every year"[141]. The practice of FGM is documented and monitored by the WHO and the UN in 26 African countries. In some countries, such as Egypt, Guinea, Sudan, Mali and Somalia, women aged between 15 and 49 who have undergone FGM exceed 90 percent[142], with peaks occurring in rural areas. In four other countries (Burkina Faso, Ethiopia, Gambia and Mauritania), FGM has been administered to the majority of women; however, the figures are not as extensive. In five other countries (Chad, Côte d'Ivoire, Guinea Bissau, Kenya and Liberia), the prevalence rate is considered average, ranging between 30 and 40 percent of the female population. In the remaining countries, the diffusion of FGM oscillates between 5 and 19 percent[143].

The age of girls subjected to FGM varies. In Egypt, over 90 percent are "mutilated" between 4 and 15 years of age. In Ethiopia, Mali and Mauritania, 60 percent of girls are subjected to the procedure before they are 5 years old; in Yemen, 76 percent of FGM is performed in the girls' first two weeks of life. Similar variations may be found within individual countries: in Sudan, for example, 75 percent of girls undergo mutilation between 9 and 10 years of age in South Darfur, while 75 percent of girls in the Kassala region between 4 and 5 years. Although constituting a minority, there are situations in which FGM, if not practiced in the first years of life, is administered in adolescence, at the time of marriage, during pregnancy or at the time of delivery[144]. Recent studies have shown a gradual lowering of the age of girls subjected to FGM, which can be explained by the greater ease of concealing these practices where they are forbidden, but also by the greater ease of overcoming any resistance on the part of the girls.

---

[140] UNICEF, "No Time To Lose: On Child Marriage and Female Genital Mutilation /Cutting". 2014. https://www.youtube.com/watch?v=h8TxXOD9X7U, accessed on 3 November 2015.

[141] UNICEF, "Female Genital Mutilation/Cutting: A statistical overview and exploration of the dynamics of change", New York, 2013. p 5. https://www.unicef.it/Allegati/MGF_Report_2013.pdf, accessed on 6 June 2016.

[142] Ministry of Health of the Italian Republic, Commission for the prevention and ban on FGM practices, "Rapporto al Ministro della salute", 9 March 2007, p. 5 (http://www.simmweb.it/fileadmin/documenti/Rapporti_ufficiali/mgf_min_salute_07.pdf, accessed on 4 February 2016.

[143] Istituto Piepoli, "Valutazione quantitativa e qualitative del fenomeno delle mutilazioni genitali in Italia", July 2009, pp. 6-7 (http://www.dirittoegiustizia.it/allegati/17/0000044486/Istituto_Piepoli_S_p_A_Ministero_per_le_Pari_Opportunita_Valutazione_quantitativa_e_qualitativa_del_fenomeno_delle_mutilazioni_genitali_in_Italia_Ricerca_117_01_2009.html, accessed on 28 March 2015).

[144] Ministry of Health of the Italian Republic, Commission for the prevention and ban on FGM practices, "Rapporto al Ministro della salute", 9 March 2007, p. 8 (http://www.simmweb.it/fileadmin/documenti/Rapporti_ufficiali/mgf_min_salute_07.pdf, accessed on 4 February 2016.

Among the practices harmful to health[145], the ACRWC does not expressly mention FGM. However, it can be considered incompatible with Article 21 ACRWC, according to which the practices that may be prejudicial to the health of the child must be abolished, and with Article 14 ACRWC, which states that every child has the right to enjoy the best attainable state of physical, mental and spiritual health.

According to Article 14(i), States Parties undertake to ensure the meaningful participation of non-governmental organizations, local communities and the beneficiary populations in the planning and management of a basic service programme for children. A measure taken by the AU to discourage practices that are harmful and conflict with human rights is the cooperation and assistance agreement with the IAC, to which observer status was granted in 1994 by the Organization of African Unity (the current AU). The IAC believes that the problem of FGM should be addressed in the context of tradition, with tools related to culture, health and human rights. In 29 African countries where genital mutilation is a traditional practice, the IAC works in collaboration with the UNFPA, WHO and UNICEF, is a member of the NGO network affiliated to the International Organisation of la Francophonie, and has intensified its actions to prevent the practice of FGM at local level.

On 20 December 2012, the UN General Assembly adopted a resolution[146] on a universal ban on FGM. The resolution, the adoption of which was promoted by the Ban Female Genital Mutilation Campaign, reflects the universal agreement FGM constitutes a violation of human rights and that all countries of the world should undertake "all necessary measures, including the promulgation and strengthening of legislation prohibiting FGM, to protect women and children from these forms of violence and to end impunity"[147]. Indeed, the law can create an environment conducive to persuading communities to abandon these practices; however, it must be complemented with other measures that guarantee their effective application.

---

[145] In medical terms, FGM poses significant obstacles to child delivery and of a physical and psychological nature; it aggravates inflammation and hinders the ordinary recovery from disease, and puts the reproductive health of women at risk. See, in this connection, Istituto Piepoli, *op. cit.*, p. 39.

[146] UNGA Resolution of 20 December 2012, UN Doc. UN doc. A/RES/67/146, ai par. 4, 12 e 14 recita: "les États à condamner toutes les pratiques nocives pour les femmes et les fillettes, en particulier les mutilations génitales féminines, qu'elles soient ou non pratiquées dans un centre médical, à prendre toutes les mesures nécessaires pour préserver les fillettes et les femmes de ces pratiques, en promulguant et en faisant appliquer une législation interdisant cette forme de violence, et à mettre fi n à l'impunité"; "Engage les États à énoncer des politiques et des règles pour assurer la mise en oeuvre effective des cadres législatifs nationaux contre la discrimination et la violence à l'encontre des femmes et des fillettes, en particulier les mutilations génitales féminines, et à établir des mécanismes de responsabilisation adéquats aux niveaux national et local pour veiller à leur respect et à leur application"; "Prie instamment les États d'allouer des ressources suffisantes à la mise en oeuvre des politiques, des programmes et des cadres législatifs contre les mutilations génitales féminines".

[147] No peace without Justice. Campagna per abolire le MGF. New York – Rome, 26 November 2012, (http://www.npwj.org/it/GHR/Campagna-Ban-FGM.html-l, accessed on 17 May 2016.

In 2011, for the first time, FGM was explicitly criminalized in Kenya[148]. Legislation is a decisive and crucial step in the protection and promotion of the rights of Kenyan women and girls, because it allows the perpetrators of these practices to be denounced. The penalties provided for by the law are strict: a prison sentence of three to seven years and a fine of 6 000 dollars for all persons practicing FGM, traditional excisors, parents, doctors and nurses (as well as their accomplices). The same penalty applies to all persons found guilty of bringing a daughter to Kenya to circumcise her, to fail to report a case of FGM or to practice FGM on a Kenyan citizen in another country. Furthermore, the Children Act allows police forces to enter premises where they believe FGM is being practiced. Physicians practicing FGM are struck off the medical registry. If a child dies after an operation (due to infection, hemorrhage, etc.), all persons directly involved risks life imprisonment. The law clearly states that the fact of declaring that FGM is a cultural or religious custom and that the victim consented does not prevent being charged with this type of crime.

The law also establishes the Anti-Female Genital Mutilation Board. The Board is supported by the Kenyan Government and envisages the participation of its ministers. However, prevention, awareness, awareness, training and information are paramount[149]. Medical professionals should be trained to not carry out these practices and information should be provided to local populations such that they refrain from contacting non-medical personnel.

In Kenya, parties, music and dances are organized to involve the population, providing an opportunity to introduce dialogue on HTP. In Sudan, midwives, health workers and doctors are mobilized to fight against FGM. Home visits and education are also used, as well as efforts to raise awareness among politicians and religious leaders. In Uganda, every year, a cultural day is organized during which positive traditional practices are praised; at the same time, a campaign against FGM was been launched, with street posters warning that it is dangerous for women's health. In Benin, traditional leaders are mobilized for awareness campaigns.

In Mali, where 85 percent of girls undergo genital mutilation, women's associations organize awareness and cultural mediation activities, hoping to change the prevailing mentality and eradicate this practice[150].

---

[148] *Prohibition of female genital mutilation act,* Law no. 32 of 2011, http://kenyalaw.org/kl/fileadmin/ pdfdownloads/Acts/ProhibitionofFemaleGenitalMutilationAct_No32of2011.pdf, accessed on 6 June 2016.

[149] WHO. Dorkenoo. "Female Genital Mutilation. The prevention and Management of the Health Complications". WHO/FCH/GWH/01.5 WHO/RHR/01.1. Geneva, 2001, p. 13 (http://apps.who.int /iris/ bitstream/10665/66858/1/WHO_FCH_GWH_01.5.pdf, accessed on 7 June 2016).

[150] Euronews Reporter. Kadi Traoro. "Excision: breaking the taboo" 4 febbraio 2011. https://www.youtube.com/ watch?v =Z-ziAaluIBo, accessed on 9 November 2015.

This multi-faceted global approach combines education against FGM with global development and debates on human rights, health, education, the economy and development in general[151].

Therefore, to implement the rules of the ACRWC and to complete all "necessary steps" (Article 1(1)) to discourage HTP (Article 1(3)), an integrated approach involving civil society is necessary, so that it too complies with the relevant legal prescriptions, and is aware of the national and international law on the subject and related sanctions.

To ensure the effectiveness of these measures, it is necessary to implement prevention activities, to launch dialogue aimed at preventing the daughters of women who are victims of FGM from being subjected to mutilation in turn; however, it is also important to assist and rehabilitate women and girls who have already undergone these practices. In addition, health workers within communities should receive guidelines, with which they can properly address these issues as they assist and rehabilitate FGM victims and to prevent recurrence of the practice. If the ACRWC's protection in this regard appears partial, the Commission's action may be essential, as already mentioned, in specifying the modalities of its correct implementation.

II.1.3   Forced marriage

Forced marriage remains a reality for millions of children – mostly girls – in Africa[152]. According to the custom of *ukuthwala*, the suitor abducts the girl from her family and then brings her back to begin marriage negotiations. This custom is followed in rural areas. Forced marriage may also occur when two families agree the marriage without consulting the girl or proceeding against her will. According to some scholars, the custom of *ukuthwala* is a "lovers' elopement", typical of rural

---

[151] GAMCOTRAP (the Gambia Committee on Traditional Practices Affecting the Health of Women and Children) was successful in working with the circumcisers who stopped practising FGM in 2007. In the first group, 18 circumcisers and 63 communities stopped FGM. In 2009, there was a significant increase, to 60 circumcisers and 351 communities. This happened after training was provided to circumcisers, those who attend births, and women leaders. From 2005 to 2006 the rate of FGM fell by 78.3 percent (http://www.equalitynow.org/partner/dr_isatou_touray, accessed on 18 July 2015. In addition, GAMCOTRAP's strategy is to advance advocacy efforts with men, women, youth and children, journalists, medical professionals, human rights organizations, politicians, and religious and community leaders (http://www.gamcotrap.gm/content / index.php?option=com_content&view=article&id=50&Itemid=74, accessed on 18 July 2015).

[152] ACERWC, "End Child Marriage Now. 25 years after the Adoption of The African Children's Charter: Accelerating our Collective Efforts to End Child Marriage in Africa", 14–15 June 2015, Johannesburg, p. 1 (http://www.acerwc.org/?wpdmdl=8515, accessed on 9 February 2016). The percentages of girls marrying before the age of 18 is: in Nigeria, 75 percent, 68 percent in Chad, 68 percent in the Central African Republic, 63 percent in Guinea, 56 percent in Mozambique, 55 percent in Mali, 52 percent in Burkina Faso, 52 percent in South Sudan, 50 percent in Malawi, 48 percent in Madagascar, 47 percent in Eritrea, 45 percent in Somalia, 44 percent in Sierra Leone, 42 percent in Zambia and 41 percent in Ethiopia. ICRW International Center for Research on Women (http://www.icrw.org/child-marriage-facts-and-figures accessed on 18 July 2015. See also UNICEF, "Matrimoni precoci. Una violazione dei diritti umani", 4 marzo 2013 (http://www.unicef.it/doc/4605/matrimoni-precoci-una-violazione-dei-diritti-umani.htm, accessed on 2 June 2016 and UNICEF, "Mauritania. Married at 13. Fighting for a divorce", https://www.youtube.com/watch?v=IiBUJtHc5T0, accessed on 2 June 2016).

populations that live according to local customs[153]. Van der Watts and Oven emphasize how over time, the practice was distorted and gradually became a criminal act[154]. Maluleke[155] claims that *ukuthwala* includes kidnapping, violence and the forced marriage of girls with much older men.

States therefore have a responsibility to protect girls from the violence, harm and abuse that this practice entails. Indeed, the practice of forced marriage violates a series of interdependent rights, such as the right to health, education, non-discrimination and protection from trafficking. Forced child marriage deprives girls of the opportunity to attend school and early pregnancies may cause numerous health complications. Girls married between the ages of 15 and 19 tend to die or develop diseases as a result of pregnancy and childbirth[156]. Child brides with early pregnancies may contract sexually transmitted diseases including HIV.

Moreover, given the price paid, the woman is considered property of the man, and is reduced to slavery and forced to submit to violence[157]. Ill-treatment and deprivation may also lead to psychological consequences resulting from to ill-treatment and deprivation[158]. As the duties deriving from marriage are not observed, the practice may be considered enslavement and trafficking pursuant to Article 29 ACRWC.

A number of socio-economic factors – poverty, stereotypes, discrimination, religion, etc. – foster marriage before the age of 18, with negative consequences for the girls involved. Because of poverty, many families prefer to raise males rather than females. Parents encourage the marriage of their daughters while they are still young, in the hope that marriage can benefit them both financially and socially. Religions and cultural and social practices justify the marriage of girls, in violation of international law on children's rights, general principles of human rights and national social policies[159].

Child marriage violates several rights enshrined in the ACRWC[160]: freedom of association (Article 8); the right to privacy (Article 10); to education (Article 11, and especially Article 11(3)(e), which requires special measures to be taken with respect to girls, to ensure equal access to education

---

[153] Koyana, Bekker, "The indomitable ukuthwala custom", *De Iure*, 2007, p. 139.

[154] Van der Watt, Oven, "Contextualizing the practice of Ukuthvala within South Africa", *South African Journal* 2012, p. 11.

[155] Maluleke, "Culture, tradition, custom, law and gender equality", *Potchefstroom Electronic Law Journal/ Potchefstroomse Elektroniese Regsblad*, 2012, p. 11.

[156] ACERWC, "Addis Ababa Declaration to End Child Marriage in Africa", adopted at the 23rd Session of the ACERWC [11 aprile 2014], para. 4. See also International Center for Research on Women. "Health and child marriage", (http://www.icrw.org/child-marriage-facts-and-figures accessed on 18 July 2015) and UNICEF, "Early Marriage. A harmful traditional practice", 6 April 2005, p. 2 (http://www.unicef.org/publications/files/ Early_Marriage_12.lo.pdf, accessed on 8 February 2016).

[157] "End Child Marriage Now", *op. cit.*, p. 7. See also Mifumi, "What price, bride price? A full documentary", 26 March 2013 (https://www.youtube.com/watch?v=Gmp4ogS1UH8, accessed on 4 November 2015).

[158] Wadesango, Rembe and Chabaya, "Violation of Women's Rights by Harmful Traditional Practices", *Anthropologist*, 2011, p.125.

[159] *Ibidem*, p. 7.

[160] *Ibidem*, p. 5.

for all sections of the community); the right to leisure, recreation and cultural activities (Article 12); the right to health (Article 14); protection from child labour (Article 15); protection against abuse and torture (Article 16); protection of the family (Article 18); parent care and protection (Article 19); protection against harmful cultural and social practices (Article 21); protection in the event of separation from parents and the family environment (Article 25); protection from sexual exploitation (Article 27); and protection from sale, trafficking and abduction (Article 29).

According to Article 21(2) ACRWC, child marriage and the betrothal of girls and boys are forbidden. In addition, States Parties must take measures to specify that the minimum age for marriage is 18 and to make registration of all marriages in an official registry compulsory.

Article 46 ACRWC states that the Commission is inspired by international human rights law and other international instruments. A confirmation of Article 21 ACRWC may be found in the Protocol to the African Charter on Human and Peoples' Rights. The Maputo Protocol is a treaty on the rights of women in Africa. It was adopted by the AU on 11 July 2003 in Mozambique, within the context of the agreements defined by the African Charter on Human and Peoples' Rights. The treaty consists of 32 articles that commit ratifying countries to adapt their internal legislation by introducing an extensive range of women's rights. Article 6 of the Protocol states "that men and women enjoy equal rights and are considered equal partners in marriage. In this regard, Member States shall take appropriate legislative measures to ensure that no marriage is concluded without the full and free consent of the two parties; the minimum marriage age for the girl is 18 years [...]; [and that] any marriage, to be legally recognized, must be concluded in writing and registered in accordance with national legislation".

Article 46 ACRWC states that for its activities, the ACERWC shall draw inspiration from international law on human rights, human rights and other international provisions. Article 21 ACRWC is confirmed in the Protocol to the African Charter on Human and Peoples' Rights (ACHPR). The Maputo Protocol is a treaty on the rights of women in Africa, adopted by the AU on 11 July 2003 in Mozambique, within the context of the agreements defined by the ACHPR. This treaty consists of 32 articles that commit ratifying countries to introduce, in their national legal systems, an extensive set of women's rights. Article 6 of the Protocol affirms that "women and men enjoy equal rights and are regarded as equal partners in marriage. In this regard, States Parties agree to enact appropriate national legislative measures to guarantee that no marriage shall take place without the free and full consent of both parties; the minimum age of marriage for women shall be 18 years; [...] every marriage shall be recorded in writing and registered in accordance with national laws, in order to be legally recognized".

The Preamble of the Protocol to the ACHPR on the Rights of Women in Africa (2003) affirms that the States Parties to the Protocol of Maputo "[recall] that women's rights have been recognised and guaranteed in all international human rights instruments, notably the Universal Declaration of Human Rights, the International Covenant on Civil and Political Rights, the International Covenant on Economic, Social and Cultural Rights, the Convention on the Elimination of All Forms of Discrimination Against Women and its Optional Protocol, the African Charter on the Rights and Welfare of the Child, and all other international and regional conventions and covenants relating to the rights of women as inalienable, interdependent and indivisible human rights". However, despite the ratification of the African Charter on Human and People's Rights and other international human rights instruments by the majority of the States Parties, and despite their solemn commitment to eliminate all forms of discrimination and practices prejudicial to women, women in Africa continue to be victims of discrimination and harmful practices. According to Article 46 ACRWC, the ACERWC shall draw inspiration for its activity also from the human rights instruments adopted by African countries. The Maputo Protocol focuses on women's rights in more detail than the ACRWC, and affirms certain guarantees that the ACRWC does not include. For example, Article 6(c) of the ACHPR encourages monogamy; Article 13(g) requires States Parties to "introduce a minimum age for work and prohibit the employment of children below that age, and prohibit, combat and punish all forms of exploitation of children, especially the girl-child"; Article 17 ACHPR establishes the right, for women, "to live in a positive cultural context and to participate at all levels in the determination of cultural policies."

Article 21 ACRWC specifies another standard of protection, stating that the betrothal of underage individuals is to be prohibited. However, in practice, in African countries, customs contrary to said article persist. For example, Egypt has drafted a reservation with regard to Article 21(2), excluding the application of the prohibition of the marriage of girls within its own legal order, as will be seen in chapter 3.

On the contrary, the laws of Ethiopia, Kenya and South Africa constitute a model of compliance with the provisions of the ACRWC.

In Ethiopia[161], Article 34 of the Constitution establishes the right to marry and found a family with free and full consent, once the age of 18 years has been attained (Family Code, Articles 6 and 7). When consent is extorted with violence or error and the spouses are under 18 years of age, the marriage shall not be valid (Family Code, Articles 13 and 14). Article 648 of the Criminal Code criminalizes marriage with a minor with a maximum term of imprisonment of three years. When the bride is under 13 years of age, the maximum imprisonment increases to seven years.

Media campaigns have been conducted in Ethiopia to ensure that the public is aware of the harmful effects of early marriages. A specialized hospital (the Hamlin Fistula International Hospital) was created for women and young people who have been victims of early marriages, to provide them with adequate cures for the health problems associated with early marriage.

The Ethiopian criminal code criminalizes the infliction of bodily or mental harm arising from HTP (Article 567), the transmission of disease through HTP when the victim has contracted a communicable disease as a result of an HTP (Article 568), and the participation in HTP (Article 569). A parent or any other person who participates in the commission of one of the specified crimes is liable to imprisonment not exceeding three months or to a fine.

---

[161] Ethiopia Initial Report on the implementation of the ACRWC, p. 118, http://www.acerwc.org/download/ethiopia-initial-report/?wpdmdl=8645, accessed on 2 June 2016.

The Ministry of Health actively participates in the eradication of HTP together with the police forces, judges, lawyers and other legal professionals. Several cases have been brought before the courts. The Ethiopian Women Lawyers Association (EWLA) provides free legal aid and legal representation to support women and also actively promotes legislative reform.

The Kenya country report[162] refers to the 2010 Constitution of Kenya. Article 53 establishes that every child has the right to be protected from abuse, neglect, and harmful cultural practices such as child marriage, FGM and violence.

As for child marriage, Article 45(2) of the Constitution establishes that marriage should not be forced and should only take place with the free consent of the marrying parties. The Children's Act of 2001 offers protection to all children from harmful social and cultural practices and prescribes sanctions for offenders.

South Africa's Recognition of Customary Marriages Act adheres to the ACWRC, and especially its Article 21(2). Indeed, it provides that both spouses must consent to the marriage. The minimum age for marriage is 18 years. If one of the parties is under 18, he or she may marry, but cannot be younger than 16 years of age. In this case too, the party's express consent is required[163]. The ACRWC and South African legislation also attribute rights to minors, considering them as subjects of rights that are capable of personally disposing thereof.

South African legislation clarifies that forced marriage also violates the principle of non-discrimination, as well as specific criminal precepts[164]. The police must arrest every person accused of *ukuthwala* and schoolteachers should report the cases that they are aware of. All cases of *ukuthwala* involving minors under 18 should be prosecuted. Parents and other persons involved in forced marriages may be prosecuted under Articles 1 and 4 of the Prevention and Combating of Trafficking in Persons Bill 2009, which prohibits the recruitment, sale, procurement, transportation, transfer, concealment, disposal of people with the use of threats, force, intimidation or other forms of coercion; or by abusing their vulnerability, for the purpose of exploitation.

South Africa has also taken concrete measures to counteract the practice of *ukuthwala*, such as cross-sector collaborations, research, advocacy, training, monitoring and evaluation, prevention services, first aid, assistance to families to meet their basic needs, and providing information on access to services, legal actions and possible reintegration[165].

---

[162] Kenya Initial Report on the implementation of the ACRWC, p. 8, http://acerwc.org/?wpdmdl=8648, accessed on 27 December 2015.

[163] See *Recognition of Customary Marriages Act* no. 120 of 1998, Article 3(1) e 12(2) (b).

[164] The *Criminal Law (Sexual Offences and Related Matters) Amendment Act* n. 32 del 2007 was enacted by the Parliament of South Africa to reform and codify the law on sexual offences. It establishes that the age of consent is 16 years.

[165] See Kwazulu Natal Department of education. "Policy guidelines for the Management of Child Abuse and Neglect in kzn". April 2010 (http://www.kzneducation.gov.za/Portals/0/Circuiars/KZN/2010/CHILD%20 ABUSE %20POLICY%20GUIDELINE%20APRIL%202010%20REVISED.pdf, accessed on 23 March 2016).

Another example is Uganda's Constitution of 1995, which expressly provides that the minimum age for marriage is 18 years (Article 31(1)), in line with Article 21(2) ACRWC; it further specifies that the basis for such a provision is to create a family from which equal rights flow for both wives and husbands in marriage and during marriage, thus also requiring the consent of both spouses. However, the widespread poverty in Uganda has contributed to the persistence of child marriages as a strategy for economic survival[166].

Zambia has one of the highest rates of child marriages in the world, with 42 percent of women having married under the age of 18. Girls who live in poverty, do not have an education and are subject to old discriminatory practices are particularly vulnerable to child marriages. In 2013, the Government of Zambia launched a nationwide campaign to end child marriage, and made the marriage of girls a top priority on its regional and international agenda. In September 2013, Zambia, together with Canada, promoted the first UNGA Resolution on the subject[167].

In 2016, the Constitutional Court of Zimbabwe decided to outlaw marriages in which both or one of the partners is under the age of 18.

The case was brought to the Court[168] by two girls, Loveness Mudzuru and Ruvimbo Tsopodzi, who had both been married off at a very young age. They accused the Government of Zimbabwe, which by law guaranteed that girls could marry at age 16 and boys at 18, of violating their rights. Now, it is up to the Government to make the new legislation known to Zimbabwe's many local communities.

Inkosi Kachindamoto was an elderly tribal leader who, in the district of Dedza (in central Malawi) canceled 330 tribal marriages between boys and girls. The woman took a decision against the tide to encourage the youths to return to school and continue to live a healthy childhood. Therefore, the gradual legislative progress made is complemented with the increasing awareness of people who claim rights in line with those enshrined in the ACRWC.

Marriage is also governed by cultural and religious norms. It is common, for example, for a daughter to be given in marriage as reparation to an offended party[169].

---

[166] According to data from the UNFPA, Uganda has a population of 34.5 million people, about 23.1 million are close to poverty and approximately 8.4 million of these (close to 24.5 percent) live in absolute poverty. The Uganda spending review conducted in 2012 by the country's Directorate of Social Protection, within the Ministry of Gender, Labour and Social Development revealed that 67 percent of Ugandans spend $1.20 a day. Where there is poverty, a young girl can be considered an economic burden and an extra mouth to feed.

[167] The UNGA Resolution on child, early and forced marriage of 17 November 2014 [UN Doc A/C.3/69/L.2/Rev.1], voted for by 109 states, strives to include the issue on the 2015 Agenda and to draft a report on the prevention and eradication of the practice.

[168] *Mudzuru, Tsopodzi v Minister of Justice, Legal & Parliamentary Affairs*. Judgment no. CCZ 12/2015 (http://www.zimlii.org/zw/judgment/constitutional-court/2016/12/CCZ%2012-15.pdf, accessed on 21 December 2016).

[169] "End Child Marriage Now", *op. cit.*, p. 13.

In this regard, the ACERWC urges States Parties to take measures to define the role of religion and culture in the well-being and development of children[170], and calls for discouraging their use in justifying child marriage. In addition, the ACERWC has also proposed legislative reforms for the next five years (starting from 2015) to abolish all regulatory provisions that justify child marriage by invoking culture, tradition, honour or religion, and to set up a monitoring and evaluation database in addition to national observatories to assess the phenomenon of child marriages. This is envisaged to ensure that attention for the emergency of child protection in this regard remains alive[171].

According to the ACERWC, African States should adopt best practices to end child marriage[172], ensure that the perpetrators of the phenomenon are punished according to the law, and establish working groups in collaboration with ministries, agencies and departments at national level to adopt cultural approaches to combat child marriage and related problems; to undertake regulatory reforms to eliminate all legal provisions that justify child marriage by invoking culture, religion, traditions, honour or religion[173]; to illustrate, in reports, the situation regarding discrimination and violence against girls; implement national programs that emphasize traditional and positive values, especially those relating to marriage, highlighting the positive values of the family and the value of children[174]; and harmonize national legislation on rights with the ACRWC, the CRC and the international and regional legal documents that prohibit child marriage.

The ACERWC has recommended that children participate in the implementation of these activities, also because Article 9 ACRWC provides that minors must be given guidance in the exercise of the rights enshrined in the ACRWC[175].

To implement the obligation contained in Article 1 ACRWC, Article 16 also provides for the adoption of educational measures aimed at protecting the child from any form of inhuman or degrading treatment, and, in particular, any form of physical injury or mental trauma. Several studies have demonstrated the importance of the role of education in overcoming child marriage, as will be discussed shortly[176].

Economic measures could also discourage the practice. If families were able to enjoy greater economic welfare through small loans, it may be possible to reduce the occurrence of child

---

[170] *Ibidem*, p. 14.
[171] *Ibidem*, p. 15.
[172] *Ibidem*, p. 18.
[173] *Ibidem*, p. 14.
[174] *Ibidem*, p. 20.
[175] *Ibidem*, p. 21.
[176] UNICEF & Innocenti Resaerch Centre. "Early Marriage", no. 7, March 2001. Florence. Pp. 2-3-6-8, (https://www.unicef-irc.org/publications/pdf/digest7e.pdf. Accessed on 06 June 2016). See also "End Child Marriage Now", *op. cit.*, p. 10.

marriages[177]. The commitment of parents and the community is considered to be a useful strategy in combating this phenomenon.

The ACERWC created a special commission on forced child marriage[178]. In the ACERWC's view[179], as a preventive social strategy, gender equality must be promoted; stereotypes must be changed; protected spaces for girls must be created; girls should be encouraged to enter education and work programs; and urgent measures must be taken to support and provide for the needs of vulnerable girls, such as underage mothers, albino girls and girls who have left school. In addition, it is necessary to support the economic capacity of families and develop programs that promote a positive, non-violent and non-discriminatory approach to education. Girls with eight or more years of school are less likely to get married early than girls who have had less than three years of schooling[180]. Education improves the autonomy of girls, gives them the opportunity to negotiate their choice of partner and to avoid premature marriage. Education also increases the aspirations of girls and allows them to find a suitable partner[181].

To address the negative practice of forced child marriage, many states have passed legislation that forbids marriage until 18 years of age, in accordance with Article 21(1)(b) ACRWC.

There are also court cases filed by girls, with the support of legal associations, to dissolve such "marriages". However, on the other hand, nothing has yet been done to obtain compensation for the girls or to prohibit the HTP of bride prices[182].

The measures recommended by the Committee on the education of girls are yet to be implemented. Therefore, it is also necessary to introduce economic measures to support families.

---

[177] Walker, "Why Ending Child Marriage Needs to be An Educational Goal: The Case for Improved Coordination Between Ending Child Marriage and Girls Education Movements in West Africa", Center for Universal Education, 2013, p. 8 (http://www.brookings.edu/~/media/Research/Files/Reports/2013/12/improving%20learning%20outcomes%20girls%20africa/walker_girls_education.pdf, accessed on 8 February 2016).

[178] Ibidem, p. 23.

[179] Saranga, Kurz, "New Insights on Preventing Child Marriage. A global Analysis of Factors and Programs", *Review by the United States Agency for International Development*, 2007, p. 10.

[180] Lloyd, Mensch, "Implications of formal schooling for girls' transitions to adulthood in developing countries", in *National Research Council, Critical Perspectives on Schooling and Fertility in the Developing World*, The National Academies Press, Washington, 1999, p. 82.

[181] Lloyd, Mensch, "Implications of formal schooling for girls' transitions to adulthood in developing countries", in *National Research Council, Critical Perspectives on Schooling and Fertility in the Developing World*, The National Academies Press, Washington, 1999, p. 82.

[182] In Bangladesh, the Dowry Prohibition Act of 1980 bans bride prices. Article 3 imposes a term of imprisonment not exceeding 5 years upon those convicted of such violation (http://bdlaws.minlaw.gov.bd/print_sections_all.php?id=607, accessed on 9 June 2016).

II.2   Handicapped children in Africa (Article 13 ACRWC)

"Disability is not related exclusively to the health of the individual or to welfare policies. On the contrary, it is a problem of citizenship, that is, of full participation in all aspects of life and of the progressive deconstruction of prejudices and stereotypes. These priorities are aimed at achieving fundamental principles such as dignity, equality and non-discrimination, individual autonomy, participation and inclusion in society, which are prerequisites to the acceptance of disability as part of human diversity."[183]

As for the implementation of the ACRWC obligations, according to Article 13 ACRWC, States Parties undertake to provide, available resources permitting, adequate assistance for the special needs of disabled children. In addition, States Parties commit to ensuring access to public buildings that built on several floors and to all other buildings that the disabled may wish to access. However, a number of regulatory gaps exist and must be noted.

It has been estimated that approximately 500 million to 600 million people in the world are handicapped (equivalent to approximately 10 percent of the world's population); of these, 150 million are children[184]. In Africa, there are 52 million disabled children and youth[185], who often encounter difficulties in accessing services because of architectural barriers and an absence of specialized teachers[186].

In the Central African Republic, 48 percent of children are disabled[187]. In Africa, there are numerous cases of children who have been traumatized or mutilated by war and war devices, such as landmines. African children with mental disabilities have been affected by diseases that have already been eradicated in the Western world. In African countries, the percentage of young people under the age of 15 who are affected by a disability ranges between 10 and 25 percent. Few of these reach adulthood. In industrialized countries, the percentage of disabled minors is between 4 and 11 percent[188].

---

[183] Rossi, "La salute mentale attraverso lo spettro dei diritti umani", 2015, p. 22 (http://www.forumcostituzionale.it/wordpress/wp-content/uploads/2015/03/rossi.pdf, accessed on 6 June 2016.

[184] UN CRC Committee, General Comment no. 9, "The rights of children with disabilities" (11–29 September 2006). UN DOC: CRC/C/GC/9, Geneva, Switzerland, p 1.

[185] Ablechildafrica. "We need education too. Disabled children in Africa and the right to an inclusive education". 2011 (http://ablechildafrica.org/wp-content/uploads/2011/03/Education-Leaflet.pdf, accessed on 20 March 2016), p .1.

[186] *Ibidem.*

[187] UNICEF. Aslam. "The State of the world's children. Children with disabilities", May 2013, E. 13. XX.1 (http://www.uis.unesco.org/Library/Documents/state-world-children-2013-children-with-disabilities-en.pdf. Accessed on 18 July 2015), p. 69.

[188] WHO. *World Report on disability 2011.* p. 30, http://www.who.int/disabilities/ world_report/2011/report.pdf, accessed on 7 June 2016.

In Africa, exclusion, prejudice and discrimination remain common for millions of disabled people[189]. Fragile states, countries in post-conflict scenarios and natural disasters often exacerbate the conditions in which the disabled live. People with disabilities have been stigmatized because of cultural and religious beliefs. Negative cultural beliefs about disability and attitudes towards disabled people remain deeply rooted in Africa[190]. In Africa, most people living with disabilities have no access or means to acquire special equipment, transportation, job opportunities, communications and information.

Article 23(3) CRC provides that disabled children must have effective access to education, health care, rehabilitation, and preparation for employment services, and must be able to benefit from these services in a manner conducive to the child's achieving the fullest social integration and personal development, including in the cultural and spiritual fields. The ACRWC affords a higher standard of protection than the CRC, because it enshrines an obligation, for States Parties, to allocate resources to the removal of architectural barriers that prevent access to multi-storey public buildings and all other places the disabled may wish to access. Article 13 ACRWC states that the "The State Parties to the present Charter shall use their available resources with a view to achieving progressively the full convenience of the mentally and physically disabled person to movement and access to public highway buildings and other places to which the disabled may legitimately want to have access to".

More generally, Article 3 ACRWC establishes the principle of non-discrimination, although it fails to mention disability as grounds for discrimination. Article 23(4) CRC, unlike the ACRWC, also provides for the exchange of relevant information in the field of preventive health care and of the medical, psychological and functional treatment of handicapped children, including through the dissemination of information concerning rehabilitation methods and vocational training services to allow States Parties to improve their capacities in this context.

The education of children is addressed in Article 11 ACRWC which provides for "special measures" for gifted and disadvantaged minors, to ensure access to education on an equal basis. According to Article 13 ACRWC, States Parties also undertake to provide handicapped children, to the extent of the available resources, adequate assistance as required, and professional training.

One of the most debated aspects is the participation of disabled children in general educational programs. The ACRWC does not refer to State Party commitments on training for teaching disabled children. The Commission on Economic, Social and Cultural Rights (CESR)[191] has stated that it is preferable to educate people with disabilities within the general education system. In fact, States Parties should ensure that teachers are trained to educate children with disabilities

---

[189] Moyi. "Access to education for children with disabilities in Uganda: Implications For Education for All". *Journal of International Education and Leadership*. 2012 pp. 2, 5.

[190] Grobbelaar-du Plessis, Van Reenen, *Aspects of disability law in Africa*, Pretoria, Pretoria University Law Press, 2011, p. 7.

[191] Committee on Economic, Social and Cultural Rights, General Comment No 5 'Persons with disabilities', 25 November 1994, U.N. Doc E/1995/22, p. 19, https://www1.umn.edu/humanrts/gencomm/epcomm5e.htm. Accessed on 8 February 2016.

within ordinary schools, and provide the necessary preparations and support required by children with disabilities, to ensure that they enjoy the same level of education as their non-handicapped peers[192].

The Western Cape High Court of South Africa examined a case on the right to education for children with severe intellectual disability[193].

The Court held that there was a violation of article 11(2) ACRWC, which provides that every mentally and physically handicapped minor has the right to special protection measures appropriate to ensure effective access to training.

The applicant argued that children with severe intellectual disabilities did not receive education and that the subsidy provided by the State was wholly inadequate to give full effect to the right to education for every child[194]. The High Court noted the legislation on the needs of children with severe intellectual disabilities did not contain express provisions requiring special schools[195]. The High Court considered that the right to basic education was a constitutional obligation towards all, and that mere cooperation with organizations did not suffice to fulfill this obligation[196]. It found that the right to basic education for children with severe intellectual disabilities had been violated[197]. The High Court thus ordered the State to take reasonable steps to achieve the right to basic education for children with severe intellectual disabilities[198].

If the ACRWC provides that the limit on covering expenses for the disabled consists in the "resources available" some States appear to wish to implement their obligations more broadly. The new Constitution of Kenya recognizes the right of all children, without discrimination based on disability, to enjoy free and obligatory basic education. Therefore, children's right to education is an immediate obligation, to be achieved regardless of whether its costs are covered,

---

[192] Committee on Economic, Social and Cultural Rights, "General Comment n 13 on the right to education, Article 13 CRC", 8 December 1999, UN Doc E/C.12/1999/10, p. 3, (http://www.refworld.org/docid/4538838c22.html. Accessed on 8 February 2016.

[193] High Court of South Africa, *Western Cape Forum for Intellectual Disability v Government of the Republic of South Africa and Government of the Province of the Western Cape*, Case no. 18678/2007, 11 November 2010 (http://www.saflii.org/za/cases/ZAWCHC/ 2010/544.html, accessed on 22 March 2016).

[194] *Ibidem*, par. 8–10.

[195] *Ibidem*, par. 18.

[196] *Ibidem*, par. 24: "Inasmuch as the state currently cooperates with and relies on organisations such as the applicant to provide education for mentally disabled children, it must be borne in mind that this does not relieve the state from its constitutional obligation. This is clear from the *Modderklip Boerdery* case in which the constitutional court held:-

"[45] ...It is unreasonable for a private entity such as Modderklip to be forced to bear the burden which should be borne by the State, of providing the occupiers with accommodation..."

[197] *Ibidem*, par. 45.

[198] *Ibidem*, par. 52.

unlike socio-economic rights[199]. Therefore, the international obligation contained in Article 13 ACRWC sets a threshold of available resources; in comparison, Kenya provides a greater standard of protection.

Articles 7(2) and 12 of Kenya's Children's Act of 2001 state that education, medical treatments and special care are to be provided free of charge or at a reduced cost, when possible[200].

In its Sessional Paper No. 1 of 2004, the Government outlined its education and training policy by recommending that education be inclusive, there being the "need [...]to strengthen mobilization and awareness programmes to eradicate taboos and beliefs associated with disability"[201].

With regard to the health sector, the ACRWC does not require for States to provide, beyond effective medical treatment, prevention measures administered by qualified personnel, nor territorial rehabilitation services. On the social level, people with disabilities are entitled to access public services, integrated structures of education and professional training. The creation of harmonized guidelines for the just and dignified treatment of children with disabilities would make it possible to monitor disability policies and practices in a fair and effective manner.

While the ACRWC does not establish a monitoring or research system to identify the needs of children with disabilities, some States have introduced one.

In Algeria[202], in accordance with the Convention on the Prohibition of the Use, Stockpiling, Production and Transfer of Anti-Personnel Mines and on their Destruction (Ottawa Treaty), a specific support program was envisaged for children injured by landmines. The program has enabled the modernization of the computer system of registration and identification of all victims of landmines and explosive devices. It is in this context that a support program for organizations working with disabled people was formulated and implemented, to increase the capacity to provide victims with assistance. The training was aimed at granting better psychological support to victims and ensuring social support and rehabilitation. Between 2005 and 2008, a study was conducted on the socio-economic impact of mines and the development of education and an accident-prevention program. In January 2010, a program titled "Education for All: Towards inclusion of children with disabilities in the Algerian educational system" for children with auditory and/

---

[199] Article 53 of the Kenya Constitution states that '[e]very child has the right ... to free and compulsory basic education'.

[200] Kenyan Children's Act. Article 7 (2): Every child shall be entitled to free basic education which shall be compulsory in accordance with Article 28 of the United Nations Convention on the Rights of the Child.
Art. 12. A disabled child shall have the right to be treated with dignity, and to be accorded appropriate medical treatment, special care, education and training free of charge or at a reduced cost whenever possible. https://www.icrc.org/applic/ihl/ihlnat.nsf/a24d1cf3344e99934125673e00508142/95bcf642e7784b63c1257b4a004f95e8/$FILE/Children's%20Act.pdf. Accessed on 7 June 2016.

[201] Kenya, Ministry of Education, Science And Technology, Sessional Paper no. 1 on a policy framework for education, training and research, October 2004, p. 7 (http://planipolis.iiep.unesco.org/upload/Kenya/Kenya%20Policy%20Framework%20 Education%20Training.pdf, accessed on 28 March 2016.

[202] Algeria Initial Report on the implementation of the ACRWC, p. 45, http://acerwc.org/?wpdmdl=8766, accessed on 27 December 2015.

or visual sensory impairments was launched within psychoeducational centres, to develop the victims' intellectual, psychological and motor skills.

In Algeria, according to Decree no. 80-59 of 8 March 1980 on the establishment, organization and operation of specialized educational centres for children with disabilities, teachers, psychologists and special needs educators offer basic primary care within the framework of the national educational program, applying appropriate teaching methods. However, it must be said that disabled children encounter difficulties in integrating back to ordinary schools after leaving these centres, mainly because of the lack of resources devoted to fostering their re-integration in such schools.

As for the information on and awareness of the situation of children with disabilities, the Government of Algeria has organized information campaigns and debates on the rights of disabled children and the problems related to their implementation. Similarly, landmine risk-awareness programs have been developed in coordination with national institutions and civil society to reduce the number of landmine victims, in accordance with the efforts to implement the Ottawa Treaty[203].

In Burkina Faso[204], an inter-sectoral committee was established to address the needs of disabled people in various sectors: education, health, training, work, sport and leisure. The State commemorates disabled people every year on 3 December, with an awareness-raising campaign to change societal behaviour towards them.

In this regard, the ACERWC noted that despite the efforts made, 99 percent of disabled persons are still illiterate. Disabled persons continue to encounter problems in accessing public buildings and school infrastructures, and discrimination against them is persistent. Therefore, the ACERWC called on the Government of Burkina Faso to undertake additional actions to foster literacy among disabled people, address the specific educational needs of disabled minors, and develop special programs to promote the education, capacity-building and socio-professional integration of disabled minors. As for the initiatives to combat the marginalization and stigmatization of handicapped children, the ACERWC suggested providing rehabilitation services with adequate budgets, sufficient to effectively take care of disabled children. A general form of protection would also derive from the law that promotes and protects handicapped children[205].

Cameroon's report emphasizes the difficulties resulting from the scarcity of state funds, which prevent meeting the needs of children with disabilities and ensuring the the quality and continuity

---

[203] It is necessary to emphasize the significant role of the 250 solidarity "cells" that have been established in remote and isolated areas of the country, to provide community health, social support, psychological and therapeutic support, mediation and social communication.

[204] Burkina Faso *Ibidem*, p. Initial Report on the implementation of the ACRWC, p. 78, http://acerwc.org/?wpdmdl=8780, accessed on 27 December 2015.

[205] Concluding Observations and Recommendations of the ACERWC on the Burkina Faso Report, p. 5, http://www.acerwc.org/?wpdmdl=8740, accessed on 19 January 2016.

of specialized institutes and staff. Cameroon[206] celebrates the International Day of Persons with Disabilities, transmitting public awareness of the fundamental rights of the disabled, and especially of children. Regarding the implementation of Article 13(3) ACRWC on handicapped persons' access to buildings, a practical guide on disabled persons' access to buildings and infrastructure was formulated; the document obtained the technical approval of all stakeholders, including representatives of associations of disabled people.

The ACERWC found the following problems: a shortage of apprenticeship centres; the failure to apply texts that grant benefits to disabled children, reducing the costs of treatment and public transport; a failure to adapt public buildings and school buildings; as well as persistent socio-cultural prejudice and discrimination within families regarding enrollment in school[207].

In its Concluding Observations, the ACERWC invited Cameroon to implement a policy to care for disabled minors, training specialized personnel and conducting a study to thoroughly determine the causes of psychomotor handicaps to reduce their high rate (22 percent) of occurrence[208].

The Congo report[209] also refers to the prevention and early detection of disability, through the development of studies and the organization of a system to improve knowledge of the causes of disability and the social conditions of disabled people, and to promote early diagnosis techniques. The implementation of services and monitoring and evaluation activities are entrusted to the National Action Plan for the Disabled, which between 2009 and 2010 provided support to 1 600 disabled people, implementing services related to sign language and Braille, literature programs for disabled adolescents and adults, and early diagnosis for the treatment of disabilities[210].

In 2004, Kenya[211] established the National Council for Persons with Disability, an association of civil society organizations that carries out awareness programs to reduce stigma and help parents of disabled children to seek medical and educational services for children with disabilities. The Council also lobbies the government to increase funding for the sector and to create more job opportunities for people with disabilities. In 2010, the Kenyan Government conducted a census of albino people, because they are subject to such severe discrimination that often, they are not enrolled in school and suffer from socialization issues. The challenges that remain concern, above

---

[206] Cameroon Initial Report on the implementation of the ACRWC, p. 35, http://acerwc.org/?wpdmdl=8781, accessed on 27 December 2015.

[207] Concluding Observations and Recommendations of the ACERWC on the Cameroon Report, p. 2, http://www.acerwc.org/?wpdmdl=8741, accessed on 19 January 2016.

[208] Concluding Observations and Recommendations of the ACERWC on the Cameroon Report, p. 2, http://www.acerwc.org/?wpdmdl=8741, accessed on 19 January 2016.

[209] Congo Initial Report on the implementation of the ACRWC, p. 20, http://acerwc.org/?wpdmdl=8796 accessed on 27 December 2015.

[210] International Monetary Fund. "Republic of Congo: Growth, Employment and Poverty Reduction Strategy Paper", IMF Publication Services, Washington D.C. August http://www.acerwc.org/?wpdmdl=8741, accessed on 19 January 2016. *Ibidem*, p. 2012, p. 44.

[211] Kenya Initial Report on the implementation of the ACRWC, p. 51, http://acerwc.org/?wpdmdl=8648, accessed on 27 December 2015.

all, social prejudice and the insufficiency of the funds allocated for the assessment, treatment, rehabilitation and provision of equipment to support disabled children.

With regard to disabled children, the ACERWC noted that only 2 percent of children with special needs are enrolled in ordinary schools and invited the Kenyan Government to take further action to provide for the education of disabled children. The ACERWC recommended that adequate rehabilitation infrastructure for disabled children be constructed and special education, capacity-building and socio-professional integration programs be developed to combat the marginalization and stigmatization of disabled children[212].

The Lesotho report[213] mentions the Building Control Act (1995), which requires that schools be constructed with ramps, to improve accessibility for those who use wheelchairs and other aids. The law entered into force with a 20-year delay, also because the national budget allocates scarce funds to addressing the needs of people with disabilities. There is also a shortage of teachers who are properly trained on the needs of the disabled. In addition, much remains to be done on the stigma associated with disability.

The Mali report[214] states that the education of disabled children is the priority of the country's program relating to persons with disabilities. Through awareness campaigns and the training of partners in the field of education, schools were opened to accept handicapped children. In 1994, the Mali Federation of Sports for Disabled Persons was created in 1994, to promote sports initiatives for people with disabilities.

In the Mozambique report[215], its Government emphasized that programs aimed at protecting mental health in pediatric services have been adopted. Moreover, specific programs have been created for the early diagnosis of diseases such as epilepsy and mental retardation. However, these programs are still geographically limited and do not meet all needs of the urban and rural communities. To ensure that children with special needs receive appropriate attention in schools, the Ministry of Education has provided 3 455 teachers with training related to teaching children with special educational needs, sign language and Braille. A number of efforts have been made to create the necessary conditions for disabled people to access public buildings.

The Parliament of Rwanda[216] reserves a special seat to a member elected to represent persons with disabilities. To discourage all forms of discrimination and violence against people with disabilities,

---

[212] Concluding Observations and Recommendations of the ACERWC on the Kenya Report, p. 4, http://www. acerwc.org/?wpdmdl=8746, accessed on 27 December 2015.

[213] Lesotho Initial Report on the implementation of the ACRWC, p. 46, http://acerwc.org/?wpdmdl=8774, accessed on 27 December 2015.

[214] Mali Initial Report on the implementation of the ACRWC, p. 52, http://acerwc.org/?wpdmdl=8782, accessed on 27 December 2015.

[215] Mozambique Initial Report on the implementation of the ACRWC, p. 50, http://acerwc.org/?wpdmdl=8650, accessed on 27 December 2015.

[216] Rwanda Initial Report on the implementation of the ACRWC, p. 20, http://acerwc.org/?wpdmdl=8653, accessed on 27 December 2015.

Article 27 of Law No. 01/2007 of 20 January 2007, on the protection of the rights of the disabled, establishes that "[a]ny person found to be a person with a disability, or to be punished with the heaviest penalty among the penalties provided for by the Criminal Code and special laws relating to such a crime".

More generally, the ACERWC noted that although States Parties have taken measures in support of disabled children, much remains to be done and has recommended that States Parties multiply schools with integrated classes for disabled children; increase the number of specialized teachers; provide rehabilitation services with adequate budgets for the effective care of children with disabilities; to provide for this issue when defining development policies; adopt and implement an action plan for the rehabilitation of people living with a disability; and adopt and implement an action plan to combat disabling diseases[217].

The report of the United Republic of Tanzania[218] contains a commitment to the early detection of major disabilities and to adopt special programs to address them, as well as implement measures to prevent disability. A special training school was created in Arusha together with the Minister of Education and Training; since 2004, 1 333 teachers have been trained and received certifications. There is a special seat in the Tanzanian Parliament for a representative of the disabled.

In the Zimbabwe report[219], the country's Government stated that it allocates 10 percent of the Basic Education Assistance Modules (BEAM) to the special needs of children with disabilities. Among the preventive measures aimed at protecting children against disability, the Public Health Act provides for the immunization of children against disabling diseases such as polio. The Zimbabwean Government is also launching programs to educate the public on preventing home accidents that can result in disability. Disability is first detected through screening measures and the use of "risk registers", especially through the monitoring of children. The Disabled Persons Act guarantees the disabled with access to education and work; participation in sport and cultural activities; prevention of discrimination; and compliance with international treaties on the well-being of disabled people. Through rehabilitation programs, disabled children in rural areas are provided with support to enhance their independence, such as orthopaedic equipment and other equipment adapted to the home environment.

Regarding the implementation of Article 13 ACRWC, the ACERWC recommended that studies be done on the causes of disability, to reduce their high incidence. Congo, Mozambique and the United Republic of Tanzania have adopted a system to study the causes of disabilities and to promote measures for early diagnosis.

---

[217] Concluding Observations and Recommendations of the ACERWC on the Rwanda Report, p. 5, h http://www.acerwc.org/?wpdmdl=8753, accessed on 27 December 2015. The ACERWC notes that wheelchairs and Braille material are provided in schools. However, specialized teachers are required and advises the Government to take the necessary measures to cover such gaps.

[218] United Republic of Tanzania Initial Report on the implementation of the ACRWC, p. 30, http://acerwc.org/?wpdmdl=8786, accessed on 27 December 2015.

[219] Zimbabwe Initial Report on the implementation of the ACRWC, p. 55, http://acerwc.org/?wpdmdl=8778, accessed on 27 December 2015.

The ACERWC also noted that disabled children tend to lack access to education, and to present a high rate of illiteracy, issues that persist also because of prejudice. The ACERWC therefore encouraged States Parties to remove cultural discrimination surrounding disabled children and discrimination in access to an education appropriate to their specific needs, by undertaking awareness campaigns on the subject of disability.

Algeria, Burkina Faso, Cameroon and Mali have organized information campaigns on the rights of disabled children.

The ACERWC also recommended that adequate budgets be allocated to meet the special needs of disabled minors and to train personnel specialized in the care and training of disabled minors. The right to health requires the provision of social services that are adequate to meet health-related needs, a personalized treatment plan, recreational services and education, as well as the allocation of resources comparable to those envisaged for other health facilities.

The ACERWC's recommendations show that the effective implementation of the ACRWC depends not only on the adoption of appropriate internal regulatory measures, but also – and often – on the availability of the financial resources required to fulfill the positive obligations set out in this area.

II.3   Article 22 ACRWC and child soldiers

The phenomenon of child soldiers is a global plague. However, Africa is certainly the continent to suffer most. According to the latest UN estimates, of the over 300 000 teenagers employed by government armies, paramilitary groups and irregular armed factions in current conflicts, approximately half may be found in Africa[220]. Children are certainly involved in wars today, being recruited by armed groups, kidnapped, tortured and reduced to slavery, and required to participate in war crimes, crimes against humanity and genocide. Many children are killed and injured every year as a result of war. However, many have also suffered from the indirect effects of conflicts, such as malnutrition and disease, lack of education, disability and the general disintegration of the social protection system. This breakdown in the physical, emotional, moral, cognitive and social development of children has long-term consequences, for children themselves and for their societies[221].

Soldiers must face the stress of combat, and reach awareness of the paradoxical "right to kill and be killed". Rigorous discipline, combined with a high risk of death or serious and disabling injuries, creates traumatic experiences and cause them to sediment deep in the psyche, adding up to the psychological consequences of leaving the family unit, which is fundamental to balanced emotional, social and cognitive growth. The inevitable loss of care and assistance is exacerbated by fact that there are no opportunities for the formative experiences of social life to occur, such as those that unfold with the simple attendance of school.

---

[220] UNGA, "Children and Armed Conflict – Report of the Secretary General", 21 December 2007, UN DOC A/62/609/S/2007/757, (http://www.unicef.org/emerg/files/childsoldiers.pdf, accessed on 20 March 2016).
[221] UNICEF & Innocenti Centro di Ricerca. "Children and Truth Commission", August 2010, p. IX, (http://www.unicef-irc.org/publications/pdf/truth_commissions_eng.pdf, accessed on 18 July 2015).

To understand the behaviour of child soldiers, it is necessary to examine the socio-cultural context in which they exist. Through indoctrination processes, some children become "adult" fighters, in a scenario wholly devoid of rules. The ACRWC protects minors from this development, which certainly does not respond to their best interest. Article 22(2) states that "States Parties to the present Charter shall take all necessary measures to ensure that no child shall take a direct part in hostilities and refrain in particular, from recruiting any child." The article requires the implementation of measures to prevent the enlistment of minors, through the implementation of Article 11 ACRWC on education and Article 12 ACRWC, which includes the right of the child to age-appropriate recreational activities.

For the younger generations of Sudan, Angola, Afghanistan, Eritrea, Congo – a list which, tragically, may grow – war is the reality they have known since birth. A situation that tends to be thought of as exceptional is absolutely normal in many parts of the world and in Africa especially.

From independence to date, most African countries have experienced civil wars and long periods of political instability, characterized by coups and continuous political change. In recent years, a new phenomenon has arisen that renders the definition of "civil war" partially obsolete: the regionalization of war. Indeed, many African wars today are the result of a "contamination": the expansion of a conflict from a single country to entire regions[222].

In these new wars, the traditional distinction between soldiers and civilians is lost and the latter have become the main victims. Most new wars are no longer fought by regular armies, that provide a period of military training and require compliance with a disciplinary code; rather, the fighters are poorly trained and wholly undisciplined militias, made up of very young individuals and, often, children[223]. Indeed, the new wars are linked to the growing weakness of many States and to the global affirmation of criminal organizations, which are increasingly ramified and that base their income on the trafficking of natural resources. In these conflicts, resort to terror and the use of child soldiers have become systematic[224].

If, on one hand, the lack of job opportunities pushes many young people to enlist, on the other, the young fighter is a "model of strength" in minds of the young, which can take hold in the

---

[222] According to many scholars, the post-Cold-War conflicts – that is, the conflicts of the era of globalization – may be clearly distinguished from the previous ones. In this regard, the English activist and scholar Mary Kaldor has coined the expression of "new wars", to underscore these aspects of discontinuity. Kaldor argues that once the era of clashes between states has ended, in the current era, conflicts seem to find fertile ground in the erosion of the state, where the latter is no longer able to exercise a monopoly over violence. According to Kaldor, the new wars have the characteristics of "internationalized civil conflicts" and are fought no longer for the purpose of territorial expansion but to pursue the interests and privileges of small groups, that are often involved in criminal activities taking place within a globalized war economy. Kaldor, "Transnational civil society", in Dunne, Wheeler, Human Rights in Global Politics, Cambridge University Press, Cambridge, 1999, pp. 195–213.
[223] Jourdan, *Generazione Kalashnikov. Un antropologo dentro la guerra in Congo*, Rome, Laterza, 2010, p. 15.
[224] Gates, Reich, *Child Soldiers in the age of fractured States*, Pittsburgh, University of Pittsburgh Press, 2010, p. 96.

"chaotic vacuum" of post-colonialism[225]. Indeed, in times of uncertainty and restlessness, two models of social success appear to have most sway among the new African generations: fervent religious persons, who are affiliated to a wider community of believers; and fighters, members of an army or militia with specific rules. These are the anthropopoietic projects that succeed in an impoverished and confused world[226].

Wars are the most dramatic aspect of the desire, of new African generations, to be protagonists in their societies and on the world stage. Mayi-Mayi, Cobra, Ninja, Cosa Nostra are but the most imaginative names of the multitude of militias that are active on the continent and in which tens of thousands of youths and children militate. Therefore, the "youth issue" occupies a fundamental position in the etiology of African wars[227].

In Africa, child soldiers are employed in armed conflicts. The estimates provided by authoritative humanitarian organizations[228] indicate that approximately 300 000 children are forced to fight in other countries, such as Angola, Rwanda, Sudan and Somalia, as well as in the Democratic Republic of the Congo and Burundi. In the last decade of armed conflicts, over 2 million children lost their lives, more than 6 million were disabled, 1 million lost their families, 12 million were made homeless and almost all of them suffer psychic traumas attributable to war[229].

Child soldiers are also recruited in Chad, Niger, Nigeria and Cameroon[230] and in the Central African Republic, Liberia, Rwanda, Sierra Leone, Uganda, Somalia, Eritrea and Ethiopia[231]. In addition, the economic and political crisis affecting many African countries has meant that enlisting – given the absence of viable alternatives – has become tempting even for children[232].

---

[225] Jourdan, *Generazione Kalashnikov. Un antropologo dentro la guerra in Congo, op. cit.*, p. 33.

[226] *Ibidem.*, p. 33.

[227] *Ibidem.*, p. 33.

[228] Save the Children, "Bambini e armi. L'istruzione per combattere la guerra", October 2008, p. 12 (http://images.savethechildren.it/IT/f/img_pubblicazioni/img32_b.pdf, accessed on 28 March 2016).
It is very difficult to estimate the number of child soldiers, because these data are difficult to obtain. Amnesty International estimates that there are 300 000 child soldiers, 40 percent of whom are girls, while the UN estimates that there are 250 000 child soldiers. L'Espresso. Quanti sono i bambini soldato nel mondo. 14 january 2015. http://espresso.repubblica.it/internazionale/2015/01/14/news/amnesty-sui-bammbini-soldato-1.195118. Accessed on 10 july 2018.

[229] Polidori, Bocco, Corvino, Fucini, Garavoglia, Giuliani, Laiso, Misso, Nacci, Punzo, Rapporto Centro studi per la difesa e la sicurezza. *Conflitti non convenzionali nell'Africa sub-sahariana.* 2008, p. 157 (http://www.academia.edu/1536841/Rapporto_Cesdis_2008_Conflitti_non_convenzionali_nell_Africa_sub-sahariana, accessed on 28 March 2016).

[230] Amnesty International, "Panoramica regionale sull'Africa subsahariana", 2015-2016 Report, p. 27, (http://www.rapportoannuale.amnesty.it/sites/default/files/2016/Africa.pdf, accessed on 28 March 2016).

[231] Nomis, Brownlees, Save the children, "Bambini e armi. L'istruzione per combattere la guerra", October 2008. p 12 (http://images.savethechildren.it/IT/f/img_pubblicazioni/img32_b.pdf, accessed on 28 March 2016).

[232] The propensity of youth to enlist is significant in the eastern regions of Congo. Jourdan, *op. cit.*, p. 78.

To understand how the ACRWC can actually be applied, it is important to identify the type of combatant that militates in the ranks of the numerous militias, armies and rebel groups of the African continent. As Alcinda Honwana argues[233], this is mostly an individual trained to inadequately equipped, who frequently, mercilessly, harasses, loots and indiscriminately kills defenceless civilians. Child soldiers fall fully within this definition: little trained or not at all, armed mostly with Kalashnikov rifles, they loot, rape and kill civilians who are often defenceless.

The kidnapping of children for the purpose of forcing them to enlist is common, to varying degrees, in almost all African conflicts. Once enlisted, they are often turned into ruthless warriors through a process of initiation into violence that involves bloody and macabre rites. This training generally uses light weapons, which are readily found in Africa, and are easily used even by children.

In this connection, the CRC and ACRWC do not provide any protection regarding the trafficking of light and heavy weapons and their use by children[234]. However, a factor that has fostered the increasing use of minors in African wars is precisely the proliferation of light weapons: guns, rifles and machine guns that, with appropriate training, even a child of 7 or 8 years can use, thus becoming a veritable "instrument of death"[235]. According to estimates by the Global Policy Forum, over 100 million small arms and light weapons are currently in circulation on the African continent (out of a total of approximately 640 million worldwide). Eighty percent of this arsenal is in the hands of rebel groups and paramilitary formations, while only 16 percent is used by regular armies[236].

The Preamble to the ACRWC states that "the child occupies a unique and privileged position in the African society and that for the full and harmonious development of his personality. the child should grow up in a family environment in an atmosphere of happiness, love and understanding". Article 22(2) ACRWC states that the States Parties must take all necessary measures to ensure that no minor directly takes part in the hostilities and, in particular, that no minor is enlisted in their armed forces.

Many international specialists continue to believe that during conflict, it is impossible to develop policies and guidelines on human rights, social protection or development. However, experience has shown that in many conflict situations, specific policies, guidelines and services can indeed be developed[237]. During wars, special attention should be given to inter-institutional coordination.

---

[233] Honwana, "Innocent & Guilty. Child soldiers as Interstitial & Tactical Agents", in Honwana, De Boeck (ed.), *Makers & Breakers. Children and Youth in Postcolonial Africa*, James Currey, Oxford, 2005, p. 34.

[234] The *Global Armed Violence Prevention Programme* (AVPP) seeks to prevent the use of weapons and is promoted by the United Nations Development Programme and the WHO (http://www.who.int/violence_injury_prevention/violence/activities/avpp.pdf, accessed on 23 March 2016).

[235] Carrisi. *Tutto quello che dovresti sapere sull'Africa e che nessuno ti ha mai raccontato.* Newton Compton Editori. Roma 2009, p. 186.

[236] *Tutto quello che dovresti sapere sull'Africa e che nessuno ti ha mai raccontato. op. cit.* p. 167

[237] Vargas-Baron. "National Policies to prevent the recruitment of child soldiers. In Gates, Reich. *Child soldiers in the age of fractured states.* Pittsburgh: University of Pittsburgh Press, 2010, p. 216

in all aspects of policy development and application. To develop and implement effective policies, a system of coordination (including governments and NGOs) is essential[238].

Specific programs were developed during war in countries such as Algeria, Eritrea and Senegal: training centres and services for young children and parents were created, helping not only the resident population but also refugees and street children[239]. Local, regional or national governments conduct these programs; however, they are usually carried out by civil society organizations, including national and international NGOs, community development organizations, universities, institutes and religious organizations[240].

Article 22(3) ACRWC provides that "States Parties [...] shall, in accordance with their obligations under international humanitarian law, protect the civilian population in armed conflicts and shall take all feasible measures to ensure the protection and care of children who are affected by armed conflicts. Such rules shall also apply to children in situations of internal armed conflicts, tension and strife."

Information systems that record the recruitment and disappearance of children are rare. It must be recalled that, contrary to Article 6 ACRWC, many children are not registered at birth. Yet such a system could help advance those national policies and service programs established to find children, enhance efforts to save them, ascertain responsibilities and evaluate which services to provide. Release programs carried out during the conflict may help encourage young child soldiers to flee[241]. Educational programs could contribute towards healing from trauma and reconciliation, because the community too must be educated to accept former child soldiers[242].

The recruitment of child soldiers, as well as its methods and results, should be researched and monitored, not only to understand the relative *modus operandi* but also to arrest those who transgress the law and taking them to justice, thus ending their impunity and preventing them from continuing their recruitment practices[243].

Article 22 ACRWC provides that States Parties must take measures to ensure that no minor directly takes part in hostilities. This provision refers to preventive measures. Therefore, each country should develop guidelines on discouraging the recruitment of child soldiers and, on the other hand, encouraging citizens to contribute to the efforts to resist and end recruitment. A public information campaign on the key elements of international treaties on children's rights and on the judgments of the International Criminal Court should be combined with information on the implementation of

---

[238] *Ibidem*, p. 217.

[239] *Ibidem*, p. 214.

[240] *Ibidem*, p. 214.

[241] *Ibidem*, p. 215.

[242] *Ibidem*, p. 216.

[243] Singer, "Talk is Cheap: Getting Serious about Preventing Child Soldier", *Cornell International Law Journal* 2004, pp. 561–586.

the ACRWC, social protection measures and policy developments in each country[244]. It is essential to use radio and mass media, to reach those child soldiers who are illiterate.

The main relevant measures include the tripartite action plan signed between the Union of Democratic Forces for Unity (*Union des Forces Démocratiques pour le Rassemblement*, UFDR), the Government of the Central African Republic and UNICEF for the reduction and elimination of the recruitment and use of child soldiers, their demobilization and reintegration, which involved the release of 200 children. Subsequently, another 450 children were released, of whom 75 percent were between 13 and 17 years of age; 10 percent were under 10 years of age. All children were reintegrated into families or communities[245]. In August 2007, the dedicated Uganda task force team met with the country's Minister of Foreign Affairs to draft an action plan to prevent the recruitment and use of child soldiers[246]. A meeting was held in Kampala on 24 August 2007 with government stakeholders, and the task force drafted an action plan which was quickly adopted by the government[247]. In Chad, the Government formed an agreement with UNICEF on the release of child soldiers from the armed forces[248]. This phenomenon raises two main problems: the repression of the recruitment of child soldiers and the repression of the crimes committed by them.

II.3.1   Voluntary and forced recruitment

Assessing the criminal liability of those who recruit or use child soldiers is regulated by two provisions of the ACRWC: Article 16 on protection against abuse and torture by the parent, legal guardian or any other person who has custody over the child, to avoid physical injury or mental trauma occurring to the child; and Article 22, according to which the States Parties take all necessary measures to ensure that no minor directly participates in hostilities and, in particular, that no minor is enrolled in their armed forces, as well as to protect and care for minors affected by conflict. Article 17 ACRWC, on juvenile justice, focuses on the rights of the accused child: Every child accused or found guilty of having infringed penal law shall have the right to special treatment in a manner consistent with the child's sense of dignity and worth and which reinforces the child's respect for human rights and fundamental freedoms of others". The law does not mention specific obligations of States Parties regarding the punishment of those who recruit child soldiers.

It also does not regulate the guarantees applicable to child soldiers in light of their socio-economic responsibilities, nor the conditions for the rehabilitation and reintegration of child soldiers.

The recruitment and use of minors under the age of 18 in hostilities is prohibited by the ACRWC. Specific provisions may also be found in the Statute of the International Criminal Court, Article 8.2 XXVI of which expressly prohibits the recruitment of minors under 15 years of age.

---

[244] "National Policies to prevent the recruitment of child soldiers", *op. cit.* p. 219.

[245] UN Secretary General, Report on "Children and armed conflict", 13 August 2007, UN Doc A/62/228, p. 8.

[246] Security Council, Resolution 1612 (2005) on Children and armed conflict, adopted on 26 July 2005.

[247] UN Secretary General, Report on "Children and armed conflict", 13 August 2007, UN Doc A/62/228, p. 11.

[248] *Ibidem.* p. 36.

According to the Statute of the Special Court for Sierra Leone, the body has no jurisdiction over minors under the age of 15. On the other hand, minors between the ages of 15 and 18 who have committed crimes must be treated with dignity, in accordance with international human rights and children's rights standards, considering their young age, promoting their rehabilitation, reintegration and assumption of a constructive role in society. According to Article 8 of the Rome Statute of the International Criminal Court, the recruitment and enlistment of children under the age of 15 in armed forces can be considered a full-fledged "war crime". Article 3 of the Optional Protocol on the Involvement of Children in Armed Conflict sets the minimum age for recruitment in armed forces at 18 years. Moreover, such criminalization has also been considered to form part of customary international law, and as such applicable in both international and internal conflicts[249].

Further details may be found in the case law of international criminal tribunals. The International Criminal Court has found Thomas Lubanga Dyilo guilty of the war crime of enlisting and recruiting children under the age of 15 in the *Forces patriotiques pour la liberation du Congo* (FPLC; Patriotic Forces for the Liberation of Congo), with regard to the hostilities protracting from September 2002 to August 2003. The ICC sentenced him to 14 years in prison, a term confirmed on appeal[250].

Thomas Lubanga was the president of the FPLC/UPC and was, at the same time, the political leader and the commander of the armed forces. He was involved in planning the military operations and played a crucial role in logistics and in the procurement of ammunition for the FPLC troops. In addition, he actively supported recruitment initiatives, also by delivering speeches to the local population. In his speech at the Rwampara military camp, he encouraged children under the age of 15 to take up arms and provide for the security of the population, after a period of

---

[249] Sam Hinga Norman, former Deputy Minister of Defence and then Minister of the Interior was indicted on 7 March 2003. Moinina Fofana, alleged National Manager for the Civil Defense Forces War and Allieu Kondewa, Minister of Cult were indicted on 26 June. On 22 February 2007, Sam Hinga Norman died of natural causes while in Dakar for treatment and the trial against him was closed on 21 May 2007. On 28 May 2008, the appeal chamber sentenced Moinina Fofana to 15 years and Allieu Kondewa to 20 years in prison for crimes against humanity, violations of Article 3 common to the Geneva Conventions, other serious violations of international humanitarian law, unlawful killings, psychological violence and mental suffering, looting and fire, collective punishment to the detriment of the population and use of child soldiers. See Special Court for Sierra Leone, Appeals Chamber, Case SCSL 04-14-A., *Prosecutor vs Fofana, Kondewa*, Judgment of 28 May 2008 (http:// www.rscsl.org/Documents/Decisions/CDF/Appeal/ 829 / SCSL-04-14-A-829.pdf viewed on 23 March 2016).
[250] International Criminal Court, *Prosecutor vs. Thomas Lubanga Dylo* [ICC-01 / 04-01 / 06- 2842], Trial Chamber, Judgment of 14 March 2012. The Court unanimously decided that Thomas Lubanga Dyilo was guilty of perpetrating war crimes comprising the enlistment of children under 15 years of age and of having used them to actively participate in hostilities from 1 September 2002 to 13 August 2003. On 10 July 2012, the Trial Chamber sentenced Thomas Lubanga Dyilo to 14 years of imprisonment. See https://www.icc-cpi. int/iccdocs/doc/doc1379838.pdf, accessed on 23 March 2015. On 1 December 2014, the appeal court upheld the judgment by a majority of judges, declaring Mr Lubanga guilty and confirming his sentence of 14 years of detention. See International Criminal Court, *Prosecutor v. Lubanga*, (ICC-01 / 04-01 / 06 A 4 A 6), Judgment on the Appeals, Judgment of 1 December 2014, https://www.icc-cpi.int/iccdocs/doc/doc1877186.pdf. Accessed on 28 March 2016.

military training. He and the other members of his staff had children under the age of 15 among their own bodyguards. In addition to the children who volunteered, others had been forcibly recruited and subject to harsh training and punishments, as shown in videos shot in the military camps of Bunia, Rwampara, Mandro and Mongbwalu[251].

According to Article 8 of the Rome Statute, "[c]onscripting or enlisting children under the age of fifteen years into the national armed forces or using them to participate actively in hostilities" is a war crime and attracts criminal liability upon its perpetrators.

It should be recalled that the ICC is the first international court to recognize a role to victims and to create a fund for them. Article 79 of the Rome Statute 79 provides for the establishment of a Trust Fund for victims, in which money and property collected through fines or forfeiture shall be transferred by order of the Court. According to Article 75 of Rome Statute, the Court establishes the principles applicable to reparation. In particular, these principles concern:

- restitution and restitution measures, where possible, that lead to the restoration of the victim's personal life, for example by returning the latter to his or her family, home or work, or by returning illegitimately taken property or assets;
- compensation for physical, mental or emotional suffering; material damage, including lost earnings and job opportunities, loss or damage to property, lost wages, other interferences related to the ability to work and loss of savings; loss of opportunities, including work, study and social benefits, loss of status and interference with legally recognized individual rights; costs associated with medical, legal, psychological and social support, including care for children with HIV/AIDS;
- rehabilitation to be granted to victims or their dependents. These remedies include medical and health services (especially for the treatment of HIV), and psychological, psychiatric, social welfare and legal services aimed at alleviating the suffering and the effects of the trauma suffered by the victims[252];

Article 16 ACRWC on protection against abuse and torture regulates the opening of judicial proceedings and investigations, the handling of the case and subsequent measures. In particular, the States Parties are required to adopt specific legislative and administrative measures to protect the child from all forms of physical injury or mental trauma, abuse, neglect or mistreatment.

The key to the judicial choice of remedial measure is the principle of adequacy or appropriateness. Indeed, in each concrete situation, it is necessary to identify the reparation that is most suitable to achieve the remedial targets, for the benefit of former child soldiers.

---

[251] The International Criminal Court found them guilty of the crime of recruiting minors under the age of 15 years. *The Prosecutor v. Thomas Lubanga Dyilo*. ICC -01/04-01/06 (http://www.icc-cpi.int/iccdocs/PIDS/publications/LubangaENG.pdf, p. 1. Accessed on 8 February 2016).

[252] Poltronieri Rossetti, "Il diritto alla riparazione per le vittime di crimini internazionali: problemi e prospettive a partire dalle decisioni della CPI nel caso Lubanga , Graduation thesis, School of Law, Universita di Trento, 2012-2013, p. 211.

Enduring problems are the scarcity of available resources and the absence of adequate remedies in case the convicted is insolvent, or has conscripted minors into the armed forces[253]. How is it possible to avoid the impecuniousness of the convicted from frustrating the reparatory expectations of the victims? In principle, this problem can be remedied in two, possibly even joint, ways[254]: providing some form of subsidiary and supplementary liability of persons other than the convicted (for example, the State); and/or creating specific bodies (typically, trust funds or reparation commissions) that possess the financial and logistical resources required to actually provide the reparation (at least those of material nature) in place of the guilty.

While the Trust Fund for Victims is the only organ apart from the ICC that can become involved in providing reparation and support to the victims, it does not have sufficient resources to adequately compensate for the convicted person's lack or absence of resources for reparation. Indeed, not only have States taken care to avoid establishing forms of additional responsibility for themselves; they have also avoided any legal obligation to make stable, periodic and specific contributions to the TFV, which is thus forced to "survive" on voluntary contributions.

Article 22 ACRWC states that the States Parties must take all necessary measures to ensure that no minor directly takes part in hostilities and, in particular, that minors are not enlisted in their armed forces. This article links to Article 8.XXVI of the Rome Statute, which provides for the punishable war crime of conscripting or enlisting children under the age of 15 in national armed forces, or making them actively participate in hostilities.

Article 22 ACRWC obliges States Parties to take all necessary measures to ensure that no person under 18 years of age is conscripted or participates in any type of hostilities, such as internal armed conflicts, tensions or civil unrest.

II.3.2 The legal responsibility of child soldiers

There are reasons behind the massive use of minors in armed conflict. One is the nature of wars that, for some years now, have transformed from clashes between states into mostly ethnic, social and economic conflicts. Therefore, they are no longer fought by regular armies, but rather by armed groups that do not distinguish military forces and civilians[255].

The distinction is important. If underage combatants are considered child soldiers, with all relevant military characteristics, and are therefore deprived of the guarantees due to minors, they may be subject to the military jurisdiction, which also envisages the death penalty. Minors may be executed for crimes committed with or without trial, in military courts, according to the same rules that apply to adults, as occurred in Somalia in 2010[256]. This has led some scholars to

---

[253] *Ibidem*, p. 272.

[254] *Ibidem*, p. 273.

[255] *Tutto quello che dovresti sapere sull'Africa e che nessuno ti ha mai raccontato. Op. cit.* p. 186.

[256] UNICEF, "Somalia, allarme ONU in aumento gli arruolamenti di bambini soldato', 12 February 2016, (http://www.unicef.it/doc/1422/aumento-di-reclutamento-bambini-soldato-in-somalia.htm, accessed on 8 February 2016).

consider that child soldiers retain the capacity to commit crimes. According to Alcinda Honwana, children exercise "tactical agency" on the immediate circumstances of the military context in which they operate, which is opposite to "strategic agency", which requires an understanding of the consequences of such actions[257]. According to MacMahan, the indoctrination received leads, instead, to their diminished capacity for agency, to an identity as a fighter that cannot exist in peacetime, according to Cohn and Goodwin-Gill[258]. Baines states that if child soldiers are held responsible for their actions, they cannot only be judged on the basis of their acts of violence, but must also be considered victims[259].

The issue of the legal responsibility of children challenges the traditional distinction between the categories of childhood and adulthood, which do not recognize that child soldiers possess typical traits of childhood, such as vulnerability, or those characteristics required to be adult soldiers, such as responsibility and ethics of war.

Article 17 ACRWC regulates the issue of juvenile justice, stating that "[e]very child accused or found guilty of having infringed penal law shall have the right to special treatment in a manner consistent with the child's sense of dignity and worth and which reinforces the child's respect for human rights and fundamental freedoms of others." Article 17(2) deals with safeguards, such as protection against inhuman and degrading treatments, the presumption of innocence and the separation of children and adults in detention. However, no reference is made to the intensity of malice, the degree of awareness that the agent should have exercised and the capacity to commit a crime that expresses the accused's moral level of participation and therefore responsibility (which can be deduced from the reasons for committing the crime), and of the life led by the offender prior to committing the offences. In the absence of any indication in these respects, child soldiers remain theoretically liable to be charged with the crimes committed.

However, the ACRWC's silence must be integrated by making reference to the principle of the child's best interest, and that of respect for the applicable rules of international humanitarian law and human rights. These prompt the conclusion that the crimes committed by child soldiers should not be punished. Indeed, they should not be charged with the crimes, because Article 22 ACRWC obliges States Parties to take all necessary measures to avoid that children participate in hostilities and be conscripted. According to the ACRWC, therefore, the phenomenon of child soldiers takes place, in itself, within a context of illegality.

Despite such a conclusion, in practice, there continue to be many cases in which child soldiers have been prosecuted, without the basic guarantees provided by juvenile justice. From October 2006 to July 2007, there were 49 cases in which children accused of participating in war conflicts

---

[257] Gordon, "Victims and Perpetrators: the Implications of the Dual Status of Child Soldiers", King's College London, 2011 (http://www.e-ir.info/2011/08/03/victims-and-perpetrators-what-are-the-implications-of-this-dual-status-of-child-soldiers/, accessed on 23 March 2016).
[258] Goodwin-Gill, Cohn, "Child Soldiers, The Role of Children in Armed Conflicts", Clarendon Press, Oxford, 1994. p. 228.
[259] Gordon. *Ibidem, op. cit.*

in the provinces of Bujumbura Mairie and Bujumbura Rural (Burundi) were detained[260]. Many of these were incarcerated for many months without trial or legal assistance[261].

Several child soldiers were arrested in 2014 by the authorities of Mali, and imprisoned without adequate protection measures, together with adults and without any rehabilitative guarantees. The charges against them were of being part of rebel guerrilla forces and of illegally possessing firearms. A large part is held in the Bamako prison[262].

Since 1994, Rwanda must ensure that the victims of genocide receive justice, on one hand, and to cope with the inadequacies of its justice system, on the other. To avoid impunity and ensure the timeliness of judicial procedures, Law no. 08/96 was enacted on judging crimes of genocide or crimes against humanity. Infractions committed by minors are considered in special chambers[263]. The creation of special bodies having exclusive competence in the field of juvenile justice is an important innovation in the Rwandan criminal system. Certain provisions refer to the rules of the Rwandan Criminal Code, which reduces punishments for children aged 14 to 18, setting the age of criminal responsibility at 14 years. This guarantees that children who were accused of genocide and up to 14 years old at the time of the imputed facts are absolved of all liability and released; and that special judges decide the cases of those who were between 14 and 18 years at the time of the facts. However, the 1996 law did not yield the desired results. At the end of 1999, only 2 406 people had been judged by the special chambers created to hear trials on crimes of genocide; in 2000, 4 454 children were still detained in Rwandan prisons[264].

According to the 2015 UN report on *Children and armed conflict*, 286 children in Somalia were detained by government forces. It was also reported that minors have been executed in public, as an intimidatory measure[265].

---

[260] UN Secretary General, Report on "Children and Armed Conflict", 21 December 2007, UN Doc. A/62/609/S/2007/757, p. 7 (http://reliefweb.int/sites/reliefweb.int/files/resources/ACB155BBA8E366968525 73DF00773AB4-Full_Report.pdf. Accessed on 23 March 2016).

[261] *Ibidem*, p. 104.

[262] La Repubblica. Nardinocchi. "Mali. La solitudine dei bambini soldato: in prigione come adulti" 21 August 2014. http://www.repubblica.it/solidarieta/dirittiumani/2014/08/21/news/mali_la_solitudine_dei_bambini_soldato_in_prigione_come_adulti-94240844/ Accessed on 18 May 2016.

[263] Rwanda Organic Law no. 8/96 of 30 August 1996 (Organic law on the organization of prosecutions for offences constituting the crime of genocide or crimes against humanity committed since 1 October 1990). See Human Rights Watch, "La loi et la réalité. Le progress de la réforme judiciaire au Rwanda", 25 July 2008, p. 26 (https://www.hrw.org/fr/report/2008/07/25/la-loi-et-la-realite/les-progres-de-la-reforme-judiciaire-au-rwanda, accessed on 31 March 2016).

[264] Panafrican News Agency, "Rwanda: Genocide Trials Await over 4,000 Rwanda Children Prisoners", 12 August 2000,(http://allafrica.com/stories/200008130011.html, accessed on 22 March 2016).

[265] La Repubblica. Rizzo, "Bambini soldato. Lo scempio di 23 paesi del mondo che li mandano in guerra", 12 February 2016. http://www.repubblica.it/solidarieta/dirittiumani/2016/02/12/news/bambini_soldato_lo_scempio_dei_23_paesi_del_mondo_che_li_mandano_in_guerra-133280386, accessed on 18 May 2016.

A system of participatory and popular justice, the *gacaca*, was established in Rwanda. This system allows for greater closeness to the population, given the fact that physical travel is difficult, because transportation is lacking and because participatory justice is a traditional mechanism of peaceful dispute settlement that bears a greater impact on the population[266].

The jurisdiction of the traditional local *gacaca* courts is limited to cases involving persons who have participated in but did not organize murders[267]. This system of justice identifies the guilty, provides remedies for the victims and strives to create a public space for dialogue, potentially also contributing to the community's process of social reconciliation. Effective participation can help to stop the cycle of violence and prevent future conflict and instability. The *gacaca* jurisdictions apply exclusively the provisions of the 2001 organic law, which created them in the first place. Article 74(1) of the 2001 organic law reaffirms the content of Article 77 of the Rwandan Criminal Code, which provides for reductions in sentences for children aged 14 to 18[268]. Providing for the possibility of placing children under 12 in rehabilitation centres is an important signal of the awareness of the need to consider children's reintegration into society[269]. Children aged 12 to 18 are given half the punishment applicable to adults[270]. Despite its limitations, the *gacaca* system is an advancement of the system, because it allowed children who, in 1994, were 14 to 18 years of age, to leave the prisons where they were kept in deplorable conditions[271].

To spare children the trauma of undergoing trial, some scholars suggest creating a reconciliation commission or adopting an amnesty law exclusively for minors, accompanied by a rehabilitation program. Indeed, the mechanisms that can be established in the aftermath of an armed conflict to adjudicate upon violations of international humanitarian law need not be exclusively judicial in nature. In Sierra Leone, non-judicial mechanisms were set up to bring about justice and social pacification, ensuring the rehabilitation and reintegration of child soldiers[272].

In Sierra Leone, the Truth and Reconciliation Commission was the first to expressly mention children in its mandate and recognized the rights and protection that must govern the involvement of children. A cooperation structure was created to link the Truth Commission with child protection agencies.

---

[266] Gaparayi. "Justice and social reconstruction in the aftermath of genocide in Rwanda: An evaluation of the possible role of the gacaca tribunals". AHRLJ (*African Human Right Law Journal*) 2001 para. 2.

[267] Stover, Weinstein, "My Neighbor, My enemy: Justice and community in the aftermath of mass atrocity", Cambridge, Cambridge university press, 2004, p. 70.

[268] Para. 2 of the same provision states that "Les mineurs qui, au moment des faits qui leur sont reprochés, étaient âgés de moins de 14 ans, ne peuvent être poursuivis, mais peuvent être placés dans des centres de rééducation".

[269] Arzoumanian, Pizzutelli, "Victimes et bourreaux: questions de responsabilité liées à la problématique des enfants-soldats en Afrique". International Review of the Red Cross, 2003, p. 850, (https://www.icrc.org/fre/assets/files/other /irrc_852_pizzutelli.pdf, accessed on 8 February 2016).

[270] Human Rights Watch. "La loi et la réalité. Les progrès de la réforme judiciaire au Rwanda", *op. cit.* p. 45.

[271] Arzoumanian, Pizzutelli. "Victimes et bourreaux: questions de responsabilité liées à la problématique des enfants-soldats en Afrique", *op. cit.* p. 850.

[272] Dignelle, Fierens, "Justice et gacaca. L'expérience rwandaise et le génocide". Belgio, Presses Universitaires de Namur, 2003, p. 100.

In Liberia, the law that established the Truth and Reconciliation Commission considered the role of children in conflict and proposed measures to protect them. A Memorandum of Understanding (MOU) between the Truth Commission and the National Child Protection Network Force serves as a basis for innovative strategies to protect the rights of children who testify at regional or institutional hearings[273]. Children have the right to express their point of view and to be considered in these processes of national reconciliation.

UNICEF has adopted criteria to determine when child and youth participation in proceedings. These criteria include: the independence and impartiality of the commission; compliance with international human rights standards; observance of the CRC and the ACRWC; the protection afforded to victims and vulnerable groups; the existence of safety guarantees for children; the provision of appropriate psychosocial support to children and to the overall community, in a spirit of reintegration and reconciliation[274].

More generally, the best interest of the child should be the primary consideration in all actions concerning children and a criterion in decisions to be taken in relation to minors, according to international standards of juvenile justice[275]. The identity of children should always be protected in truth commissions and in judicial proceedings. Truth commissions should not mention children who have committed crimes in its final reports; it should not consider children in such a way as to determine their criminal responsibility; children must be treated with dignity and respect; child protection should envisage techniques that include policies and procedures that safeguard their physical, psychological and spiritual well-being; the participation of children in truth commissions should focus on reintegration, reconciliation and other processes of transactional justice; the truth commission should understand the root causes of the violations of children's rights to ensure the adoption of a long-term holistic approach towards achieving children's civil, political, social, economic and cultural rights.

This system of guarantees specifies the "special treatment" to which the child is entitled pursuant to Article 17(2) ACRWC, in particular Article 17(2)(iii): every child "shall be afforded legal and other appropriate assistance in the preparation and presentation of his defence". However, the article mentions only the impartial tribunal as a judicial organ and not alternative forms of justice, nor alternative penalties to prison. Likewise, it does not specify special measures for girls and nor how witness depositions should be given. However, these measures can be traced back to the general clause of the best interest of the child.

The truth commission is most effective when it complements other transactional justice processes, such as judicial proceedings and reparation programs. While such commissions can require the community to commit to documenting of violence and seeking reconciliation, it cannot take

---

[273] UNICEF & Innocenti. Siegrist. "Children and Truth Commission". Florence, August 2010, p. XII (http://www.unicef-irc.org/publications/pdf/truth_commissions_eng.pdf, accessed on 22 July 2015).

[274] *Ibidem*, p. X.

[275] *Ibidem*, p. XII.

judicial measures concerning criminal liability[276]. Truth commissions can establish non-judicial responsibility and decide on rehabilitation and reconciliation measures[277].

Some countries have decided not to prosecute child soldiers. In 1995, the director of Justice and Peace Commission, an NGO from Liberia, described the attitude of Liberian society to the question of the criminal responsibility of child soldiers as follows: "No child soldier has ever been nor is being held accountable/prosecuted for his/her participation or commission of crimes during our civil war. Our society does not intend to punish children for their part in atrocities. The general move is rather to have them rehabilitated"[278]. And he explained the juridical and cultural reasons for such a position: "This desire not to prosecute children is in pursuance of the Convention on the Rights of the Child as well as our national laws which perceive children as being innocent, and below consent. Culturally, responsibility for wrongs is put on the parents or those who led the children into the commission of crimes rather than the children themselves"[279].

Liberia is a model of justice in the treatment of child soldiers, in accordance with Article 17 ACRWC on juvenile justice, which provides that special treatment, compatible with dignity and value as a minor, be accorded.

The position of Liberia also contextualizes the issue with reference to the responsibilities of adults in involving children in conflicts, as provided by Article 22 ACRWC, which requires States to take measures to prevent the involvement of minors in armed conflicts.

Article 40(2) CRC states that States Parties shall ensure that every child suspected or accused of a criminal offence is entitled to the presumption of innocence until his guilt has been legally established. Similar provision is made in Article 40 ACRWC.

In other countries, child soldiers have been tried for their crimes, often casting doubt on whether the minimum safeguards of juvenile justice are respected. For example, in 2000, six child soldiers were arrested in the Democratic Republic of the Congo. Five were declared guilty of conspiracy against the government, while the rest were convicted of murder. The Court imposed the death penalty upon all[280]. The children did not have legal representation. Kasongo[281], a 14-year-old soldier, was executed in January 2000, half an hour after conclusion of his trial before a special military court. In May 2001, the authorities of the Democratic Republic of the Congo reported to the UN Committee of the Rights of the Child that a number of child soldiers who had been

---

[276] *Ibidem*, p. XI.

[277] *Ibidem*, p. 27.

[278] Samuel K. Woods II, Director of the Justice and Peace Commission, letter to Chen Reis (14 December 1995, quoted in Arzoumanian, Pizzutelli, "Victimes et bourreaux: questions de responsabilité liées à la problématique des enfants-soldats en Afrique", *op. cit.* p. 846).

[279] *Ibidem*.

[280] Coalition to stop the use of child soldiers. Guest. Child soldiers global report. 2008. London. http://www. child-soldiers.org/global_report_reader.php?id=97. Accessed on 28 March 2016.

[281] Amnesty International, Coordinamento pena di morte. "Non uccidete il futuro. Stop alle esecuzioni di minorenni September 2009, p. 1 (www.amnesty.it/flex/cm/pages/ServeAttachment.php/L/11/.../ BLOB%3AID%3D35, accessed on 8 February 2016).

sentenced to death had been pardoned, while failing to mention the execution of Kasongo. Said Committee asked the country "to ensure compliance with Article 37(a) CRC and that no person under the age of 18 be sentenced to death"[282].

This shows that child soldiers continue to undergo proceedings that fail to take into account their vulnerability and the best interest of the child. Before deciding whether to prosecute child soldiers, judicial bodies must exercise their discretion on how to proceed[283]. In reaching this decision, the prosecution should be guided by the child's best interest, determined according to the principles of the ACRWC and the CRC, by evaluating the child's maturity, his or her moral development and the availability of alternative reconciliation mechanisms.

Article 7 of the Statute of the Special Court for Sierra Leone (SCSL) states that the child must be "treated with dignity and a sense of worth, taking into account his or her young age and the desirability of promoting his or her rehabilitation, reintegration into and assumption of a constructive role in society."[284]. In accordance with international law, the Statute of the SCSL provides for child soldiers at Article 7[285]. Instead of imposing terms of imprisonment, the SCSL only orders rehabilitative measures: care, assistance, supervision, counselling, fostering, educational and vocational training programs, reformatories, and disarmament, demobilization and reintegration programs overseen by child protection agencies.

In Rwanda, the minimum age to incur criminal liability is 14 years. However, the Public Prosecutor of the International Criminal Tribunal for Rwanda decided that children from 14 to 18 should not be brought before the ICTR, nor be called to testify[286].

---

[282] UN. CRC Committee, UN DOC: CRC/C/SR.705, 31 May 2001, para. 48; (docstore.ohchr.org/ SelfServices/ FilesHandler.ashx?enc, visionato il 09-06-2016). UN. CRC Committee, UN DOC: CRC/C/SR.706, 3 June 2002, para. 13; (tbinternet.ohchr.org/_.../Download.aspx?...CRC%2FC%2FSR.7, accessed on 09 June 2016). NU. Comitato CRC,CRC/C/15/Add.153, 9 July 2001, para. 75 (tbinternet.ohchr.org/_.../Download.aspx?... CRC%2FC%2F15%2, accessed on 9 Jun 2016).

[283] Jallow. "Prosecutorial discretion and international criminal law" *Journal of International Criminal Justice* 2005, p 145.

[284] Article 7 of the Statute of the SCSL.

[285] 1. The Special Court shall have no jurisdiction over any person who was under the age of 15 at the time of the alleged commission of the crime. Should any person who was at the time of the alleged commission of the crime between 15 and 18 years of age come before the Court, he or she shall be treated with dignity and a sense of worth, taking into account his or her young age and the desirability of promoting his or her rehabilitation, reintegration into and assumption of a constructive role in society, and in accordance with international human rights standards, in particular the rights of the child; 2. In the disposition of a case against a juvenile offender, the Special Court shall order any of the following: care guidance and supervision orders, community service orders, counselling, foster care, correctional, educational and vocational training programmes, approved schools and, as appropriate, any programmes of disarmament, demobilization and reintegration or programmes of child protection agencies.

[286] Children and Truth Commission, *op. cit.* p. 17.

States should draw up maps to identify those areas where conflicts, at-risk groups and potential recruitment agents are concentrated, and intervene accordingly to prevent the recruitment of minors[287]. Likewise, light weapons traffickers and those who support them must be punished[288].

The ACRWC does not establish rehabilitation measures for child soldiers. Instead, the CRC (Article 39) states that States Parties shall take all appropriate measures to facilitate the physical and psychological recovery and social reintegration of every child who is the victim of an armed conflict.

Often, these commitments to advance the recovery and physical and psychological rehabilitation (including prostheses) of child soldiers are carried out by associations, and not by States.

Article 22 ACRWC provides that States Parties shall take all necessary measures to ensure that no minor takes part in the conflicts or is enlisted. The phenomenon of child soldiers demonstrates, therefore, the interdependence of the rights enshrined in the ACRWC. indeed, it is only by implementing Article 6 on the registration of children at birth, and Article 11 on education, that it will be possible to prevent the recruitment of child soldiers. Registration at birth enables searching for children and verifying the age of those enlisted. Education offers training for life in civil society, based on the values expressed at Article 11(d): "the preparation of the child for responsible life in a free society, in the spirit of understanding tolerance, dialogue, mutual respect and friendship among all peoples ethnic, tribal and religious groups".

The ACRWC does not contain provisions on the treatment to be accorded to child soldiers in the trials against them, nor does it suggest any alternatives to formal proceedings. On the other hand, countries such as Rwanda, Liberia and Sierra Leone introduced such provisions into their legal systems, thus assuring greater guarantees to children than envisaged at international level. In addition, the ACRWC does not provide for rehabilitation measures. However, these may be inferred from the CRC. There remains the issue of the implementation of rehabilitation, which should be done by countries, also on the basis of guidelines; instead, it is actually done by NGOs, which enjoy significant discretion in this context.

Some countries, such as Congo[289] and Rwanda[290] have created a demobilization program for former child soldiers, aimed at their reintegration into families. However, the reports do not discuss any policies put in place to prevent the recruitment of child soldiers.

---

[287] Anselmi. "Il fenomeno dei bambini soldato quando l'educazione è progettualità di cambiamento". Graduation thesis. Degree in "operazioni di pace, gestione e mediazione dei conflitti". Università degli studi di Firenze. 2006-2007, p. 86. http://gruppocrc.net/IMG/pdf/TESIbambinisoldato.pdf.

[288] *Ibidem*, p. 92.

[289] Congo Initial Report on the implementation of the ACRWC, p. 103, http://www.accrwc.org/download/congo_initial_report_acrwc/?wpdmdl=8796, accessed on 2 June 2016.

[290] Rwanda Initial Report on the implementation of the ACRWC, p. 38, http://www.acerwc.org/download/rwanda-initial-report/?wpdmdl=8653, accessed on 2 June 2016.

II.4 Article 23 ACRWC: the protection of refugee and displaced children

Violence in Darfur, lawlessness in Somalia and the civil war in the Sahrawi Arab Democratic Republic, Uganda, Côte d'Ivoire and Chad, as well as the recent history of violence in the Democratic Republic of the Congo, Sierra Leone, Liberia and Guinea make Africa one of the most unstable continents in the world. Political instability in countries such as Zimbabwe, Rwanda, Burundi, the Central African Republic, Ethiopia and Eritrea has caused massive social dislocation, the result of the migration of people seeking refuge from danger[291]. At the end of 2005, the total number of people in Africa who had sought refuge outside their own country was of approximately 2.6 million, while the total number of refugees (internationally displaced persons, or IDPs) is just under 12 million[292].

However, although these forced migrations affect all members of the population, their impact on minors is particularly significant. The UN High Commissioner for Refugees has estimated that, of the population that has fled across borders, at least 45 percent are children under 18 years of age, while more than 60 percent of refugees are children[293]. Given their young age and absence of guardians, refugee children are particularly at risk of illegal military recruitment, sexual exploitation and abuse, child labour, difficulties in accessing basic education and care, and even death[294]. Considering their great vulnerability, refugee children require a high level of protection and assistance.

Although a multitude of refugee children live on the continent and their vulnerable state has been recognized, the African human rights system did not initially envisage a special protection regime to deal with their particular situation. The protection of refugees in the African system is provided by the AU, the OAU Convention Governing the Specific Aspects of Refugee Problems in Africa and the African Charter on the Rights of Peoples. However, these instruments do not carve out special protection for refugee children, leaving the matter to receiving states and international refugee organizations.

With the entry into force of the ACRWC, fundamental and far-reaching changes were made in the protection of children in general and refugee children in particular. Article 23 ACRWC states that States Parties shall take all appropriate measures to ensure that each refugee and displaced child receives the protection and humanitarian assistance in the enjoyment of the rights set out in this Charter and other international human rights and humanitarian instruments to which the States are parties, to alleviate their difficult situation. There is no indication on the nature

---

[291] Samra, Bernstein, Birkenes, Eschenbacher, Faret, Foaleng, McCallin, Kok, Nadig, Skwarska, Thienig, Walicki, Zeender, "Internal displacement, Global overview of trend and developments in 2006", Internal Dispacement monitoring centre, April 2007, p. 23 (http://www.internal-displacement.org/assets/publications/2007/2007-global-overview2006-global-en.pdf, accessed on 8 February 2016).

[292] *Ibidem*, p. 51.

[293] *Ibidem*, p. 183.

[294] UNGA. "Protection and Assistance to Unaccompanied Refugee Minors". 19 December 2001, UN Doc. A/Res/56/136, par. 6 (http://www.un.org/en/ga/search/view_doc.asp?symbol=A/RES/56/136, accessed on 09 June 2016).

of such "appropriate measures": the situations in which refugee children find themselves must be assessed on a case-by-case basis, and the answers continuously re-evaluated in light of the particular situation at hand.

The principle of non-discrimination obliges States Parties to grant to all children, without discrimination, the rights enshrined in the ACRWC. Thus, any child who falls under the jurisdiction of a State enjoys all rights established in the ACRWC regardless of political opinion, citizenship, immigration status or other state[295]. In fact, in relation to refugee children, the ACRWC obliges States to ensure that they enjoy the rights established in the ACRWC itself and in the other international instruments to which they may be party (Article 23(1) ACRWC). In particular, the host country is obliged to provide a minimum set of essential guarantees, such as food, adequate health care and hospitalization if required, and is obliged to ensure that children are adequately safe and free from dangers deriving from the situations they have fled. States must also guarantee the continuity of children's education[296]. The state thus undertakes to facilitate the expeditious normalization of children's situations. Where the receiving state is unable to guarantee this, it must make use of its diplomatic powers to obtain international aid from other regional or international partners[297].

As for family reunification, when children are separated from the adult caring for them, the ACRWC does contain special provisions. According to Article 23(2), States Parties shall assist international organizations having the mandate of protecting and assisting refugees, in their efforts to perform child protection and assistance activities, and to find the parents or close relatives of unaccompanied refugee children, to obtain the information required to return them to their families. Recognizing the centrality of the family in the education of children is a priority in family reunification, as a primary response in family separation. This responds to the best interest of the child, because within their families, children are generally better protected from risks such as exploitation and sexual abuse, military recruitment, child labour or lack of access to education[298]. Therefore, the ACRWC promotes family reunification as a primary option. However, even family reunification must consider the best interest of the child. Reunification may not be in the best interest of the child if the parents or relatives are partly or wholly responsible for crimes: in the Rwandan genocide, for example, many family members were responsible for killing their own relatives. Thus, when a child escapes from a HTP, such as forced marriage or genital mutilation, in which family members were involved, reunification must be considered with great caution.

---

[295] Chimni. "International Refugee Law: a Reader". Sage Publications, New Dehli. 2000, p. 200.

[296] UNHCR (2004) "Education Forum Initiative: Innovative Strategic Partnerships in Refugee Education", March 2004, p. 7 (http://www.unhcr.org/408e06224.pdf, accessed on 5 February 2016).

[297] Kaime. "The protection of Refugee Children Under the African Human Rights System: Finding Durable Solutions in International Law". In *Children's Rights in Africa*. Sloth Nielsen (ed.), Ashgate, 2010, p. 189.

[298] In May 2007, UNHCR conducted an assessment visit, with Rwandan authorities, to the refugee camps, to verify reports on the recruitment of child soldiers and to raise awareness within the refugee community, while ensuring the greater involvement of local authorities, increasing controls over children leaving the camps and bringing to justice those who recruited children. The Government of Rwanda undertook an investigation following the recruitment of an 8-year-old boy from the Kiziba camp. See UN Secretary General, Report on "Children and armed conflict", 21 December 2007, UN Doc UN Doc, A/62/609 / S/2007/757, p. 10 (http://watchlist.org/wordpress/wp-content/uploads/SG-annual-report-2007.pdf. Accessed on 28 March 2016).

It should be noted that reunification does not only entail the repatriation of the unaccompanied minor to his or her country of origin; the best interest of the child may require reunification in the place where the child is currently found[299]. For example, during the 2006 war in Somalia between the federal government and the Islamic militias, Kenya repatriated refugees including Somali children. Clearly, returning to a country in the throes of war was not in the best interest of the children.

With regard to alternative treatments, Article 23(3) ACRWC states that where parents or legal guardians or relatives cannot be found, unaccompanied refugee children should be granted the same protection as any other child who has been permanently or temporarily deprived of his or her family for any reason. According to these provisions, states must ensure that children who are without parents, permanently or temporarily, receive alternative forms of family care, such as adoption or entrustment to institutions working for the protection and care of children[300].

In relation to the provision of alternative care for unaccompanied refugee children, the ACRWC demonstrates a preference for accommodation that safeguards the minor's ethnic, religious or linguistic origin. Article 25(3) states that if a child is to be placed in a shelter or given up for adoption, in considering the best interest of the child, it should be recalled that it is desirable to ensure educational continuity for the child, and that the child's ethnic, religious and linguistic roots should be taken into account. However, in the best interest of the child, accommodation that offers cultural continuity with the customs and traditions of the country of origin could be excluded if the other guarantees provided by the ACRWC are no longer assured.

The right to identity envisaged by Article 6 ACRWC guarantees to each child the right to the name, the right to be registered immediately after birth, and the right to acquire a nationality. The commitment of the States Parties to fulfill the duty to register pursuant to Article 6 ACRWC relates to the adoption of mechanisms that can ensure the registration of children immediately after birth and that children are not illegally deprived of their names or their origin[301]. In relation to refugee children, the right to identity and registration of children is of paramount importance. The registration of children helps to trace family members for reunification purposes, and to protect the cultural, racial, linguistic and religious identity that informs the process of determining

---

[299] "The protection of Refugee Children Under the African Human Rights System: Finding Durable Solutions in International Law" *op. cit.* p. 19.

[300] Article 25(2)(a) ACRWC: States Parties to the present Charter: (a) shall ensure that a child who is parentless, or who is temporarily or permanently deprived of his or her family environment, or who in his or her best interest cannot be brought up or allowed to remain in that environment shall be provided with alternative family care, which could include, among others, foster placement, or placement in suitable institutions for the care of children".

[301] The ACERWC has emphasized that these rights are critical to the child's identity because it is only through registration that it is possible to guarantee that the existence of a child is guaranteed by law (Nowak, 1993, p. 432).

the best interest of the child. These provisions require states to identify, register and document refugee children to the greatest extent possible[302].

UNICEF[303] has called on the international community to address the root causes of the huge migration of desperate children, making firmer diplomatic efforts to end conflicts and provide the necessary humanitarian support and development in the countries of origin: in other words, a greater commitment to relocate refugees from war-torn countries, to reduce the likelihood that they will resort to dangerous routes and are caught by human traffickers.

Analysing the effectiveness of Article 23 ACRWC, according to which the ACRWC recognizes that the States Parties shall take all appropriate measures to guarantee that refugee minors enjoy the rights enshrined in the ACRWC itself and in any other international humanitarian and humanitarian instruments to which the States are party. Such rights concern medical care and education services, as well as registration at birth. Article 23 ACRWC requires States and international organizations having a mandate to protect and assist refugees to collaborate with one another.

State reports illustrate the measures taken to ensure that children in refugee camps receive basic services such as food, medical care and education.

The crucial issues concern registration at birth, family reunification and safety in the refugee camps.

In the Algeria report[304], the *Integral de Salud Infantil Sahrawi – Pisis* program, jointly executed by the UN High Commission for Refugees (UNHCR) and the World Food Program (WFP) establishes strict protocols to improve the health and nutritional status of children under five years of age in refugee camps. Such protocols include vaccinations, treatment of the most common diseases, efforts to prevent malnutrition, and monitoring of hygiene and nutrition standards.

Burkina Faso[305] provides for repatriation with free transportation. The care envisaged for repatriated children consists of vaccinations (meningitis, tetanus, measles) and psychological assistance.

Cameroon[306] gives refugee children food, medical care, education, school fees, school supplies and uniforms.

---

[302] Steinbock, "Unaccompanied Refugee Children in Host Country Foster Families", *International Journal on Refugee Law*, 1996, p. 21. See also UNHCR, "Refugee Children: Guidelines for Their Protection and Care", 1994, http://www.unhcr.ch/, accessed on 29 October 2006. P. 124

[303] UNICEF. "Bambini migranti e rifugiati. Dall'Europa più azioni condivise ed equa ripartizione degli oneri", 5 settembre 2015 (http://www.unicef.it/doc/6411/bambini-migranti-e-rifugiati-unicef-da-europa-pi-azioni-condivise-e-equaripartizione degli-oneri.htm.5, accessed on 5 February 2016).

[304] Algeria Initial Report on the implementation of the ACRWC, p. 56, http://acerwc.org/?wpdmdl=8766, accessed on 27 December 2015.

[305] Burkina Faso Initial Report on the implementation of the ACRWC, p. 116, http://accrwc.org/?wpdmdl=8780, accessed on 27 December 2015.

[306] Cameroon Initial Report on the implementation of the ACRWC, p. 57, http://acerwc.org/?wpdmdl=8781, accessed on 27 December 2015.

The Congo has established a voluntary repatriation program, in cooperation with the UNHCR. In 2007, several children[307] have benefited from this program; however, 8 000 people, including approximately 5 000 children, have refused repatriation and remain in the long-term refugee category.

In Ethiopia[308] in December 2012, the Ministry of Interior, in partnership with the UNHCR, launched a project to register refugee children in civil registers, as part of a larger intervention. Proclamation no. 409/2004 of 2004, on Refugee Proclamation, grants special rights to all refugees. The measure is in accordance with the UN and AU conventions on refugees. Article 2(8)(b) expressly states that children are automatically eligible, as members of refugee families. Article 12 ensures family unity and their right of access services.

Ghana[309] collaborates with other agencies to provide refugee children with special protection, shelter, food, psychological assistance and other forms of emotional support necessary for their survival. The Ghanaian immigration services handle the applicable immigration procedures, in cooperation with the Department of Social Protection.

In Liberia[310], several efforts have been made to facilitate the reunification of unaccompanied children. The Liberia Repatriation, Reunification and Resettlement Commission (LRRRC) has the mandate to work with the international community on issues of internal separations and dispersal arising from armed conflicts, civil wars or natural disasters. The LRRRC has worked with the international community and local civil society organizations to address the issues relating to family reunification. Article 23 ACRWC declares that States should refer to organizations to trace the parents or close relatives of unaccompanied refugee minors, and to obtain the necessary information to return them to their families.

In collaboration with the UNHCR, the LRRRC provides for the repatriation of families with children born in exile and who have been raised in refugee camps, as well as for the reception (and related legal and social assistance) of those refugees who wish to remain in Liberia[311].

In the Mali report[312], the main problem highlighted with regard to the condition of unaccompanied children is the lack of professionalism in identifying them and assuring the necessary social

---

[307] Congo Initial Report on the implementation of the ACRWC, p. 102, http://acerwc.org/?wpdmdl=8796, accessed on 27 December 2015.

[308] Ethiopia Initial Report on the implementation of the ACRWC, p. 100, http://acerwc.org/?wpdmdl=8645, accessed on 27 December 2015.

[309] Ghana Initial Report on the implementation of the ACRWC, p. 51, http://acerwc.org/?wpdmdl=8775 (accessed on 27 December 2015).

[310] Liberia Initial Report on the implementation of the ACRWC, p. 14, http://acerwc.org/?wpdmdl=8651 (accessed on 27 December 2015).

[311] Palmisano, Momodu. UNHCR. "Completes repatriation of 155,000 Liberians". 4 January 2013. http://www.unhcr.org/50e6af089.html. Accessed on 19 May 2016.

[312] Mali Report on the implementation of the ACRWC, p. 94, http://acerwc.org/?wpdmdl=8782, accessed on 27 December 2015.

assistance. The Government, together with UNICEF, has developed a "Training manual for unaccompanied and separated children" program[313].

In the Mozambique report[314], the Government noted the creation of the National Institute for the Assistance of Refugees (INAR), which ensures that refugee rights are protected, such as access to education by refugee children, medical care, social security and the right to recreation, as well as protection against torture and degrading treatment, abuse and other forms of practices that are detrimental to their development.

The Namibia report[315] emphasizes that measures have been adopted to guarantee the right of refugee children to medical care. Primary and secondary education is free and guaranteed to all children, including refugee children. An agreement with the UNHCR guarantees prenatal and post-natal care to mothers. Child cannot be repatriated if suitable accommodation cannot be guaranteed upon his return, and in the absence of judicial authorization. Refugee children cannot be detained, except in extreme cases, and in any case, cannot be detained with adults. The only exception is where refugee families are detained; in this case, the children cannot be separated from adult family members.

In Nigeria[316], the National Population Commission (NPopC), in cooperation with the African Refugee Community, ensures that all refugee children in the country are registered, regardless of the circumstances of their birth.

In Rwanda[317], the Ministry for Disaster Management and Refugees Affairs (MIDIMAR) was created in 2010, to ensure the implementation of the National Refugee Policy and to monitor and evaluate the efficiency of the management of refugee camps and the observance of refugees' rights and social welfare.

In Zimbabwe, with regard to refugee children, the Government and other development partners seek to facilitate family reunion and reunification. Refugee children are registered and acquire the nationality of their parents[318].

As for the effectiveness of Article 23 ACRWC, states such as Burkina Faso, Cameroon, Ghana, Mozambique and Namibia provide basic humanitarian assistance in the form of medical treatment

---

[313] International Red Cross Committee. Kellenberger. "Inter-agency, Guiding Principles on unaccompanied and separated children". January 2004. http://www.unicef.org/protection/IAG_UASCs.pdf, accessed on 27 December 2015.

[314] Mozambique Initial Report on the implementation of the ACRWC, p. 65, http://acerwc.org/?wpdmdl=8650, accessed on 27 December 2015.

[315] Namibia Initial Report on the implementation of the ACRWC, p. 81, http://acerwc.org/?wpdmdl=8652, accessed on 27 December 2015.

[316] Nigeria Initial Report on the implementation of the ACRWC, p. 59, http://acerwc.org/?wpdmdl=8784, accessed on 27 December 2015.

[317] Rwanda Initial Report on the implementation of the ACRWC, p. 37, http://acerwc.org/?wpdmdl=8653, accessed on 27 December 2015.

[318] Zimbabwe Initial Report on the implementation of the ACRWC, p. 28, http://acerwc.org/?wpdmdl=8778, accessed on 27 December 2015.

and food. Ghana also refers to psychological assistance, while only the Cameroon report mentions to the right to education as per Article 11 ACRWC. It is clear that only the reports of Zimbabwe and Liberia refer to measures taken for the purpose of family reunification.

Therefore, according to Article 2(2), States Parties must act and work with with international organizations mandated to protect and assist refugees in carrying out their child protection and assistance activities, to track down the parents or close relatives of unaccompanied refugee children, and to obtain the information required to return them to their families. Monitoring efforts should be included in their reports.

Regarding the report of the United Republic of Tanzania, the ACERWC expressed concern that the family tracing program is not conducted by the State Party itself but by the country's Red Cross. There is also a lack of clear and up-to-date information necessary for reunifying children with their families. The ACERWC urged the State Party to pass specific legislation and establish appropriate and effective mechanisms in this regard[319].

In Liberia, too, repatriation took place 23 years after the end of the war. Therefore, the children who were born in refugee camps became adults therein the refugee camps[320].

Refugee children, according to Article 22 ACRWC on the right to receive protection and humanitarian assistance within the framework of the rights recognized by the ACRWC itself, may benefit from medical treatment (Article 14), birth registration (Article 6), education (Article 11) and recreational activities (Article 12).

Several States have taken steps to achieve family reunification, including through cooperation with humanitarian organizations. However, much remains to be done regarding the safety of children in refugee camps, especially with regard to unaccompanied minors, who are most liable to recruitment by military rebels[321], contrarily to Article 22 ACRWC.

II.5   Child trafficking in Africa

A 2002 UNICEF study[322] analysed child trafficking in eight African countries: Benin, Burkina Faso, Cameroon, Côte d'Ivoire, Gabon, Mali, Nigeria and Togo. In Africa, 68 percent of victims

---

[319] Concluding Observations of the ACERWC on the United Republic of Tanzania Report, p. 10, http://www. acerwc.org/?wpdmndl, accessed on 2 February 2016.

[320] "Completes repatriation of 155,000 Liberians". *op. cit.*

[321] UNICEF. Atzori. "I bambini della guerra", June 2000, p. 22 (https://www.unric.org/html/italian /children/ TEMI3.PDF, accessed on 09 June 2016).

[322] UNICEF & Centro di ricerca Innocenti di Firenze. Pais. "Child Trafficking in West Africa. Policy responses". April 2002. p. 7 (http://www.unicef-irc.org/publications/pdf/insight7.pdf. Accessed on 5 February 2016).

of trafficking are children: trafficking is done mainly for sexual exploitation, labour exploitation, organ trafficking and slavery[323].

Article 29 ACRWC on the sale, trafficking and abduction of children calls on States Parties to take appropriate measures to prevent the kidnapping, sale and trafficking of minors for any purpose or in any manner by any person, including their parents and legal guardians. However, the ACRWC does not give a detailed definition of "trafficking" and "sale" of children, such that the elements of the offences are unclear.

Gose[324] notes that the inclusion of parents and legal guardians in Article 29 ACRWC as potential agents of trafficking translates to a higher level of protection for children[325]. However, the ACRWC does not specify which measures should be taken in this regard.

In Chad, for example, children are sold and enslaved[326]. Teenagers may be sold by their parents for a sum of 10 000 to 15 000 CFA francs (between 15 and 23 euros) to Arab farmers from the north. Others may be exchanged for a calf. The practice of child shepherds began in the 1970, during the Sahel drought and, because of widespread poverty, soon spread throughout the southern part of the country. The practice consists in selling children to a breeder, to keep the latter's flock. In return, the breeder pays the family a sum between 10 000 and 15 000 francs CFA (between 15 and 23 euros) or can be paid with a calf. The "contract" is valid for one year. However, many children end up working for their Arab masters for three years, in extremely harsh and difficult conditions, especially if one considers that such shepherds may be as young as eight years old. They are forced to graze and watch the flock even at night, and in all weathers. Malnourished and ill-treated, they eat and sleep on the ground among the oxen and are exposed to snake bites and to the attacks of the animals of prey that inhabit the southern region of Chad. They are often punished and beaten, especially if an animal is lost. In some cases, these children, already weak because of their working conditions[327], die. According to a number of humanitarian agencies located in Chad, today there are approximately 2 000 child shepherds under the age of 8, sold off by their parents and then enslaved by their masters.

---

[323] United Nation Office on Drugs and Crimes, Kangaspunta, Sarrica, Johansen, "Global report on trafficking in persons", December 2012, p. 10 (https://www.unodc.org/documents/data-and-analysis/glotip/ Trafficking_in_Persons_2012_ web.pdf. Accessed on 5 February 2016).

[324] Gose, "The African Charter on the Rights and Welfare of the Child, Bellville: Community Law Centre". University of the Western Cape, 2002. p. 66.

[325] Article 29: Sale, Trafficking and Abduction
States Parties to the present Charter shall take appropriate measures to prevent:
    (a) the abduction, the sale of, or traffick of children for any purpose or in any form, by any person including parents or legal guardians of the child;
    (b) the use of children in all forms of begging.

[326] US Department of State. "Trafficking in Persons Report – Chad", 19 June 2012 (http://www.refworld.org/ docid/4fe30cd83c.html, accessed on 12 January 2016).

[327] Peace Reporter. "Bambini pastori". 18 January 2005 (http://it.peacereporter.net/articolo/1055/ Bambini+pastori, Accessed on 19 March 2016).

In Benin, Article 166 of the Labour Code[328] limits the minimum age for employment to 14 years. However, there are cases of children working from the age of 6[329]. The largest group of child labourers consists essentially of minors who have either left school or never enrolled. The most common form of child labour is that of "vidomegon", or child entrustment. *Vidomegons* are children who have been entrusted by their parents to a third party or a person called an intermediary, with the aim of giving them an education or work. Once considered a sign of traditional solidarity between parents and members of the same family, *vidomegon* has now become a lucrative phenomenon of child placement, by intermediaries who benefit from remuneration while the children provide free labour in plantations or markets, and are susceptible to mistreatment. The phenomenon has now assumed the dimensions of a veritable criminal enterprise, which involves organizations involved in both national and cross-border child trafficking[330]. Internal trafficking is a submerged work activity; international trafficking is done by means of a supply-chain organization which benefits organized crime.

The absence of preventive and coercive national measures is exacerbated by the problem of the permeability of borders, resulting from regulatory and institutional shortcomings. In Africa, in recent years, there have been increasing efforts to raise awareness on the issue, so that legislation can be enacted to combat child trafficking and provide for the rehabilitation and repatriation of the victims of trafficking. At the 2002 session of the Labour and Social Affairs Commission, the AU reiterated the intention to eliminate child trafficking as an operational priority[331]. Other African initiatives to combat child trafficking include the Action Plan adopted by the Economic Community of West African States (ECOWAS) in December 2001 and the Action Plan adopted in Libreville in December 2000 by the Sub-Regional Consultation on the Development of Strategies to Fight Child Trafficking for Exploitative Labour Purposes in West and Central Africa.

Another aspect of this problem that emerges in South Africa is the trafficking of refugees. Cape Town has been identified as the main destination of refugee trafficking[332]. The Molo Songololo Report states that in the context of child trafficking, in South Africa, girls are the primary target and the main traffickers are parents and local criminal gangs[333].

---

[328] Law no. 98-004 of 27 January 1998, Labour Law Code (http://www.ilo.org/dyn/natlex/docs/WEBTEXT/49604/65115/F98BEN01.htm, accessed on 7 June 2016).

[329] UNICEF. "Report di progetto "contro il traffico di bambini" in Benin risultati conseguiti 2008-2009" (http://www.unicef.it/Allegati/benin_report.pdf, accessed on 9 June 2016).

[330] Unicef. "Report di progetto "Contro il traffico di bambini" in Benin. 2009" (http://www.unicef.it/doc/608/report-progetto-benin-traffico-bambini.htm accessed on 19 March 2016).

[331] Unicef, Innocenti Research Centre, "Trafficking in human beings, especially women and children in Africa", 2005, p 1.1 (http://www.unicef-irc.org/publications/pdf/insight9e.pdf, accessed on 23 March 2016).

[332] International Organization for Migration, Martens, Pieczkowski, Van Vuuren-Smythe, "Trafficking in Women and Children for Sexual Exploitation in Southern Africa", April 2003, p. 13 (http://www.childtrafficking.org/pdf/user/iom_south%20_africa_research.pdf, accessed on 9 June 2016).

[333] Molo Songololo, "The trafficking of children for Purposes of Sexual Exploitation: South Africa" Cape Town. 2000, p. 2 (http://www.atria.nl/epublications/2000/trafficking_of_children.pdf, accessed on 29 March 2016=.

Article 35 CRC states that to counter trafficking and child trafficking, States must take all appropriate national, bilateral and multilateral measures. Article 29 ACRWC, instead, on trafficking, does not specify the measures to be taken. As regards the provisions actually made in this context, African states appear somewhat varied.

Nigeria was the first African country to adopt anti-trafficking legislation in 2003 and to set up an anti-trafficking agency, the National Agency for Prohibition of Traffic in Persons and Other Related Matters (NAPTIP).

A recent study of six countries of southern Africa[334] has emphasized that South Africa is the only state that has adopted specific legal provisions on child trafficking: the Children's Act of 2005 defines child trafficking in detail[335]. Article 11 of the law establishes penalties for trafficking without documents, referring to the states' national laws[336].

Some international instruments may be of assistance when seeking to interpret the concepts of the ACRWC[337]. In particular, the Additional Protocol to the United Nations Convention against Transnational Organized Crime (Palermo Protocol) establishes that "trafficking in persons" consists of: the recruitment, transport, transfer, hosting or hosting of a child for exploitation purposes. As for the notion of exploitation, reference can be made to the ACRWC provisions on the employment of minors (Article 15) and sexual exploitation (Article 27).

---

[334] Thompson. "Legal and Practical Obstacles to Prosecution of Child Labour Exploitation in Southern Africa", paper presented at Conference on "Reducing Exploitative Child Labour, Johannesburg, Sud Africa, July 2006 (http://www.queensu.ca/samp/migrationnews/article. php?Mig_News_ID=3196&Mig_News_Issue=18&Mig_News_Cat=1, accessed on 9 June 2016).

[335] Article 1 of the Children's Act 2005 defines child trafficking as "recruitment, sale, supply, transportation, transfer, harbouring or receipt of children, within or across the borders of the Republic: (a)By any means, including the use of threat, force or other forms of coercion, abduction, fraud, deception, abuse of power or the giving or receiving of payments or benefits to achieve the consent of a person having control of a child; or (b)Due to a position of a child facilitated or secured through illegal means. Likewise, exploitation is defined in the same section as: "exploitation", in relation to a child, includes: (a) All forms of slavery or practices similar to slavery, including debt bondage or forced marriage; (b) Sexual exploitation; (c) Servitude; (d) Forced labour or service; (e) Child labour prohibited in terms of section 141; and (f) The removal of body parts."

[336] Article 1 of the Children's Act 2005 sets out punishments: "Where appropriate and without prejudice to applicable international conventions, such measures shall include establishing the obligation of commercial carriers, including any transportation company or the owner or operator of any means of transport to ascertain that all passengers are in possession of the travel documents required for entry into the receiving State. Each State Party shall take the necessary measures, in accordance with its domestic law, to provide for sanctions in cases of violation of the obligation set forth in paragraph 3 of this article."

[337] The UN Protocol on the Prevention, Suppression and Persecution of Trafficking in Human Beings, especially Women and Children is one of the three Palermo Protocols (the others are the Protocol against the trafficking of migrants by land, sea and air and the Protocol on the fight against illicit manufacture and trafficking of firearms, their parts and components and ammunition), adopted by the UN in Palermo in 2000. The Protocol on trafficking was adopted by the UN in Palermo in 2000 and entered into force on 25 December 2003. It has been ratified by 154 States.

Article 15 ACRWC on child labour protects children from economic exploitation and from doing work that involves a likelihood of harm or the risk of disturbing their education or compromising their health or physical, mental, spiritual, moral and social development. However, the law does not provide protection in many cases, such as: full-time work at a very young age, dangerous work environments, excessive working hours, psychological, verbal, physical and sexual abuse, forced labour, poor or no wages, working and living on the streets in poor conditions, inability to escape the vicious circle of poverty, failure to access education.

Article 27 ACRWC on sexual exploitation is formulated in broad terms, that can thus encompass all forms of exploitation. Indeed, it commits States Parties to protecting children from all forms of sexual exploitation and abuse and regarding all sexual activity.

While some states do not regulate trafficking, others have introduced specific precise bans. Burkina Faso does not have laws that prohibit the trafficking of children or adults; Mozambique has no national provisions to prosecute traffickers of human beings. On the other hand, in 2008, the United Republic of Tanzania promulgated the Anti-Trafficking in Persons Act, a law that prohibits all forms of trafficking. The penalties are imprisonment (up to 20 years) and fines, ranging from 5 million to 50 million shillings, depending on the type of trafficking[338]. In addition, the law provides for crimes that refer to the trafficking of children or the disabled, adoption for sexual or labour exploitation and offences that may be committed by religious leaders or other authorities[339]. Zimbabwe's Trafficking in Persons Act 2014 also provides for information campaigns to be conducted in the media, as well as international cooperation programs for people vulnerable to child trafficking due to poverty and to the lack of opportunities[340].

---

[338] Anti-Trafficking in Persons Act della Tanzania, 2008 Section 4(3). "Where a victim of trafficking in person is a child, consent of the child, parent or guardian of the child shall not be used a defence in prosecution under this Act regardless of wheter there is evidence of abuse of power, fraud, deception or that the vulnerability of the child was taken advantage of" (http://www.immigration.go.tz/downloads/Anti-trafficking%20in%20Person%20 Act% 202008.pdf, accessed on 07 June 2016).

[339] *Ibidem.* Section 6(2)(a): "The trafficked person is a child or a disabled person."

[340] Article 9 of the Prevention of Trafficking in Persons Act states that: "States Parties shall establish comprehensive policies, programmes and other measures: (a) to prevent and combat trafficking in persons; and (b) to protect victims of trafficking in persons, especially women and children, from revictimization, 2. States Parties shall endeavour to undeltake measures such as research, information and mass media campaigns and social and economic initiatives to prevent and combat trafficking in persons. 3. Policies, programmes and other measures established in accordance with this article shall, as appropriate, include cooperation with non-governmental organizations, other relevant organizations and other elements of civil society, 4. States Patties shall take or strengthen measures, including through bilateral or multilateral cooperation, to alleviate the factors that make persons, especially women and children, vulnerable to trafficking, such as poverty, underdevelopment and lack of equal opportunity, educational, social or cultural measures, including through bilateral and multilateral cooperation, to discourage the demand that fosters all forms of exploitation of persons, especially women and children, that leads to trafficking. 5. States Parties shall adopt or strengthen legislative or other measures, such as educational, social or cultural measures, including through bilateral and multilateral cooperation, to discourage the demand that fosters all forms of exploitation of persons, especially women and children, that leads to trafficking."

Similarly, Malawi has shown real commitment in combating trafficking, both in law and in practice. Malawi has adopted criminal legislation that prohibits all forms of trafficking through various legislative acts, including the Employment Act and Articles 135 to 147 and 257 to 269 of the Penal Code, and that criminalizes forced labour, prostitution and reduction in slavery. These rules protect children up to 14 years of age. The Malawi Government has also opened drop-in centers to provide medical care, legal assistance, shelter, food and training for victims of trafficking and sexual violence. In this case too, the ACRWC does not provide for reception and rehabilitation measures for child victims of trafficking. However, such assistance can be deduced from the principle of the best interest of the child.

In 2005, Nigeria enacted a federal law that prohibits trafficking. The country has undertaken numerous initiatives to combat the phenomenon, providing for the training of investigators and using a computerized database on criminal trafficking and establishing an anti-trafficking network with other 11 states[341].

West African countries have implemented multilateral and bilateral cooperation agreements with their neighbouring countries, to gather information by means of electronic databases[342]. For this reason, a number of African states have successfully adopted this model. In Gabon, an ad-hoc interministerial committee set up an action platform: the Libreville Common Platform of Action[343]. The Ethiopian Government has also responded to an increase in traffic with the organization of an interministerial committee on trafficking in women and children[344].

Article 29 ACRWC adds a prohibition on begging, conceived as a new form of trafficking. This is an advancement in protection with respect to the CRC, because in Article 29, begging is mentioned together with sale, trafficking and abduction. Indeed, the minor can be exploited and forced to beg for profit (benefitting third parties)[345], thus being denied ACRWC rights such as the right to education in accordance with Article 11. Article 20 ACRWC also provides that States Parties, taking into account their available resources and the national situation, shall take all necessary measures to assist parents or other persons responsible for minors and, in case of need, provide material assistance programs and support, in particular food, clothing and housing.

---

[341] US Department of State, Brown, Donnelly, Eterno, Flood, Kennelly, Gaetan,Goode, Goedrich, Hall, Keena, Menares Bury, Miller, Neumann, Norin, O'Neill Richard, Patel, Pierce, Pike, Sharifi, Sigmon, Sims, Stevens, Taylor, Tetschen, Topping, Yousey, Zeitlin. "Trafficking in Persons Report", June 2006, p. 251 (http://www.state.gov/documents/organization/66086.pdf, accessed on 09 June 2016).

[342] Southern African development community, "Regional Trafficking Person Data Collection and Database Management Training", 24 February 2005 (https://www.sadc.int/news-events/events/regional-trafficking-person-data-collection-and-database-man/ accessed on 9 June 2016).

[343] UNICEF. Common Platform for Action of the Sub-Regional Consultation on the Development of Strategies to Fight Child Trafficking for Exploitative Labour Purposes in West and Central Africa 22–24 February 2000, Libreville, Gabon (http://www.unicef.org/media/newsnotes/platform.pdf, accessed on 9 June 2016).

[344] US Department of State. "Ethiopia. Trafficking in person report", 2013 (http://www.state.gov/j/tip/rls/tiprpt/countries/2013/215460.htm, accessed on 9 June 2016.

[345] Kadjar-Hamouda. Terre des Homme. "Kids as commodities? Child trafficking and what to do about it". May 2004. P. 27 (http://www.terredeshommes.org/wp-content/uploads/2013/06/commodities.pdf, accessed on 8 February 2016).

As regards the international instruments aimed at eradicating the phenomenon, the agreement concluded in 2000 by Côte d'Ivoire and Mali to combat the cross-border trafficking of children, although recent instability in Côte d'Ivoire has prevented the implementation of the agreement.

Another African agreement, between Benin and Côte d'Ivoire on trafficking in children envisages repatriation between Togo, Ghana, Benin and Nigeria[346]. Nigeria has also developed bilateral cooperation agreements with European destination countries. For example, Nigeria and the Italian government have negotiated a "Re-admission Agreement", that allows for cooperation on the return of deported illegal immigrants from Nigeria. The two governments also have a collaboration agreement with the United Nations Interregional Crime and Justice Research Institute (UNICRI) to strengthen their local and national tools to reduce the trafficking of children and young women from Nigeria to Italy. In addition, two National Task Forces Against Trafficking have been created, composed of representatives of the ministers of the interior and justice of Nigeria and Italy, the national police forces, NGOs and relevant experts, to improve bilateral cooperation[347].

The ACERWC examined the reports of 42 African countries that contained a description of national policies on child trafficking in 18 countries. In its recommendations, the ACERWC referred especially to the promotion of cooperation agreements between countries, the ratification of international legal instruments, the revision and reform of legal frameworks, the strengthening of laws and the implementation of educational programs on awareness-raising and issues related to human trafficking, together with reintegration programs for victims. The ACERWC recommended the facilitation and reunification of child victims with their families and the provision of adequate care and rehabilitation programs[348].

An interesting measure undertaken at the African States' discretion to effectively combat trafficking concerns the creation of local committees, together with the decentralization of anti-trafficking activities. The measure was explored in a joint UNICEF – Benin government research project[349]. The first village committee in Benin was created in August 1999 in the prefecture of Ze, Dogbo and Agbangnizoun, in the south of the country. Child trafficking is common in the area. There are now more than 170 committees that carry out a wide range of activities. The committees provides special surveillance on the movements of children in their villages, spreads awareness and compiles reports on cases of child sexual abuse and suspicious departures of children exposed to trafficking. In addition, the committees monitor the reintegration of child victims of trafficking once they return to the village. When a child leaves the village, the committee proceeds to a rapid investigation and alerts the police, together with the youth protection team. In many cases, these rapid interventions have prevented the trafficking of children to neighbouring countries. The committees have the advantage of on-site supervision, thereby encouraging self-initiated

---

[346] UNICEF & Innocenti centro di ricerca. Rossi. "Trafficking in human beings, especially women and children in Africa". September 2003. p. 38 (http://www.unicef.org/media/files/insight8e.pdf, accessed on 7 June 2016).

[347] *Ibidem*, p. 40.

[348] *Ibidem*, p. 41.

[349] *Ibidem*, p. 44.

protection of local children. The committee also provides efficient recording of deaths, births and marriages in the villages. This makes it possible to compensate for the shortcomings of the civil register and to better understand the current situation and movements of children[350].

Trafficking is a complex phenomenon that involves many stakeholders at various institutional levels. The involvement of several ministers in the formulation and implementation of anti-trafficking policies requires an integrated national policy and the effective mobilization of resources to facilitate real international cooperation. Although the ACRWC does not refer to what type of measures should be introduced to combat trafficking, African states appear to be increasingly active in combating the phenomenon.

In particular, States should continue in their efforts to implement anti-trafficking information campaigns, in addition to decisive measures taken by states to impose sanctions on traffickers, intermediaries, but also for minor participants.

II.6   Conclusions

The ACRWC has the merit of breaking some taboos on traditional practices that are harmful to the health and well-being of minors, expressly prohibiting them, as in the case of forced marriages (Article 21 ACRWC) or inviting States Parties to implement all measures necessary to discourage HTP (Article 1). Article 1 ACRWC does not define what customs, traditions, cultural or religious practices are negative, such as FGM.

On the other hand, the ACRWC recognizes positive African heritage as a source of inspiration for ACRWC rights. It is then for its interpreters and the ACERWC to balance traditional African heritage and the "counter-limits" posed by the ACRWC itself.

Many African states appear to have fulfilled their obligations under the ACRWC to discourage HTP. States Parties, given their discretion in the field, have issued not only legislative, but also cultural types of measures, and have formed interregional and international cooperation agreements.

As for the effectiveness in combating HTP according to Article 21 ACRWC, States Parties have made significant efforts in accordance with a multidisciplinary legislative, health and cultural approach, also with the help of NGOs. In the case of genital mutilation, for example, in addition to information campaigns, NGOs have used local staff as cultural mediators in discouraging the practice. In the case of forced marriage, some women broke with the tradition and appealed to the courts. These are positive examples in promoting a change in mentality. In the case of handicapped minors, the path ahead remains long; in addition to taking measures against the stigma associated with the disabled, it is necessary to allocate more resources and invest in qualified personnel to meet the special needs of children with disabilities, and invest in studies and

---

[350] UNICEF. "Child Trafficking in West Africa: Policy Responses" *op. cit.*, p. 14 (http://www.unicef-irc.org/publications/pdf/insight7.pdf, accessed on 9 novembre 2015).

prevention. With regard to the phenomenon of child soldiers, preventive measures concern greater educational and work opportunities, as well as ensuring not only international but also national justice, and the certainty of punishment of those who violate the ban imposed by Article 22 ACRWC on the recruitment of minors in armed conflicts. For refugee children there is no special dedicated body. The remaining problems concern registration at birth and family reunification. In child trafficking, bilateral and multilateral cooperation is often effecting, considering that the routes involve several states: the countries of origin, transit and destination. However, States must provide a unique and detailed definition of the notion of trafficking.

Progress has been made since 1990 in the implementation of the ACRWC, also thanks to the monitoring and recommendations made by the ACERWC to States in their country reports. This will be explored in the next chapter.

CHAPTER

III

THE ACERWC AND ITS CONTRIBUTION TO THE GRADUAL IMPLEMENTATION OF THE ACRWC

III.1   Role and functions of the ACERWC

In July 2001, as established by Article 32 ACRWC, the ACERWC was established[351], with the mandate to promote and protect the rights enshrined in the ACRWC. The ACERWC is a body of the AU and, in accordance with the provisions of Article 33 ACRWC, is composed by eleven members of the highest morality, integrity, impartiality and competence in all matters concerning the rights and welfare of the child.

The members of the ACERWC are appointed by the Conference of Heads of State and Government on the basis of a list of persons indicated by the States Parties (Article 34); they remain in office for five years and cannot be re-elected; they do not represent their own State of origin but sit on a personal basis. The ACERWC cannot include two or more experts of the same nationality.

According to Article 11(2) of the Rules of Procedure adopted by the ACERWC, "The position of a member of the ACERWC is incompatible with any activity that might interfere with the independence or impartiality of such a member or the demands of the office such as working in any intergovernmental organisation, UN Agencies, or a Cabinet Minister or Deputy Minister, member of parliament, Ambassador, or any other politically binding function".

The ACERWC meets twice a year, usually in May and November in Addis Ababa, Ethiopia. The ACERWC reports to the Conference of Heads of State and to the AU every two years.

The mandate of the ACERWC is specified in Article 42 ACRWC. It provides that the ACERWC has the tasks of promoting and protecting the rights enshrined in the ACRWC, supervising their application and monitoring compliance therewith, and interpreting the ACRWC's provisions at the request of the States Parties, AU institutions or any other institution, developing and formulating principles and rules to protect the rights and well-being of children in Africa, collecting documents

---

[351] The first members of the ACERWC were elected by the XXXVII Conference of Heads of State and Government of the AU, held in Lusaka, Zambia, in July 2001.

and information, commissioning interdisciplinary assessments on existing problems in Africa in the field of children's rights and protection, making recommendations to governments and, finally, carrying out any other activity that may be entrusted to it by the Conference of Heads of State or Government, the President of the Commission or any other AU body.

Articles 43 to 45 ACRWC describe the powers conferred upon the ACERWC to complete its tasks. Pursuant to Article 43, the ACERWC has the power to receive and examine the reports of States Parties on the measures taken to implement the provisions of the ACRWC and the progress made in the exercise of the rights enshrined therein. States do not always present their reports on a timely basis, despite the numerous calls to that effect by the ACERWC.

The ACERWC has wider powers than those of the CRC Committee. Not only is it empowered to examine the reports of States Parties; it also has the power to receive individual and interstate communications (Article 44). These communications, which involve the States Parties, may concern any matter dealt with by the ACRWC. The ACERWC also has the power to conduct investigations (Article 45) while the CRC Committee only has the power to examine the reports received. Furthermore, the ACRWC also establishes an individual complaint procedure. Any individual, group or NGO recognized by the AU, a State Party or the UN can file a complaint with the ACERWC. The ACERWC may also, on its own initiative, investigate or investigate facts leading to the presumption that violations of the rights of a child in a State Party have been committed. Indeed, Article 45 ACRWC provides that the ACERWC may use any appropriate means to investigate any matter concerning the ACRWC. To do so, it may request that States Parties provide all relevant information concerning the application of the ACRWC and use any appropriate method of investigation, to ascertain which measures have been taken by the States to apply the provisions of the ACRWC.

The ACERWC has carried out investigations against states that are not parties to the ACRWC. The individual communication procedure provided for by the ACRWC is considerable progress with respect to the UN CRC. In fact, the latter does not provide for filing litigation proceedings on violations of children's rights recognized by the CRC. The only mechanisms envisaged are oriented towards the diplomatic promotion of the rights proclaimed in the CRC itself.

Following the example of other international bodies, the ACERWC can only deal with a specific communication when internal remedies have been exhausted and no other international "jurisdiction" has been involved. It is therefore an exclusive report, that prevents the applicant from resorting to all international or regional bodies at the same time, to avoid them from competing on the same issue.

Countries that have ratified the ACRWC must submit initial reports to the ACERWC within two years of ratification of the ACRWC and every three years thereafter.

The ACERWC itself has formulated guidelines[352] on the preparation of States Parties' periodic reports. According to Article 43 ACRWC, the reports must contain sufficient information on the implementation of the ACRWC in the country in question and indicate, where appropriate, the factors and circumstances that hinder compliance with its obligations. States Parties must report the important changes that have occurred. The information provided by the States Parties in their reports on the implementation of each ACRWC provision should also include statistical data referring to the age, sex and disability of minors, to highlight the significant changes that may have occurred[353] and to make adequate and informed decisions on planning interventions, allocating resources, and providing and monitoring services.

III.2   The ACERWC's relationship with the Commission and the African Court

The mandates of the ACERWC and of the African Commission on Human Rights are clearly defined in their foundational documents. The mandate of the ACERWC refers in particular to the rights of the child, while that of the Commission is linked to the rights of humans and peoples in general. The ACERWC and the Commission must therefore establish complementary relations in the implementation of their mandates, which overlap in part. The modalities of this close cooperation should become the subject of an agreement between the ACERWC and the Commission[354].

According to Article 63 of the Rules of Procedure of the African Commission, any human rights institution can request the African Commission to include, on its agenda for the Ordinary Session, a human rights issue[355]. Thus, the ACERWC could turn to the Commission if it must deal with issues concerning the application of human rights in Africa.

The Commission, according to Article 45 of the African Charter on Human and People's Rights, cooperates with other African or international institutions that are interested in the promotion and protection of human beings and peoples.

The ACERWC's regulations envisage discussion, during the ordinary sessions, of issues submitted by AU bodies[356]. Therefore, mechanisms do exist that provide for the possibility of a link between the Commission and the ACERWC.

---

[352] ACERWC State Party Reporting Guidelines, http://acerwc.org/?wpdmdl=8694. Accessed on 5 February 2016.

[353] *Ibidem*, p. 15.

[354] Boukongou. "Le systéme africain de protection des droits de l'enfant. Exigences universelles et pretentions africaines", *Cahiers de la recherche sur les* droits *fondamentau*, 2006, p. 106.

[355] African Commission on Human and Peoples' rights, "Rules of Procedure" (http://www.achpr.org/files/instruments/rules-of-procedure-2010/rules_of_procedure_2010_en.pdf, accessed on 10 May 2016).

[356] *Ibidem*, rule 6(f): "The provisional agenda for each ordinary session shall be prepared by the Secretary in consultation with the Chairperson of the Committee, in conformity with the relevant provisions of the Children's Charter, and shall include: (f) Any item proposed by the Policy Organs of the AU. (http://www.acerwc.org/download/acerwc_revised_rules_of_procedure/?wpdmdl=8810, accessed on 3 June 2016).

As regards the relationship between the ACERWC and the African Court of Human and Peoples' Rights, the ACERWC has the mandate to interpret the provisions of the ACRWC, while the Court has jurisdiction over cases filed before it in light of the Charter of Peoples' Rights. In terms of interpretation, Article 3.1 of the Protocol to the African Charter on Human and People's Rights on the creation of an African Court of Human and Peoples' Rights (1998) states that "The jurisdiction of the Court shall extend to all cases and disputes submitted to it concerning the interpretation and application of the Charter, this Protocol and any other relevant Human Rights instrument ratified by the States concerned (Article 3(1)). The Court provides an authoritative interpretation of the African Charter on Human and Peoples' Rights and of other instruments for the protection of human rights ratified by the States; the ACRWC may be included among these.

According to Article 42(c), the ACERWC is mandated with interpreting the rules of the ACRWC at the request of the States Parties, AU institutions or any other institution recognized by the AU or a Member State.

Therefore, both the Court and the ACERWC may interpret the Charter. The problem is thus one of coordination, between their respective competences regarding the interpretation of the ACRWC[357]. On the procedural level, it is hoped that the *lex specialis* of the ACRWC would be enhanced[358]. The African Charter on Human and Peoples' Rights is more general in scope, while the ACRWC has a specific scope. To resolve the question of the overlapping jurisdiction and the risk of conflicting interpretations of the Charter by the Court and the ACERWC in issues concerning the rights of the child, such issues could be the subject of a preliminary reference, by the Court to the ACERWC[359]. The ACERWC could issue a non-binding opinion on the interpretation of the Charter. However, such a mechanism has yet to be implemented. Likewise, all broader issues beyond the narrow scope of children's rights could be referred by the ACERWC to the Commission or the African Court of Human and Peoples' Rights[360].

In the ACERWC's Rules of Procedure, Article 48 discusses the ACERWC's competences[361], although it does not provide for references to other bodies.

Article 4 of the Protocol to the African Charter on Human and Peoples' Rights on the creation of an African Court of Human Rights and Peoples affirms that: "At the request of a Member State of the AU, the AU, any of its organs, or any African organization recognized by the AU, the Court may provide an opinion on any legal matter relating to the Charter or any other relevant human rights instruments, provided that the subject matter of the opinion is not related to a matter being

---

[357] Maffei. "Sistema africano e meccanismi di controllo", in L.Pineschi (ed), L*a tutela internazionale dei diritti umani*, Giuffrè, Milan, 2004, p. 690.

[358] *Ibidem*, p. 100.

[359] *Ibidem*, p. 106.

[360] Boukongou, "Le systéme africain de protection des droits de l'enfant. Exigences universelles et pretentions africaines", *op. cit.* p. 106.

[361] The ACERWC's Rules of Procedure are available at http://www.acerwc.org/download/acerwc_revised_rules_of_procedure/?wpdmdl=8810, accessed on 3 June 2016.

examined by the Commission. [...] The Court shall give reasons for its advisory opinions provided that every judge shall be entitled to deliver a separate of dissenting decision".

This synergy and reciprocity of the procedures would strengthen the African system of protection of human rights. Currently, the Court enjoys a broad jurisdiction and stands independently of the ACERWC; it is not obliged to request the ACERWC's opinion.

III.3 Investigations

The ACERWC has the institutional power to carry out investigations. Article 45 (1) ACRWC states that "[t]he Committee may, resort to any appropriate method of investigating any matter falling within the ambit of the present Charter, request from the States Parties any information relevant to the implementation of the Charter and may also resort to any appropriate method of investigating the measures the State Party has adopted to implement the Charter."

Many African states have experienced civil wars, military dictatorships, human rights violations on a mass scale and genocide[362]. These situations also involve minors; therefore, the ACERWC's power to investigate is an important tool to verify compliance with the ACRWC. The ACRWC does not govern investigative activities. However, the related procedures are outlined in the ACERWC's guidelines[363].

Investigations are missions sent by the ACERWC to a State Party to the Charter to gather information on the situation of children's rights therein. The ACERWC may undertake two types of investigative missions[364]: a) investigations on any matter, referred to the ACERWC, that denounces serious and systematic violations of the rights of the child in a State Party; b) investigations undertaken on its own initiative. The ACERWC may also undertake an investigation mission upon invitation by the State concerned[365]. In case a State Party refuses to accept a fact-finding mission on its territory, the State concerned must indicate the reasons for such refusal within a reasonable time. This may appear to be a mild measure; nevertheless, it can promote cooperation with the ACERWC. The ACERWC takes note of the reasons given by the State and reports on the matter to the Assembly of the African Union, which will then decide on the further measures to be taken. The States Parties will endeavour to adopt a policy of welcoming investigative missions to their respective territories[366].

Egypt, despite having ratified the ACRWC on 29 November 2006, is the only State that has formulated a reservation on the ACERWC's institutional powers of investigation pursuant to

---

[362] Okechukwu, "The challenges of international criminal prosecution in Africa". *Fordahm International Law Journal*, 2008, p. 343.

[363] ACERWC. Guidelines on the conduct of missions (http://www.acerwc.org/?wpdmdl=8668. Accessed on 31 March 2016).

[364] *Ibidem*. Article 3.

[365] *Ibidem*. Article 4.2.

[366] *Ibidem*. Article 4.3.

Article 45(1); therefore, Egypt has preliminarily refused all missions of the ACERWC. This translates into an absence of interlocutors within the State party, that the ACERWC may refer to regarding the observance of the ACRWC's rules and any violations thereof. However, this reservation does not appear to comply with the general reservation regime, as will be seen below.

The purpose of the investigations is to evaluate the general situation of children's rights in the given country; clarify the facts and establish the responsibilities of the individuals within the State and families towards children who have suffered from the violations; promote and support the implementation of rights and well-being by the various institutions of the country, in accordance with the ACRWC[367].

Based on the information gathered, the ACERWC prepares recommendations[368] on the implementation of the ACRWC or on the violations of children's rights encountered in the State Party visited.

The ACERWC's recommendations are sent to the relevant State Party, with the measures to be taken. The recommendations may also be sent to other public and private institutions responsible for monitoring and implementing the rights of the child recognized by the ACRWC. The ACERWC may also invite specialized institutions and civil society organizations to provide information on the monitoring and implementation of the ACRWC in the areas in which the ACERWC is empowered to investigate[369].

The ACERWC may request the State Party to include, in the subsequent report, made pursuant to Article 43 ACRWC, information on the measures taken following the ACERWC's recommendations as formulated after the mission[370].

The ACERWC submits a report on its activities to the Conference of Heads of State and Government at its ordinary sessions[371]. Mezmur[372] emphasizes the role of the Department of Peace and Security of the AU in implementing the ACERWC's recommendations. The African Commission on Human and Peoples' Rights is asked to take all appropriate measures to implement the ACERWC's recommendations. However, the scholar notes that the ACRWC does not require the Commission to inform the ACERWC on the actions taken[373].

Article 45(2) ACRWC requires the ACERWC to submit a report on its activities to the Conference of Heads of State and Government at its ordinary sessions. After the reports have been examined

---

[367] *Ibidem*, Article 2.

[368] *Ibidem*, Article 23.

[369] *Ibidem*, Article 27.

[370] *Ibidem*. Article 26.

[371] Article 45(2) ACRWC: "The Committee shall submit to each Ordinary Session of the Assembly of Heads of State and Govenrment every two years, a report on its activities and on any communication made under Article 44 of this Charter."

[372] Mezmur, "African Committee of Experts on the Rights and Welfare of the Child. An Update. The Recent developments", *African Human Rights Law Journal*, 2006, p. 565.

[373] *Ibidem*.

by the Conference of Heads of State and Government, they are published by the ACERWC. The ACRWC does not refer to further obligations on the part of the Conference of Heads of State or Government towards the ACERWC.

Compared to the powers of the CRC Committee, those of the ACERWC are broader and more aligned with the sociopolitical situation of the African states. Such a context made it necessary to endow the ACERWC with the power to investigate human rights violations involving minors. To date, the ACERWC has conducted two investigations, in two third states: the Central African Republic and South Sudan. These countries have not ratified the ACRWC, although they have willingly agreed to collaborate with the ACERWC in its investigation. Therefore, the third states gave their consent, in line with Article 34 of the Vienna Convention on the Law on Treaties. Both governments were sent the minutes of the resolution with which the ACERWC ordered the investigation into the countries. Both South Sudan and the Central African Republic accepted the ACERWC's mission[374].

According to Article 35 of the Vienna Convention, "[a]n obligation arises for a third State from a provision of a treaty if the parties to the treaty intend the provision to be the means of establishing the obligation and the third State expressly accepts that obligation in writing". By consenting to the ACERWC's mission, third states are bound by Article 45 ACRWC with regard to the investigations carried out in their territory. As for States Parties, they consent to investigations into the measures taken by a State party with the ratification of the ACRWC. The ACERWC submits a report on its activities to the Conference of Heads of State and Government. The States will ensure that the ACERWC's reports are widely disseminated in their respective countries.

According to Ockechkwu[375], the mass atrocities that have ravaged Africa originate from sociopolitical problems that were not managed satisfactorily and were caused by isolation, injustice, corruption and ethnic hatred. All this led many individuals to participate in violence. The causes of the conflicts are thus much greater than mere individual deviance, residing rather in the defective structures of society as a whole. The best African approach, then, is to address the manifestations and the root causes of mass atrocities at the same time.

In this regard, if the ACRWC provides for the transmission of the ACERWC's investigation reports to the Conference of Heads of State of the AU, it should also provide for an agreement with a regional criminal institution.

---

[374] ACERWC. Report on the Advocacy Mission to assess the situation of children in South Sudan. Agosto 2013. http://www.rcfworld.org/docid/545b4c384.html, p. 2; ACERWC. Report on the Advocacy Mission to assess the situation of children in Central African Republic, http://www.acerwc.org/download/advocacy-mission-to-central-african republic/?wpdmdl=9478, p. 2.
[375] Ockechkwu, "The Challenges of International Criminal Prosecutions in Africa", op. cit, p. 351.

Marirakiza[376] advocates the creation of a regional African criminal court[377], as the courts of individual African states often fail to fight impunity. The state of impunity remains alarming in Africa, despite many African states having ratified the Statute of the International Criminal Court. Indeed, despite the terrible atrocities that have been perpetrated in Africa, many countries, such as Burundi, Somalia, and Côte d'Ivoire, have not committed to prosecute the relevant crimes. According to Marirakiza, the International Criminal Court and an African Criminal Court would be complementary, achieving a combined effect that can make prosecution more effective[378].

The powers conferred upon the ACERWC are therefore limited. However, its cooperation with a regional criminal court is not excluded.

It is in the interest of Africa to fight impunity, to the extent that this phenomenon undermines the establishment and entrenchment of democratic regimes based on the rule of law and respect for rights[379].

The Malabo Protocol, establishing a new Section within the African Court of Justice and Human Rights devoted to criminal matters, provides for specific crimes related to the sociopolitical context of the African continent that the Statute of the African Criminal Court does not provide. However, the Protocol has not yet come into force.

According to Paredi[380], two important levels to African criminal justice may be identified: an international level and a national level, which are both present and relevant in the current system of international criminal justice. It is equally well known, however, that the "enforcement" of criminal law at both of these levels has been seriously cast into doubt. On one hand, criticism of international tribunals is diffuse, in particular as regards the high costs they involve and their distance (in all senses) from the place where the relevant crimes were perpetrated. These disadvantages are, to some extent, amplified by the fact that these tribunals play a small, albeit

---

[376] Marirakiza, "L'Afrique et le systeme de justice penale international", *African Journal of legal studies*, 2009, p. 29.

[377] The creation of an African criminal court may have legal basis in Article 26 of the African Charter on Human and Peoples' Rights: "State Parties to the present Charter shall have the duty to guarantee the independence of the Courts and shall allow the establishment and improvement of appropriate national institutions entrusted with the promotion and protection of the rights and freedoms guaranteed by the present Charter."

[378] It seems clear that, to the extent that the Rome Statute assigns, to the International Criminal Court, a function that complements the jurisdictions of the States Parties, reserving to the latter the primary responsibility to take criminal action against the individuals responsible for the most serious international crimes, the substantive criminal law of these countries must be adequately equipped to effectively prosecute these crimes. Pividori, *Il principio di complementarietà della corte penale internazionale e il processo di adattamento degli ordinamenti interni*, Editoriale scientifica, Naples, 2016, p. 20. http://padis.uniroma1.it/bitstream/10805/2570/1/Tesi_dottorato_pividori_finale_1106_intestazioni.pdf. Accessed on 13 April 2016.

[379] Marirakiza, "L'Afrique et le systeme de justice penale international", *op. cit.* p. 52.

[380] Società italiana di diritto internazionale e di diritto dell'Unione europea. Paper presented at the *Primo incontro italo-francese tra dottorandi di diritto internazionale e dell'Unione europea*. 1 July 2014. Paredi. "Una soluzione africana ad un problema africano. La Corte penale internazionale e l'Unione africana tra conflitto e prospettive di giustizia penale regionale". p. 19. http://www.sidi-isil.org/wp-content/uploads/2014/06/PAREDI-Paper-Courmayeur.pdf. Accessed on 11 May 2016.

important, role in fighting the impunity of international crimes. Precisely because of these considerations, local courts assume significance, and indeed it is now common thought that the future of international criminal justice lies within the states themselves. The role of the AU in encouraging states to prosecute international crimes is a viable option, including with the cooperation of the ACERWC.

According to the Protocol on the Statute of the African Court of Justice and Human Rights, the Court has three Sections: general affairs, human and peoples' rights, and international criminal law. Article 28 of the Protocol provides for crimes peculiar to Africa, linked to its geopolitical context: unconstitutional change of government; piracy; terrorism; mercenary forces; corruption; money laundering, human and drug trafficking; trafficking of hazardous waste, and illicit exploitation of natural resources.

The Assembly of Heads of State and Government of the African Union may extend the consent of States Parties to the jurisdiction of the Court to incorporate further crimes, for the purpose of reflecting developments in international law. For example, the Statute of the African Court of Justice and Human Rights does not envisage crimes relating to arms trafficking; the ACERWC considered this to be a crucial issue during its investigation into the violation of children's rights in South Sudan.

Regional criminal justice offers a number of advantages. Crimes that are not regulated or insufficiently regulated in international law, such as those related to the responsibility of child soldiers, could be envisaged. For example, Article 22 ACRWC, which regulates juvenile justice, does not deal specifically with child soldiers[381].

If an African court were endowed with the jurisdiction to repress international crimes in Africa, the ACERWC would become an important body in the development and improvement of African international criminal law on the involvement of children in armed conflicts. Indeed, the ACERWC was established with the specific aim of promoting universal values and the principles of international law, in light of the historical and cultural conditions in Africa.

According to Article 3 of the guidelines on investigations, the ACERWC is responsible for ascertaining responsibility for violations of human rights against minors, and for co-operating with other international and regional institutions and organizations involved in the promotion and protection of children's rights and welfare. According to Article 42 ACRWC, the ACERWC may also carry out any other activity entrusted to it by the Conference of Heads of State and Government of the AU or by any other body of the AU or the UN. Therefore, in light of Article 42 ACRWC, the ACERWC could collaborate with bodies engaged in international and regional criminal justice. According to Article 45 ACRWC, the ACERWC publishes reports and transmits them to the Conference of Heads of State and Government; it could consider transmitting them to regional and international criminal justice bodies, as well.

---

[381] Marirakiza. "L'Afrique et le systeme de justice penale international", op. cit, p. 42.

The Protocol to the African Charter on Human and Peoples' Rights, on the creation of an African Charter on Human and Peoples' Rights, states that the Court completes the mandate to protect of the African Commission on Human and Peoples' Rights (Article 4). According to Article 45 ACRWC on investigations, the ACERWC can use any appropriate method to investigate any matter concerning the ACRWC. Therefore, during its investigations, should the ACERWC recognize violations of children's rights arising from the list of crimes provided for at Article 28 of the Protocol, it could resort to the African Criminal Court by providing it with the report of the investigation. Currently, the ACERWC is tasked with identifying culprits of violations of human rights towards minors. However, it has not established any agreements with regional criminal institutions to which submit investigation reports on specific African crimes leading to violations of children's rights. Therefore, the effectiveness of its deterrence activity is so limited, even though such effectiveness is necessary to implement its other task of promoting and supporting the implementation of the ACRWC in the areas where the investigations done.

According to Article 2 of the UN Convention on Special Missions, "[a] State may send a special mission to another State with the consent of the latter, previously obtained through the diplomatic or another agreed or mutually acceptable channel", while Article 3 of the same provides that the functions of a special mission are to be determined with the mutual consent of the sending and the receiving States.

In both cases, the minutes of the ACERWC's resolution on the investigation mission were sent to the third States and the States gave their consent to the mission.

Given the legal framework, the ACERWC's two missions address, to the third States, conclusions and recommendations, in addition to an invitation to ratify the ACRWC. The missions also provide indications for the States Parties to the ACRWC, because they explain how violations may occur or how the ACRWC's obligations should be implemented.

III.3.1   The ACERWC investigation into children involved in armed conflicts in the Central African Republic

The ACERWC stressed the importance of conducting a detailed assessment of the situation of children in the Central African Republic, as children are the category of people who were affected the most by the armed conflict. This position is in line with adopted by the AU Peace and Security Commission in the efforts to meet the needs of children in accordance with the rights established under the AU's various human rights instruments, which include: the African Charter on Human and Peoples' Rights; the Convention Governing the Specific Aspects of Refugee Problems in Africa; and the Convention for the Protection and Assistance of Internally Displaced Persons in Africa.

In 2014, the ACERWC conducted an investigation to protect child victims of armed conflict in the Central African Republic and to assess the impact of armed conflicts on children.

Article 45 ACRWC states that the ACERWC may use any appropriate method to investigate any matter concerning the ACRWC. Therefore, the ACERWC investigating violations of children's rights in the Central African Republic, which has not ratified the ACRWC, extends the protection of minors, who are in any case addressees of the ACRWC's rights, to those in a State that has not ratified the ACRWC.

With a resolution on the situation of children in the Central African Republic adopted during its 23rd Ordinary Session (7–16 April 2014) in Addis Ababa, the ACERWC approved the conduct of the investigation, to improve the protection of children's rights and to establish responsibilities regarding the children involved in armed conflicts[382].

The ACERWC sent a note-verbale to the Government of the Central African Republic, which accepted and welcomed the mission[383].

The ACERWC delegation met the country's Minister of Social Affairs, Minister of Justice, Minister of National Defence and War Veterans; as well as the committee responsible for security reform, disarmament, demobilization and reintegration program; the prefect of Haute-Kotto and Ouham; the AU mission to the Central African Republic; UN agencies including UNICEF and UNHCR; Save the Children and other national and international NGOs[384].

The ACERWC delegation appreciated the Government's efforts to cooperate with national and international NGOs. However, it noted that the State does not have the authority to guarantee the well-being of the general population and of children in particular. The national situation remains fragile and is characterized by multiple, interdependent and cumulative violations of children's basic rights[385].

The delegation noted that many schools were burned and destroyed, and school supplies stolen. The schools had not been rebuilt and, in rural areas especially, were occupied by armed groups. For 1 million children, primary education is not guaranteed. Many children prefer to be involved in processing gold rather than going to school, because of the shortage of teachers and the lack of safety. Teachers have not resumed activities because of the conflict and fears for their own safety[386].

The ACERWC delegation considered that the psychological support[387] provided to child victims of violence in refugee camps was insufficient to restore their sense of trust[388].

---

[382] ACERWC. Mission Report of the ACERWC to assess the Situation of Children Affected by the conflict in Central African Republic, p. 2 (http://www.acerwc.org/?wpdmdl=9478, accessed on 29 March 2016).

[383] *Ibidem*, p. 3.

[384] *Ibidem*, p. 6.

[385] *Ibidem*, p. 8.

[386] *Ibidem*, p. 9.

[387] The UNHCR, in partnership with International Medical Corps, has set up socio-psychological assistance services to help victims to deal with trauma immediately (http://www.unhcr.it/news/repubblica-centrafricana-lunhcr-condanna-fermamente-il-rapimento-di-rifugiati-congolesi-da-parte-dei-ribelli-lra, accessed on 22 April 2016).

[388] ACERWC. Mission Report of the ACERWC to assess the Situation of Children Affected by the conflict in Central African Republic, p. 14 (http://www.acerwc.org/?wpdmdl=9478, accessed on 29 March 2016).

In particular, the delegation noted the lack of state authority in administering justice. Of the six courts on the territory of the Central African Republic that deal with juvenile justice, only one, in the capital Bangui, is operational, and lacks sufficient human resources[389].

There is thus a need to rebuild the judicial system in general, and restore the synergy between the various organs of the State, if the responsibility of those who have violated children's rights is to be effectively established[390].

As for the general situation and the dynamics and causes of the involvement of children in armed conflicts, the information obtained by the ACERWC shows that 10 000 children have been recruited and exploited by two rival armed organizations: the Seleka and the anti-Balaka. The delegation heard testimonies from children who committed crimes against the rival group to avenge the killing of their parents or members of their own families. The children also explained that although their parents lived in the same camp, they decided to live with the leaders of the armed groups, who provided them with safety and food[391].

The delegation received information on over 550 000 children suffering from mental disorders and psychological distress, having been victims, authors or witnesses of emotionally unbearable scenes. During the meeting with the children, the delegation learned that the children desire change and to reintegrate into society, performing socio-professional activities[392].

The ACERWC delegation recalled in positive terms the activity of "peer education", in which children sensitize the children who have been recruited by armed groups, deemed to yield positive results in improving the situation of child victims of armed conflicts. However, this activity is limited in scope, because schools are closed and the resources for providing socio-professional activities are insufficient; therefore, there are few alternatives for children who support disarmament[393].

Although approximately 8 000 combatants have undergone the Disarmament, Demobilization and Reintegration (DDR) process[394] between 2009 and 2014, the circulation and supply of weapons and arsenals among rebel groups has not changed. The ACERWC strongly recommended that

---

[389] *Ibidem*, p.14.

[390] *Ibidem*, p. 15.

[391] *Ibidem*. p. 17.

[392] *Ibidem*. p. 17.

[393] *Ibidem*. p. 18.

[394] Disarmament is the collection, documentation and elimination of light and heavy weapons held by combatants and the civilian population. Demobilization is the formal and controlled divestiture of combatant activity by the armed forces and groups, including a reintegration phase providing short-term assistance to former combatants. Reintegration is the process by which former combatants acquire civilian status, gain employment and, therefore, a sustainable income. The goal of the DDR process is to contribute to security and stability in post-conflict environments so that recovery and development can begin.

national authorities put in place the National Security Sector Reform program as soon as possible, to re-establish an efficient security and justice system and ultimately achieve long-term stability[395].

The ACERWC also noted that the Central African Republic had ratified the ACRWC – a copy was signed on 6 July 2002 by President Ange Felix Patassé – but the ratification document was never filed. The delegation considered it urgent to proceed with the ratification of the Court, and recalled that the Central African Republic authorities regretted the lack of ratification and were ready to remedy the situation[396].

The delegation concluded that certain urgent issues relating to the protection of the children's rights remained. In particular, it was deemed necessary to restore: the state system ensuring security; the basic social system for health, education, justice, disarmament, demobilization and for the reintegration of children involved in armed groups; psychosocial care for child victims of violence and socio-economic activities, with a view to create an environment functional to the well-being and rights of children[397]. This list demonstrates the urgency of improving coordination efforts between African bodies to protect human rights in general.

The ACERWC delegation noted that there is little clarity regarding the mechanism for coordinating government implementation efforts and non-governmental initiatives to protect children affected by the conflict. It called for the creation of a high-level coordination structure, with a definite mandate on human rights the financial and technical resources required to function effectively to promote the rights of children in the various sectors, at both national and local levels. Furthermore, the State should thoroughly assess the needs of vulnerable children and adopt a budget that could progressively and increasingly support children's rights[398].

The ACERWC was also concerned by the scarce budgetary resources and by the fact that the social sectors dealing with children's issues depend on funding from external donors, whose contributions cannot be guaranteed in the long term and, indeed, have been decreasing[399]. The ACERWC strongly encouraged the authorities to continue their efforts to ensure reform of the security sector and the establishment of a system of juvenile justice and the adoption of a code of child protection.

The ACERWC recommended developing training in child rights for professional groups working with children, such as law enforcement officers, judges, teachers, lawyers, health workers, social workers and prison staff[400].

---

[395] ACERWC. Mission Report of the ACERWC to assess the Situation of Children Affected by the conflict in Central African Republic, *op. cit.* p. 20.

[396] *Ibidem.* p 21.

[397] *Ibidem.* p 24.

[398] *Ibidem.* p 26.

[399] *Ibidem.* p 25.

[400] *Ibidem.* p 26.

The ACERWC called on the State to take concrete steps to protect children from sexual abuse and child prostitution, and to effectively study all cases of child sexual abuse to ensure that victims receive the best possible protection and that perpetrators are brought to justice and punished. To this end, the State must adopt an appropriate investigative system when children are involved, as well as policies and programs for the prevention, rehabilitation and social reintegration of victims[401].

In the process of security reform, the State must also take all necessary measures to prevent the recruitment and use of children in armed groups, investigating these recruitment activities in an effective and systematic manner, and provide child victims with the psychological and rehabilitative assistance they need, with the support of the UN.

The ACERWC then recommended that the State provide assistance to refugee children, with particular attention to unaccompanied children who have been separated from their families, ensuring that a particular mechanism is put in place to protect and assist them[402].

The ACERWC devoted particular attention to the lack of measures to implement the ACRWC, especially with regard to Article 16 thereof, according to which States must take legislative, administrative, social and educational measures to protect minors if judicial measures are taken against them. Finally, the ACERWC invited the State to devote budget resources to support psychosocial interventions, recalling the general principle of the Preamble to the ACRWC according to which the child holds a unique and privileged position in African society.

The ACRWC declares that states should take action, both with preventive measures to avoid children from taking part in hostilities and, in particular, that no child is enlisted in military forces (Article 22(2)). According to Article 22(3), instead, States Parties must take all possible measures to protect and care for children affected by armed conflict.

To prevent the phenomenon of child soldiers, the ACERWC recommended enhancing the efficiency of the judicial system, especially with regard to the imputation of responsibility, and that the State itself take into its care child victims suffering from post-traumatic stress disorder during disarmament, with resources being allocated for the purpose. Finally, the ACERWC recommended urgent efforts to re-establish the education sector and to provide for its safety, to ensure observance of Article 11 ACRWC.

After monitoring the human rights violations occurring in the Central African Republic, the ACERWC did not expressly referred to the ACRWC in its recommendations as the Central African Republic did not ratify it. However, the ACERWC stressed the urgent need to implement measures to assure the wellbeing and rights of children in the Central African Republic. The measures are inspired by the principles of the ACRWC.

---

[401] *Ibidem.* p 28.

[402] *Ibidem.* p 28.

The ACERWC therefore called for ratification of the ACRWC, appreciating the dialogue held with the high authorities, which allowed for a better understanding of the situation of children in the country. As long as the ACRWC is not ratified, the ACERWC's recommendations remain a simple admonishment, a moral warning. On the other hand, they are implicitly and indirectly useful to the States that have ratified the ACRWC, for which its norms are mandatory.

III.3.2   The ACERWC investigation into violations of children's rights in South Sudan

During its 23rd Ordinary Session (7–16 April 2014, in Addis Ababa), the ACERWC[403] decided to undertake a mission to improve the protection and responsibility towards children involved in armed conflicts in South Sudan. The mission sought to verify the impact of armed conflicts on children in South Sudan and determine the country's capacity and resources for prevention and support to children involved in armed conflicts.

The ACERWC sent a note-verbale to the Government of South Sudan, which accepted and welcomed the ACERWC's mission with the stated objectives.

The ACERWC's inquiry into violations of children's rights in South Sudan was completed in 2014.

The mission assessed the impact of armed conflicts on children in South Sudan and the determination of appropriate responses, also with regard to the prevention of the involvement of children in armed conflicts. The ACERWC collaborated with UNICEF, Save the children, the UNHCR, UNMISS, the AU Liaison Office in Juba, and national institutions: the Minister of Foreign Affairs of the Republic of South Sudan, the Commission on Human Rights in South Sudan, the National Commission on Disarmament, Demobilisation and Reintegration of South Sudan, the Minister of Social Development and the SPLA Child Protection Unit.

The ACERWC received reports of serious violations of the rights of children who were victims of armed conflict in 2013[404]. The violations monitored included killings, recruitment and use of child soldiers by armed groups, violence, and attacks in schools and shelters. The escalation of the recruitment of children into armed groups had become a national emergency. The ACERWC noted that girls were involved in the recruitment by armed groups.

During the conflict, 1 200 schools were closed. More than 75 schools had been occupied by the armed forces. The situation of education has become so serious that many children no longer have access to education. The effect of this situation is that an entire generation risks losing the knowledge on which the economy of the future is based[405].

---

[403] ACERWC. Report on the Advocacy Mission to assess the Situation of Children in South Sudan, August 2014, p. 2 (http://www.acerwc.org/download/report-of-the-advocay-mission-to-south-sudan/?wpdmdl=9490, accessed on 22 April 2016).

[404] *Ibidem*. p. 10.

[405] *Ibidem*. p. 18.

The ACERWC welcomed South Sudan's intention to ratify the ACRWC, took note of the Children's Act of 2008 and urged the state to implement legislative measures as soon as possible[406].

However, the ACERWC delegation noted that many protection issues must still be addressed, such as the reintegration of separated children, disarmament, demobilization and reintegration of child soldiers, and support for communities affected by violence. The ACERWC therefore strongly recommended that the AU, its member states and the international community take all necessary measures to reduce the flow of weapons in South Sudan, in the interests of children and to achieve effective disarmament. The ACERWC also urged the SPLM-IO (Sudan People's Liberation Movement in Opposition) to honor the commitment[407] made in Addis Ababa to desist from mobilizing child soldiers and demobilizing those already involved.

Regarding kidnapping and sexual violence, the ACERWC stressed the importance of conducting investigations and trials and of protecting victims with psychosocial assistance and support services. This is important if the peace process is to take place and the responsibilities of those who have committed crimes established[408].

In this context, the ACERWC also stated that the Government of South Sudan and international actors must define urgent strategies for the development of education for young children, in the interest of ensuring a future for children[409].

With regard to humanitarian aid, the ACERWC has called for the AU to make every effort to negotiate with the rebel groups on the arrival of humanitarian aid in the areas they controlled by them[410]. The ACERWC also encouraged the creation of a Children's Parliament, where the voices of the children of South Sudan could be heard[411].

In the investigation, the ACERWC also appeared to be working on a political assessment of the Government, stigmatizing arms trafficking, which was allegedly not sufficiently central in South Sudan's policies, despite being a crucial issue regarding which to ensure effective protection for children involved in armed conflicts.

The ACERWC's investigation of South Sudan denounces the malnutrition, lack of schools and health services, while its recommendations concern emergency measures. The ACERWC's recommendations concern humanitarian interventions, negotiations with rebels for the cessation of hostilities, disarmament, measures for the reunification of former child soldiers, interventions for heal trauma and resort to international organizations for the purpose of cooperating with the Government of South Sudan.

---

[406] *Ibidem.* p. 21.

[407] *Ibidem.* p. 24.

[408] *Ibidem.* p. 25.

[409] *Ibidem.* p. 26.

[410] *Ibidem.* p. 26.

[411] *Ibidem.* p. 26.

Therefore, the ACERWC's recommendations underscore some ACRWC principles, such as the protection of the family environment (Article 25), the protection of children from armed conflicts (Article 22), and the protection of physical, mental and spiritual health (Article 14).

III.4   State reservations

Although they may have ratified the ACRWC, some states have entered reservations on some articles. It is therefore necessary to examine whether these reservations is discretionary, on the part of States, or if the reservations must pass the ACERWC's scrutiny to be legitimate. To date, four States have formulated reservations on the ACRWC.

The Charter does not refer to States' power to formulate reservations; this is not the case with the CRC, which at Article 51(2) states that "[a] reservation incompatible with the object and purpose of the present Convention shall not be permitted." Article 19 of the Vienna Convention makes similar provision. Likewise, Article 20(2) of the International Convention on the Elimination of All Forms of Racial Discrimination states that "A reservation incompatible with the object and purpose of this Convention shall not be permitted, nor shall a reservation the effect of which would inhibit the operation of any of the bodies established by this Convention be allowed. A reservation shall be considered incompatible or inhibitive if at least two thirds of the States Parties to this Convention object to it."

As the ACRWC is silent in this respect, the rules of the Vienna Convention regarding the formulation of reservations apply.

Botswana has made a reservation on the definition of "child" as per Article 2 ACRWC, according to which a child is a human being under the age of 18. Botswana, failing to approve the definition of the term, does not define with certainty the age until which children may benefit from the rights established by the ACRWC. Because the ACRWC aims to protect the rights of minors under the age of 18, such a reservation affects the very purpose of the ACRWC and, according to the regime of customary international law, should be considered as incompatible.

Egypt[412], for its part, does not consider itself to be bound by Article 21(2) ACRWC, which prohibits child marriages and betrothals. In practice, this reservation allows for the HTP of child marriage to continue, in contradiction with the general purpose of Article 1 ACRWC to discourage all negative practices that are incompatible with ACRWC rights, without exception. Therefore, also this reservation should be considered incompatible.

Article 19 of the Vienna Convention does not allow for the formulation of reservations that are incompatible with the object and purpose of the treaty in question. In this case, the ban on child marriage is expressly provided for at Article 21 ACRWC and is an essential aspect of the ACRWC itself.

---

[412]   The reservations made to the ACRWC may be viewed at http://www.acerwc.org/reservations/ (accessed on 10 April 2016).

It should also be recalled that, in similar terms, the Committee[413] on the Elimination of Discrimination against Women considered that Articles 2 and 16[414] were fundamental provisions of the Convention on the Elimination of All Forms of Discrimination Against Women. In particular, it affirmed that Article 2 of said Convention is central to the object and purpose of the treaty[415], and that reservations to the provision would thus be invalid. The article affirms that States Parties condemn discrimination against women in all its forms, and agree to pursue by all appropriate means and without delay a policy aimed at eliminating discrimination against women. Article 16 of the same Convention establishes that States Parties take all appropriate measures to eliminate discrimination against women in all matters relating to marriage and family relationships. More specifically, according to the Committee, the States Parties that have ratified the Convention agree that discrimination against women in all its forms should be condemned and that the strategies established in Article 2(a) to 2(g) are to be implemented to eliminate discrimination[416]. Similarly, the Committee has established that the reservations on Article 16 for national, traditional, religious or cultural reasons are incompatible with the Convention and not permitted[417]. According to the Committee, reservations on the state of inequality of women in the world would allow some countries to ratify the Convention without really supporting its essence[418]. The Committee has therefore argued that reservations to the Convention indicate a lack of true commitment and willingness to accept women's rights, and a desire to continue the subjugation of women[419]. A similar observation may apply to the reservations made by Egypt and Botswana. Egypt has also formulated a reservation on Article 39(a) to 39(e) ACRWC, concerning the special treatment of children whose mothers are in prison. This reservation appears to be in contradiction with the principle of non-discrimination enshrined in Article 3 ACRWC. However, it does not seem to be blatantly contrary to the object and purpose of the ACRWC, because the

---

[413] Commission on the Elimination of Discriminatiom against Women. "Report of the Committee on the Elimination of Discrimination against Women" 21 August 1998, U.N. Doc A/53/38/ Rev 1 (http://www.un.org/womenwatch/daw /cedaw/reports/18report.pdf, accessed on 9 June 2016).

[414] Article 2 of the Convention on the Elimination of All Forms of Discrimination Against Women states that: "Parties condemn discrimination against women in all its forms, agree to pursue by all appropriate means and without delay a policy of eliminating discrimination against women and, to this end, undertake: (a) To embody the principle of the equality of men and women in their national constitutions or other appropriate legislation if not yet incorporated therein and to ensure, through law and other appropriate means, the practical realization of this principle. According to Article 16, "States Parties shall take all appropriate measures to eliminate discrimination against women in all matters relating to marriage and family relations and in particular shall ensure, on a basis of equality of men and women". Article 16(2) states that "[t]he betrothal and the marriage of a child shall have no legal effect, and all necessary action, including legislation, shall be taken to specify a minimum age for marriage and to make the registration of marriages in an official registry compulsory".

[415] Commission on the Elimination of Discriminatiom against Women. "Report of the Committee on the Elimination of Discrimination against Women",op, cit, p. 49.

[416] *Ibidem.*

[417] *Ibidem.*

[418] Keller, "Impact of States Parties Reservation to the Convention on the Elimination of All Forms of Discrimination against Women", *Michigan State Law Review*, 2014, p. 315.

[419] Commission on the Elimination of Discrimination against Women. "Report of the Committee on the Elimination of Discrimination against Women",op, cit, p. 49.

aspect could be considered secondary to the protection afforded by the ACRWC, although the ACERWC has considered the issue in a General Comment[420].

Finally, Egypt has made a reservation to Article 44 ACRWC, which allows the ACERWC to receive communications, and to Article 45(1), which concerns the possibility for the ACERWC to conduct investigations in the States Parties[421], effectively depriving the ACERWC of the institutional powers conferred upon it in view of the socio-political situation of the African continent. The ACERWC has yet to express itself in a General Comment on the reservations made by States.

The Optional Protocol to the Convention on the Elimination of All Forms of Discrimination against Women, which came into force in 2000, provides for an investigation procedure that allows the relevant Committee to undertake investigations in cases of serious and systematic violation of women's rights. The Optional Protocol includes a reservation clause that allows States, after ratification or approval, to declare that they do not accept the investigation procedure. To date, four States have made use of the clause: Bangladesh, Belize, Colombia and Cuba[422]. This provision may lead one to conclude that the Egyptian reservation was validly made, because it is not contrary to the substantive object and purpose of the ACRWC.

In *Rawle Kennedy v. Trinidad and Tobago*[423], the Human Rights Committee addressed the question of the validity of Trinidad and Tobago's reservation, which excludes[424] the Committee's jurisdiction with regard to the evaluation of communications in accordance with the Optional Protocol to the International Covenant on Civil and Political Rights. The Committee stated that the function of the Optional Protocol is to allow for complaints, filed within the rights of the Covenant, to be examined by the pertinent Committee[425]. Furthermore, the decision states that it is the Committee – and not the State Party – that determines the validity and effectiveness of the reservation[426].

Another decision supports the same principles. On 27 May 1992, Chile ratified the Protocol to the Covenant on Civil and Political Rights, with a reservation as to communications that can

---

[420] ACERWC. General Comment No. 1 (Article 30 of the African Charter on the Rights and Welfare of the Child) on "Children of Incarcerated and Imprisoned Parents and Primary Caregivers", 2013 (http://www.acerwc.org/download/general_comment_on_article_30_of_the_acrwc_english/?wpdmdl=8597, accessed on 3 June 2016).

[421] The reservation made by Egypt regarding Article 24 on adoption is being reviewed; an analogous reservation has already been removed with regard to the CRC.

[422] Keller, Ulfstein, *UN Human Rights Treaty Bodies. Law and Legitimacy. Protection of economic and social rights. Studies on human rights convention*, Cambridge, Cambridge University Press, 2012, p. 219.

[423] Human Rights Committee, *Kennedy v. Trinidad and Tobago*, Communication n. 845/1999, 2 November 1999, UN Doc. CCPR/C/67/D/845/1999.

[424] *Ibidem*. Par. 4.1.

[425] *Ibidem*. Par. 6.6.

[426] *Ibidem*. Par. 5.

be received by the Committee. In *Elgueta vs Chile*[427], the Human Rights Committee stated that it is the only international body that can interpret the statement issued by Chile regarding the Covenant and the Optional Protocol, and that there is no reason why the Committee should automatically accept the interpretation, provided by a state, on its own intentions. It is the Committee's prerogative to evaluate the legal effects, in light of the purpose and object of the international instrument to be applied. The ratification, states the Committee, constitutes a recognition of the Committee's competence. The Protocol does not authorize a restriction of the Committee's competences. Therefore, Chile's declaration is incompatible with the purpose and object of the treaty[428]. In other words, reservations that have the effect of limiting the procedural powers of a human rights supervisory body could also be considered invalid.

To return to the Egyptian reservation on the ACERWC's procedural powers, its result is to exclude certain categories of children from all forms of protection, thus leading to a a state of opposition with the object and purpose of the ACRWC.

Mauritania has expressed reservations regarding Article 9 ACRWC, which states that every child has the right to freedom of thought, conscience and religion, and parents, in accordance with said provision and, where appropriate, legal guardians, have a duty of guidance and guidance in exercising this right, taking into account the development of the child's ability and his or her best interest. It can only be concluded that this type of reservation does not protect the child's development in line with the principles of the ACRWC and his or her best interest, thus infringing one of the fundamental protections of the ACRWC.

Sudan does not consider itself bound by Article 10 ACRWC, which affirms that no child shall be subjected arbitrarily or illegally to interference in his or her private life, home or correspondence, nor to attacks on his or her honour and reputation; Article 11(6) on the right of girls who become pregnant to complete their studies; and Article 21(2), on the prohibition of child marriage. The reservation on the arbitrary or illegal interference in the private life of the child is the premise for the reservations on child marriage and the continuation of girls' education. These reservations affect, in particular, the rights of girls and contrast with the general principle of the best interest of the child. As such, they are incompatible with the object and purpose of the ACRWC. More generally, this opposition is confirmed by scholarship, who emphasize that the special nature of human rights treaties must be respected by assessing the compatibility of reservations with the object and purpose of the treaties, by an independent body, in a centralized manner, for the protection of human rights. Goodman also states that invalid reservations would annul the ratification instrument entirely[429]. Mujuzi[430] argues that the Protocol to the African Charter on Human Rights does not include any provision on reservations, which however does not mean that

---

[427] Human Rights Committee, *Elgueta vs Chile.*, Communication no. 1536/ 2006, Decision of 28 July 2009, p. 11.

[428] *Ibidem*. I.8.

[429] Goodman, "Human Rights Treaties, invalid reservation and State Consent", American Journal of international law, 2002, p. 531.

[430] Mujuzi, "The protocol to the African Charter On Human and People's Rights on the rights of women in Africa: South Africa's reservation and interpretative declarations", *Law, democracy & development*, 2008, p. 46.

reservations cannot be formulated. According to Baderin[431], this essentially means that reservations are possible because they are subject to the relevant international rules, and that the Protocol does not prohibit reservations to encourage the participation and adaptation of States Parties, despite possible cultural and legal differences, as long as they do not jeopardize the object and purpose of the treaty.

The International Law Commission has dealt with this subject in its work on reservations to treaties[432], underscoring the indivisibility, interdependence and interrelation of the rights enshrined in human rights treaties: "To assess the compatibility of a reservation with the object and purpose of a general treaty for the protection of human rights, account shall be taken of the indivisibility interdependence and interrelated of the rights set out in the treaty as well as the importance that the right or provision which is the subject of the reservation."[433]

The International Law Commission has not completed the work on the issue, nor has it published comments on this particular recommendation, which could be the subject of a future amendment. However, it has commented on the competence to assess reservations relating to human rights as against the criteria of compatibility with the object and purpose of the treaty[434].

Given the silence in this respect of the ACWRC and the ACERWC[435] on questions concerning reservations and their compatibility with the aims of the ACRWC, the debate on the reservations made by African States to the ACRWC has yet to be resolved. In this case, the only path is to refer to the general regime and practice of other human rights bodies.

In the case of the Charter's reservations, the States have behaved as if they had full discretion in choosing which rights are covered by the reservation. In any case, this discretion can only be limited by the general international rules governing reservations to treaties. Finally, it is considered that in light of the practice followed by other similar bodies, the ACERWC is empowered to make conclusive decisions on the reservations to the ACRWC.

III.5   The relationship with the UN Committee on the Rights of the Child

According to Paragraph 24 of the Reporting Guidelines applicable to the CRC, if a State Party has already submitted its report to the CRC Committee, that State party will be invited to add information on the provisions of the ACRWC.

---

[431] Baderin, "Recent Developments in the African Regional Human Rights Systems", *Human Right Law Review*, 2005, pp. 123–124.

[432] International Law Commission, "Report of the International Law Commission, 60th Session", *Official Records of the General Assembly. A/63/10* (http://legal.un.org/ilc/documentation/english/reports/a_63_10.pdf, accessed on 9 June 2016).

[433] *Ibidem*. p. 173.

[434] *Ibidem*. p. 173.

[435] Article 47 concerns only signature, ratification and adherence.

The Rules of Procedure of the ACERWC state that, if a State Party's initial report has already been examined by the UN CRC Committee, the final remarks and recommendations of the CRC Committee will be taken into consideration by the ACERWC at time of compilation of the list of questions to be submitted to the government in question, and at the time of drawing up its final observations and recommendations.

To enhance efficiency, the Committee of Experts and the UN Committee should engage in direct consultative cooperation and discussion on issues concerning children's rights, as the report to be submitted to the ACERWC can complete the report that has already been presented to the UN Committee, incorporating the new and specific elements of the African Charter[436].

The provision examined thus ensures that the decisions of the two bodies do not conflict.

III.6 The General Comment on Article 30 ACRWC: children with parents or legal guardians in prison

Pursuant to Article 42 ACRWC, the ACERWC has the power to give an authoritative interpretation of the ACRWC. This mandate is carried out through General Comments. To date, the ACERWC has released three General Comments. The first concerned Article 30 ACRWC on the children whose parents or guardians are in custody.

In view of the importance of the issue, the ACERWC decided to prepare its first General Comment to support the States Parties and other stakeholders in the effective implementation of Article 30 ACRWC, which states that:

"1. States Parties to the present Charter shall undertake to provide special treatment to expectant mothers and to mothers of infants and young children who have been accused or found guilty of infringing the penal law and shall in particular:

   (a) ensure that a non-custodial sentence will always be first considered when sentencing such mothers;
   (b) establish and promote measures alternative to institutional confinement for the treatment of such mothers;
   (c) establish special alternative institutions for holding such mothers;
   (d) ensure that a mother shall not be imprisoned with her child;
   (e) ensure that a death sentence shall not be imposed on such mothers;
   (f) the essential aim of the penitentiary system will be the reformation, the integration of the mother to the family and social rehabilitation."

---

[436] ACERWC. States Parties Reporting Guidelines, p. 8 (http://acerwc.org/?wpdmdl=8694, accessed on 09 June 2016).

The General Comment on Article 30 ACRWC was adopted by the ACERWC in November 2013, and stated that in cases involving pregnant women and mothers of young children, primarily, measures should always be taken into account that do not entail custody. Rather, alternatives to detention should always be considered, in accordance with Article 30 ACRWC, which provides for "special treatment" to be accorded to pregnant mothers and mothers of young children. Indeed, the rights of children who live in prison with their mothers are violated, and they are susceptible to psychological problems, health problems and difficulties in accessing education[437].

The General Comment is important especially because it provides an interpretation of some terms of Article 30 ACRWC on the children of detained mothers. The term "mother"[438] also includes the child's father or, in case these have died or fallen ill, the relatives of the extended family who have custody of the child, such as grandparents. "Imprisonment" means the custodial measure as well as informal detention, such as in detention centres, secret prisons or unofficial places of detention.

The ACERWC recalled that the best interest of the child should be the primary consideration in relation to all actions involving the children of parents who violate the law. In particular, the States Parties must ensure that criminal proceedings affecting the parents are to be prioritized decided upon quickly, because often, there is a long delay resulting from the custodial measure. Ideally, care should be provided immediately following arrest. Whether a given cure is appropriate should be decided on a case-by-case basis, with reference to the principle of the best interest of the child[439]. Treatment should be supervised and reviewed periodically. Human rights institutions and other independent institutions should be encouraged to participate in monitoring the treatment and conditions of children living in prison with their mothers. States are required to create and implement laws and policies to ensure the best interest of the child, at all stages of judgment. The ACERWC has invited Mozambique to extend the special treatment accorded to mothers as per Article 30 ACRWC from the moment of arrest until final conviction[440]. For example, Sudan[441] prohibits the detention of pregnant or nursing mothers; the trial against such women is postponed by two years.

States Parties should also establish legislative and administrative mechanisms to ensure that the decision for the child living in prison with his mother is subject to judicial review. The criteria for making this decision should develop and include consideration of the individual characteristics

---

[437] ACERWC. General Comment No. 1 (Article 30 of the African Charter on the Rights and Welfare of the Child) on "Children of Incarcerated and Imprisoned Parents and Primary Caregivers" 2013, adopted by the ACERWC during the 22nd Ordinary Session (4–8 November 2013), ACERWC/GC/01 (2013), p. 4. http://www.acerwc.org/download/general_comment_on_article_30_of_the_acrwc_english/?wpdmdl=8597, accessed on 7 June 2016.

[438] Ibidem p. 8.

[439] UN Guidelines for the Alternative Care of Children, 24 February 2010, Articles 48 and 82 (http://www.unicef.org/protection/alternative_care_Guidelines-English.pdf. Accessed on 4 February 2016).

[440] Concluding Observations and Recommendations of the ACERWC on the Mozambique Report, p. 8, http://www.acerwc.org/?wpdmdl=8749, accessed on 27 December 2015.

[441] Sudan Initial Report on the implementation of the ACRWC, p. 54, http://acerwc.org/?wpdmdl=8654, accessed on 27 December 2015.

of the child, such as age, sex, maturity level, the quality of the relationship with the mother, and the existence of valid alternatives within the family.

Legislative and administrative measures should then be adopted to ensure that imprisoned minors maintain direct contact with parents or care providers and other family members, especially during early childhood and the entire period of imprisonment. Article 30(1) ACRWC refers to special treatment for pregnant women and mothers of young children. However, it does not specify the age up to which the child can remain in prison with his or her mother. The reference to "young" age leaves this to the discretion of individual States Parties, especially as the ACERWC has also refrained from specifying an age.

In their reports, States Parties describe the measures taken and the maximum age of children in this respect; it is evident that the practice differs between states. The Algeria report[442] notes that, according to Law no. 05-04 of 6 February 2005, mothers can keep their children with them for up to three years. According to the Burkina Faso report[443], children of mothers in prison can be near their mother until the age of two[444]. Ethiopia[445] sets the age limit[446] at 18 months. Gabon, with Article 48 of Law no. 55/59 of 15 December 1959, states that women may be allowed to keep children with them up to 4 years[447]. In Ghana[448], prison authorities have indicated that when children reach the age of approximately one and a half years and are ready to be weaned, members of their family are required to retrieve them. Otherwise, the children are sent to a child shelter; they remain there once their mothers have finished serving their sentence, when reunification with their children is authorized. According to Kenya's Prison Act[449], children can stay in prison with their mother up to four years. In Lesotho[450], the Correctional Services Operational Guidelines provide that mothers may stay with their children up to the age of two, when the child is returned

---

[442] Algeria Initial Report on the implementation of the ACRWC, p. 62, http://acerwc.org/?wpdmdl=8766, accessed on 27 December 2015.
[443] Burkina Faso Initial Report on the implementation of the ACRWC, p. 124, http://acerwc.org/?wpdmdl=8780, accessed on 27 December 2015.
[444] Article 167 of the Kiti Law of 1 December 1998 on pregnant detainees. See also Burkina Faso Initial Report on the implementation of the ACRWC, p. 124, http://acerwc.org/?wpdmdl=8780, accessed on 27 December 2015.
[445] Ethiopia Initial Report on the implementation of the ACRWC, p. 107, http://acerwc.org/?wpdmdl=8645, accessed on 27 December 2015.
[446] As per the Federal Prisons Commission Establishment Proclamation No. 365/2003 cited in the Ethiopia Initial Report on the implementation of the ACRWC, p. 107, http://acerwc.org/?wpdmdl=8645, accessed on 27 December 2015.
[447] Gabon Initial Report on the implementation of the ACRWC, p. 150, http://acerwc.org/?wpdmdl=8773, accessed on 27 December 2015.
[448] Ghana Initial Report on the implementation of the ACRWC, p. 102, http://acerwc.org/?wpdmdl=8775, accessed on 27 December 2015.
[449] Kenya Initial Report on the implementation of the ACRWC, p. 96, http://acerwc.org/?wpdmdl=8648, accessed on 27 December 2015.
[450] Lesotho Initial Report on the implementation of the ACRWC, p. 69, http://acerwc.org/?wpdmdl=8774, accessed on 27 December 2015.

to the care of the extended family until the mother is released from prison. In Mozambique[451], mothers with children are placed in separate prisons, where they can take care of their children. According to the law, children can stay with mothers for up to three years. Nigeria[452] provides that children may stay with their mothers up to 6 years in a special centre for mothers, under the Child's Rights Act[453]. Rwanda[454] has set up Early Childhood Development Centres for children under three years of age who live with their mothers in prison. In South Africa[455] according to Article 26(d) of the Correctional Service Act Regulations, pregnant mothers must be able to access health services before, during and after birth; such services are guaranteed up to two years of age. In Liberia[456], Article XII, Paragraph 6.1 of the Children's Law states that "No expectant mother or a mother of a child below the age of 5 shall be imprisoned with her child. If necessary, the confinement of a convicted expectant mother or a mother of a young child shall be in a separate prison facility with her child where the child can continue to enjoy the nurture of her or his biological mother, including, where appropriate, being breastfed by such mother. Where there is no such facility, in the best interest of the child, the child shall be placed in a caregiver facility".

There is heterogeneity in the practice followed by States in their interpretation of what constitutes "young" age as per Article 30 ACRWC. Generally, this age can be assumed to range between 18 months and 6 years. Such a difference, however, causes discrimination in the protection of children depending on their country of origin.

While Zimbabwe[457] periodically grants amnesties to nursing mothers, and mothers in prison are entitled to pre- and post-natal care administered by permanent prison staff, in other African states, legislation does not always comply with the ACRWC. Even Cameroon violates Article 30: mothers cannot stay with their children in prison, even if they are still nursing[458]. In Senegal[459], in 2008, 15 nursing women and their children received an apology from the Minister for the family and received medical and nutritional products and clothing.

---

[451] Mozambique Initial Report on the implementation of the ACRWC, p. 68, http://acerwc.org/?wpdmdl=8650, accessed on 27 December 2015.

[452] Nigeria Initial Report on the implementation of the ACRWC, p. 145, http://acerwc.org/?wpdmdl=8784, accessed on 27 December 2015.

[453] Child's Rights Act 2003, Articles 221–225, http://www.unicef.org/nigeria/ng_publications_Childs_Right_Act_2003.pdf, accessed on 9 June 2016.

[454] Rwanda Initial Report on the implementation of the ACRWC, p. 3, http://acerwc.org/?wpdmdl=8648, accessed on 27 December 2015.

[455] South Africa Initial Report on the implementation of the ACRWC, p. 70, http://acerwc.org/?wpdmdl=8787, accessed on 27 December 2015.

[456] Liberia Initial Report on the implementation of the ACRWC, p. 16, http://acerwc.org/?wpdmdl=8784, accessed on 27 December 2015.

[457] Zimbabwe Initial Report on the implementation of the ACRWC, p. 61, http://acerwc.org/?wpdmdl=8778, accessed on 27 December 2015.

[458] Cameroon Initial Report on the implementation of the ACRWC, p. 61, http://acerwc.org/?wpdmdl=8781, accessed on 27 December 2015.

[459] Senegal Initial Report on the implementation of the ACRWC, p. 88, http://acerwc.org/?wpdmdl=8788, accessed on 27 December 2015.

The ACERWC noted that a regulatory gap existed in this context according to Senegal's report, as women who committed crimes continue to be imprisoned with their child(ren). The ACERWC called on the Senegalese government to ban the detention of mothers with their child(ren) and invited it to respect the ACRWC. The ACERWC encouraged resort to by the President of the Republic, to obtain benefits during nursing[460].

The ACERWC urged South Africa to build a separate prison facility for mothers and to provide basic services, such as play areas, equipment and cribs that could foster children's development, as per Article 30(b)[461].

The ACERWC [462] noted that in Sudan, mothers are still imprisoned with their children. The ACERWC recommended that the Government take urgent measures to create detention facilities that complied with Article 30 ACRWC and apply alternatives to detention for pregnant women and mothers imprisoned with their children.

More generally, the ACERWC recalled that the principle of non-discrimination against children (Article 3 ACRWC) provides that children should not be treated on the basis of their parents' actions, nor as their extension. In particular, children living in prison should not be treated as prisoners themselves, and should therefore be free to leave the facility and participate in external activities, in compliance with relevant safety standards. Furthermore, mechanisms to protect children from all forms of physical and psychological abuse in prisons should be put in place. Therefore, children should receive the same services and the same education as children who are not in prison, and States Parties should ensure the registration at birth of children born in prison, as required by Article 6 ACRWC. For example, in Algeria, the law[463] provides that civil registration and birth certificates cannot include any indication on mother's imprisonment or detention (Article 52). During the time in prison, children should receive good-quality health care on an ongoing basis and their development should be monitored by a prison psychologist and a child development specialist. However, in this regard, the ACERWC has stressed that none of the state reports mention any such measures.

The implementation of Article 30 ACRWC also implies monitoring the effect on children of a possible custodial sentence. If the custodial sentence concerns the primary care provider, the judge must ensure that the children receive adequate care while the care provider is in prison.

---

[460] Concluding Observations and Recommendations of the ACERWC on the Senegal Report, p. 6, http://www.acerwc.org/?wpdmdl=8755, accessed on 2 February 2016.

[461] Concluding Observations and Recommendations of the ACERWC on the South Africa Report, p. 6, http://www.acerwc.org/?wpdmdl=8754, accessed on 2 February 2016.

[462] Concluding Observations and Recommendations of the ACERWC on the Sudan Report, p. 7, http://www.acerwc.org/?wpdmdl=8757, accessed on 2 February 2016.

[463] Article 52 of Law no. 05-04 of 6 February 2005. See the Concluding Observations and Recommendations of the ACERWC on the Algeria Report, p. 68, http://www.acerwc.org/?wpdmdl=8766, accessed on 27 December 2015.

If it is appropriate to impose a non-custodial sentence, the court must determine the appropriate punishment, keeping in mind the best interest of the child[464].

For example, in Algeria, a temporary stay of execution may be granted to a pregnant mother or one having a child under 24 months of age[465]. In the United Republic of Tanzania[466], many alternative measures to prison are available, such as suspension of the sentence, probation, social services or fines. However, if the judge decides to impose a custodial sentence in light of the seriousness of the offense, the children will be put in jail with their mothers, and there are no specific provisions on the rights of the children.

Regarding the implementation of Article 30(c) ACRWC on special facilities for the detention of mothers, the Burkina Faso report[467] states that, with the 2002–2006 National Action Plan for Justice Reform, there has been a progressive implementation of separate quarters for minors and mothers, as well as social services, within the country's penitentiary facilities. Ghana's prison services have also launched reforms to this effect; for example, the prison authorities of Nsawam[468] have set up a children's unit in the women's section, with nursing facilities, for use by imprisoned mothers. In addition, children born in prison and those who have arrived with their mother in prison no longer share cells, as that exposed children to risks and dangers for their health.

Article VII, Section 6, paragraph 6.1 of the Children's Law of Liberia prohibits the detention of expectant mothers or mothers with children under the age of five. Convicted mothers should be placed in separate facilities, where they can continue to care for their children properly. However, the ACERWC has expressed concern on the difficulties encountered in translating the law into reality, and therefore has called on States Parties to establish appropriate mechanisms within the police forces and in prisons to effectively implement the right, in the best interest of the child[469].

With regard to Burkina Faso's report, the Commission found that children up to two years of age are in jail with their detained mothers. The food and hygiene conditions foster the risk of infections and diseases of all kinds. This does not comply with Article 30 ACRWC. The ACERWC recommended that punishments of a different nature be imposed, and encouraged the creation of special institutions for the detention of mothers[470].

---

[464] Costitutional Court of South Africa, *State v M.*, Case n. CCT 53/06 para. 36 (http://www.saflii.org/za/cases/ZACC /2007/18.html, accessed on 29 March 2016).

[465] Law no. 05-04 of 6 February 2005, cited in the Initial Report of Algeria (http://acerwc.org/?wpdmdl=8766, accessed on 27 December 2015).

[466] United Republic of Tanzania Initial Report on the implementation of the ACRWC, p. 64, http://acerwc.org/?wpdmdl=8786, accessed on 27 December 2015.

[467] Burkina Faso Initial Report on the implementation of the ACRWC, p. 14, http://acerwc.org/?wpdmdl=8780, accessed on 27 December 2015.

[468] Ghana Initial Report on the implementation of the ACRWC, p. 103, http://acerwc.org/?wpdmdl=8775, accessed on 27 December 2015.

[469] Concluding Observations and Recommendations of the ACERWC on the Liberia Report, p. 13, http://www.acerwc.org/?wpdmdl=8747, accessed on 2 February 2016.

[470] Concluding Observations and Recommendations of the ACERWC on the Burkina Faso Report, p. 7, http://www.acerwc.org/?wpdmdl=8740, accessed on 19 January 2016.

Under Article 30(1)(e) ACRWC, States parties must ensure that the death penalty is not imposed on pregnant women or mothers of young children. The exclusion of the death sentence against such mothers is also enshrined in the Protocol on the Rights of Women in Africa (Article 4(1)(j)). States Parties must inform the child if his or her parent or guardian has been imprisoned and received the death sentence, as well as provide for the child's future if the father or the mother is executed[471]. States Parties should also observe the Safeguards Guaranteeing Protection of the Rights of those Facing the Death Penalties, adopted by the UN Economic and Social Committee and approved by the UNGA in 1984, on basic guarantees in cases involving the death penalty. Furthermore, for States Parties that maintain the death penalty, it is of utmost importance that the best interest of the child is considered when the death sentence is issued to the parent or care provider[472].

Thus, for example, Article 118 of Eritrea's Transitional Penal Code[473] provides that a death sentence should not be enforced against pregnant women and mothers of young children under three years of age. In these cases, the death penalty is commuted to life imprisonment. In Ghana[474], Article 312 of Law no. 30 of 1960[475] states that a pregnancy test must be administered to mothers sentenced to death. If the test is positive, the sentence will commuted to life imprisonment. However, there are no express provisions on the revision of detention punishments for mothers with young children, unless the court exercises its discretion in this regard.

Article 30(1)(f) requires the prison systems of States Parties to strive essentially for the re-education and reintegration of the mother within the family, and her social rehabilitation. Only the Sudan report states, in this regard, that imprisoned mothers receive psychosocial support[476]. As mentioned above, Egypt does not consider itself bound by the relevant ACRWC provisions, having made a reservation on Article 30, subsections (a) to (e), on the special treatment of children of detained mothers.

The ACERWC recommended that States Parties, in collaboration with non-state agencies and civil society organizations, widely disseminate the General Comment to governments, criminal justice departments and those responsible for implementing the ACRWC. It should be sent to those who work with children, such as judges, lawyers, legal practitioners, teachers, social workers, public or private welfare institutions, as well as all children and civil society.

---

[471] The UN Human Rights Council adopted REsolution 19/37 on the rights of the child: A/HRC/RES/19/37 (http://ap.ohchr.org/Documents/dpage_e.aspx?b=10&se=126&t=11. Accessed on 27 December 2015).

[472] ACERWC. General Comment adopted during the 22nd Ordinary Session (4–8 November 2013), ACERWC/GC/01 (2013), p. 25.

[473] Eritrea Initial Report on the implementation of the ACRWC, p. 89, http://acerwc.org/?wpdmdl=8797, accessed on 27 December 2015.

[474] Ghana Initial Report on the implementation of the ACRWC, p. 102, http://acerwc.org/?wpdmdl=8775, accessed on 27 December 2015.

[475] Criminal procedure code of 1960, Criminal Law no. 30 (and procedure relating to other offences), http://www.wipo.int/ wipolex/fr/text.jsp?file_id=315286, accessed on 19 March 2016.

[476] Sudan Initial Report on the implementation of the ACRWC, p. 39, http://acerwc.org/?wpdmdl=8654, accessed on 27 December 2015.

The ACERWC has specified the components of such special treatment: participating in external activities; health and psychological care; and adequate nutrition and hygiene.

The ACERWC monitors the content of Article 30 ACRWC, which, however, appears to be focused more on the special treatment accorded to mothers, being intended to provide them with guarantees on following their children (alternative measures to detention, special detention centres, prohibition on the death penalty, rehabilitation and reintegration). However, the ACERWC also mentions some children's rights enshrined in the ACRWC, which must be guaranteed even within the prison: the right to education (Article 11), registration at birth (Article 6), nutrition, hygiene and health, psychological care (Articles 5 and 14) and outside activities (Article 12).

III.7   The General Comment on Article 6 ACRWC: the right to registration, birth, name, and nationality

Article 6 ACRWC states that every child shall have the right, from birth, to a name. Every child must be registered immediately after birth. Every minor has the right to acquire a nationality. States Parties to the ACRWC shall undertake to ensure that their constitutional legislation recognizes the principles according to which a child shall acquire the nationality of the State in the territory of which he was born if, at the time of the child's birth, he is not granted nationality by any other State in accordance with its laws.

The right to registration at birth is one of the rights that appears to not be implemented by the States Parties. According to a UNICEF report[477], 50 million children every year are not registered. Asia and sub-Saharan Africa together account for 79 percent of all unregistered births. In Africa, only small states such as Mauritius and Seychelles have complete registrations of births, deaths and causes of death.

The General Comment on Article 6 ACRWC is addressed to all stakeholders that perform a role in the implementation of the ACRWC and, especially, the rights enshrined therein. Its recipients are, therefore, the agencies of the States Parties, parliaments and judicial offices, civil society organizations, academics, lawyers and civil registry authorities[478].

The ACERWC considers that the right to a name, to registration at birth and to the acquisition of nationality constitutes a pillar of personal identity[479]. As for the implementation of the rights enshrined in Article 6 ACRWC, States Parties should respect, protect, promote and fulfill children's rights, in accordance with their obligations under Article 1 ACRWC which requires that necessary steps to be taken to adopt legislation and other measures required to give effect to

---

[477] UNICEF, "Strengthening birth registration in Africa. Opportunities and Partnerships", 2010, p.5, (http://www.unicef.org/esaro/Technical_paper_low_res_.pdf, accessed on 27 December 2015).

[478] ACERWC. General Comment on Article 6 ACRWC. ACERWC/GC/02 (2014). p. 5, (http://www.acerwc.org/download/general_comment_article_6_name_and_nationality/?wpdmdl=8606, accessed on 9 June 6 2016).

[479] *Ibid*, p. 12.

the ACWRC. The States Parties must therefore guarantee the right to registration by establishing a suitable administrative organization that enables them to exercise this right effectively.

The reports of the African states provide significant data on the situation of birth registration in different countries. In Lesotho, in 2011 only one third of the children born received a birth certificate (38.6 percent)[480]; the Registration of Births and Deaths Act of 1973 provides for the registration of births and deaths within three months of the event, while Article 6(2) ACRWC requires that every child be registered immediately after birth.

Similarly, in Nigeria, Law no. 69 of 1992 stipulates that registration is free within 60 days of birth, and not (only) immediately, as provided for by the ACRWC[481]. 70 percent of the 5 million children born each year in Nigeria are not registered at birth. 49 percent of mothers living in urban areas registered their children, while only 20 percent of those in rural areas did the same[482].

Birth registration in Liberia in 2008 was of 4 percent for children under the age of five. In 2012, the Government of Liberia, with the support of UNICEF, began a general birth registration program aimed at the construction and decentralization of birth registration facilities even in rural areas, communities and locations without hospitals, clinics and health[483].

According to the Sudan report, Article 28 of the Civil Rolls Act of 2001 provides legal guarantees for immediate registration at birth[484]. Article 29 makes birth registration a legal duty and specifies the individuals responsible for registration, such as the head of the family. Article 42 also provides for criminal sanctions to be imposed upon those who violate the duty to register.

In the Uganda report[485], it is specified that Article 18 of the Constitution provides for the registration of each birth. The Birth and Death Registration Act establishes that registration of births and deaths must take place within six months of the event.

In the United Republic of Tanzania[486], only 19 percent of births are recorded, there being great disparity between urban and rural areas resulting from scarce awareness of the importance of registration and the costs of the procedure. These envisage fees for late registration, the cost of the certificate itself and usually the travel costs to reach the relevant office. In this regard, the

---

[480] Lesotho Initial Report on the implementation of the ACRWC, p. 27, http://acerwc.org/?wpdmdl=8774, accessed on 27 December 2015.

[481] Article 6(2) ACRWC: "Every child shall be registered immediately after birth".

[482] Nigeria Initial Report on the implementation of the ACRWC, p. 6, http://acerwc.org/?wpdmdl=8651, accessed on 27 December 2015.

[483] Liberia Initial Report on the implementation of the ACRWC, p. 6, http://acerwc.org/?wpdmdl=8651, accessed on 27 December 2015.

[484] Sudan Initial Report on the implementation of the ACRWC, p. 24, http://acerwc.org/?wpdmdl=8654, accessed on 27 December 2015.

[485] Uganda Initial Report on the implementation of the ACRWC, p. 16, http://acerwc.org/?wpdmdl=8790, accessed on 27 December 2015.

[486] United Republic of Tanzania Initial Report on the implementation of the ACRWC, p. 18, http://acerwc.org/?wpdmdl=8786, accessed on 27 December 2015.

ACERWC noted that there are no implementation mechanisms that make the compulsory registration of birth effective, adding that such registration should be free. The ACERWC urged the State Party to take urgent measures to resolve this situation, ensuring the availability of all required measures and equipment to facilitate mandatory registration at birth as per Article 6 ACRWC[487].

South Africa[488] has taken measures to protect and promote birth registration rights. These rights are disregarded for many children, especially those affected by HIV and AIDS, because of stigma and discrimination[489], and those living in poverty and in rural areas, because of the distance from the registration centers and the lack of awareness of the importance of birth registration to acquire legal capacity.

In Kenya[490], only 56 percent of rural children are registered at birth. The Kenyan Government has improved mobile registration services, especially for nomadic communities. However, additional resources and staff are necessary to facilitate registration. In areas where refugees are present, with UNHCR intervention, the coverage rate can be very high. The Government has launched a project that applies and uses special technology to document births. In this project, managers use mobile phones with a special application to send short messages to the registry office, thus recording the birth. In certain areas, a lack of awareness of the need for birth registration and religious and socio-cultural conditions hinder the registration of births and deaths. The Government has promoted awareness campaigns among parents and communities on birth registration. Despite these efforts, the ACERWC called for the adoption of various measures to deal with the situation[491].

In Burkina Faso, birth registration and certificates are regularly organized throughout the territory, thanks to concerted action of the State, its bilateral and multilateral partners, NGOs and civil society. To facilitate birth registration, registry offices have been opened in maternity wards[492]. Still, only one child in three was registered at birth and 5 million children were not registered at birth[493]. On 16 June 2004, during the celebrations of the Day of the African Child, national-level efforts were made to improve the rate of birth registrations and the issuance of birth certificates. Several activities and actions were conducted: the official launch, on 9 December 2004, of a birth

---

[487] United Republic of Tanzania Initial Report on the implementation of the ACRWC, p. 9, http://acerwc. org/?wpdmdl=8752, accessed on 27 December 2015

[488] South Africa Initial Report on the implementation of the ACRWC, p. 34, http://acerwc.org/?wpdmdl=8787, accessed on 27 December 2015.

[489] UNICEF, De Bruin – Cardoso, Mampane, "Civil Registration and Children in the Context of HIV and AIDS in Africa". 2008, p. 1 (http://www.unicef.org/Birth_registration_in_the_context_of_HIV_and_AIDS. pdf, accessed on 5 February 2016).

[490] Kenya Initial Report on the implementation of the ACRWC, p. 6, http://acerwc.org/?wpdmdl=8648, accessed on 27 December 2015.

[491] Concluding Observations and Recommendations of the ACERWC on the Kenya Report, p. 3, http://www. acerwc.org/?wpdmdl=8743, accessed on 5 February 2016.

[492] Burkina Faso Initial Report on the implementation of the ACRWC, p. 38, http://acerwc.org/?wpdmdl=8780, accessed on 27 December 2015.

[493] *Ibidem*, p. 32.

registration campaign in 14 provinces; strengthening of the the registry system; the creation of a national birth registration committee, composed of representatives of the State and its public and private partners; the elaboration of a 2004 Action Plan having the objective of allowing 75 percent of the provincial populations to receive a birth certificate. The main obstacle is the geographical and financial inaccessibility of the registries, which are averagely 30 km away from populations.

In its report, Ethiopia[494] referred to its Criminal Code, which punishes the act of concealing a child's birth. Article 656 of the Code criminalizes the omission to register the birth of a child or to report its abandonment. Such offences are punishable by a fine or a term imprisonment not exceeding 1 month. Law 301 of 1965 on the registration of births and deaths established the current system of registration. The law provides for the mandatory registration of births and deaths in all regions of the country. To make records accessible to a large part of the population, the register of births and deaths has offices in regions, districts and communities.

In the Rwanda report[495], reference is made to Article 8(1) of Law no. 14 of 4 June 2008 on registration of the population, which provides that all are required to declare the birth of their child within 30 days of birth. An obligation to register births also exists in the legislation of Zimbabwe[496]. However, scholarship[497] states that the failure to register births is tolerated by the legislator, which, in certain legal provisions, uses expressions such as "of the age of (...) or apparently of the age of", which allows certain state institutions to consider the subject as a child or as an adult as convenient.

Indeed, the absence of a registry makes it difficult to determine the age of the person in question. In the absence of proof by registry officials, proof of age is obtained indirectly through baptismal certificates, medical certificates or witness statements. However, often, not even this procedure is followed, and decisions on the age of children are taken arbitrarily. For example, in the Code of Child Criminal Law of the Democratic Republic of the Congo, the judge must assess the age of the child based on physical and psychological parameters that are all but objective[498]. Also, in

---

[494] Ethiopia Initial Report on the implementation of the ACRWC, p. 45, http://acerwc.org/?wpdmdl=8645, accessed on 27 December 2015.

[495] Concluding Observations and Recommendations of the ACERWC on the Rwanda Report, p. 10, http://www.acerwc.org/?wpdmdl=8653, accessed on 2 February 2016.

[496] Zimbawbe Initial Report (http://www.acerwc.org/download/zimbabwe_initial_report_under_the_acrwc/?wpdmdl=8778, accessed on 15 March 2016). P. 26.

[497] Boukongou "Le système africain de protection des droits de l'enfant. Exigences universelles et prétentions africains», *op. cit.* pp. 97–108.

[498] Article 15 of the Decree of 6 December 1950 on "Enfance délinquante", Bulletin Officiel, 1951, p. 91, states that: "À chaque stade de la procédure, le juge est assisté de l'officier du ministère public, magistrat de carrière. Il vérifie l'identité et l'âge de l'enfant, fait une enquête sur son état physique et mental, ainsi que sur les conditions sociales et morales dans lesquelles il vit. Il soumet l'enfant à une visite médicale".

Lesotho, the Child Care and Protection Bill of 2004 provides a similar procedure to ascertain the age of the child[499].

Several factors explain this state of affairs: poverty, lack of education, discrimination against women, belonging to certain indigenous ethnic groups, or groups of migrants and refugees, or the state administration's failure to decentralize.

The ACERWC noted that improving the birth registration system increases the visibility of many disadvantaged children and enhances their protection against harmful practices. Registration at birth establishes the legal existence of a child and fulfills an essential condition for the enjoyment of other rights during his or her childhood. Legal existence allows the child to access health, social security and educational services; the child's registration is proof of his or her age, against various potential abuses such as trafficking, sexual abuse, child marriage, child labour and enlistment in the armed forces. Proof of age is important for children involved in crimes, to benefit from justice as appropriate to their needs and to their specificities and special protection measures. It constitutes an irrefutable proof of birth, providing protection against the risk of disinheritance that affects orphans and children born outside of wedlock. Finally, the right to birth registration is related to the right of children to know and be recognized by their parents[500].

On a practical level, the greatest obstacle to the effective realization of the right to nationality in Africa is the lack of a national civil registry system. In this regard, the ACERWC mentioned the AU Conference of Ministers responsible for Civil Registration and Statistics Systems (CRVS)[501]. In its General Comment, the ACERWC noted that the right to a name, to registration of birth and to nationality could not be fully implemented in the absence of an organized CRVS-related system in the States Parties[502].

The ACERWC specifically expects that States Parties that have not established civil registries will create one, and comply with the standards required by the ACRWC, through legislative reforms[503]. The ACERWC believes that the existence of up-to-date legislation on civil registration is fundamental for the fulfillment of the child's right to a name and birth registration. This legislation should: regulate the role of government agencies involved in the civil registry; establish the time period for birth registration (although Article 6 ACWRC indicates that birth registration must take place immediately); give indications on the attribution of names and surnames; regulate

---

[499] "Where the probation officer is uncertain as to the probable age of the child or person, or where the age of a child or person is in dispute, the probation officer must cause the child or person to be taken to a medical officer for assessment of age unless the child or person has already been taken to the medical officer by the police under section 85, in which case the provisions of section 87 apply."

[500] Doek. *In the best interests of the child: Harmonising laws in Eastern and Southern Africa* (African Child Policy Forum 2007), p. 17 (http://www.africanchildforum.org/clr/Harmonisation%20of%20Laws%20in%20 Africa/Publications/supplementary-acpf-harmonisation-es_en.pdf, accessed on 7 June 2016).

[501] ACERWC. General comment on Article 6 ACRWC. *Op. cit.* (http://acerwc.org/?wpdmdl=8606, accessed on 07 June 2016, p. 4).

[502] *Ibidem*, p. 6

[503] *Ibidem*, p. 6

the use of technology to ensure that civil status records retain their evidentiary value; set rules regarding costs, access to and privacy of data, as well as delays in registration procedures; and specify the information to provide on the birth certificate and the information required to obtain copies of the birth certificate[504]. Furthermore, States must establish rules to ensure that the first copy of the birth certificate is free and registered; provide measures to prevent and combat fraud and forgery of birth register information; and set specific rules on the use of digital technologies in recording or storing birth registration data. The official registration of a child at birth, at administrative and state levels, must give rise to a permanent and official record of the existence of the child[505].

The ACERWC considered the identity of the child as fundamental in ensuring his or her survival, development and protection. For example, comprehensive information on births facilitates government efforts to plan prevention campaigns for diseases such as malaria, neonatal HIV and other diseases that contribute to child mortality. This is essential in implementing Article 14 ACRWC on health and medical services.

Proof of identity through the birth registration system may be essential to provide education-related services or social services, and may also contribute to the prevention and protection of harmful practices that particularly affect children. The statistical system can contribute to the prevention of trafficking in children, as well as their sexual exploitation, early marriage, illicit adoption, and forced enlistment.

In its General Comment, the ACERWC also introduced the concept of registrations of death. Although not specifically requested by the ACRWC, it is part of the recommendation on the CRVS system in Africa. In fact, systems of recording deaths allow for the evaluation of information on causes of death and for verification of the causes of child deaths; this, in turn, enhances efforts to protect children, especially where child deaths occur on a massive scale, such as among refugees and displaced persons.

Furthermore, being registered is of fundamental importance for the child, to enable him or her to benefit more generally from the protection of the ACRWC. It is the age of the child that determines whether he may be considered criminally responsible. The birth certificate is the primary document that attests the minimum age for criminal responsibility. The ACERWC notes that failure to register children deprives them of the protection of Articles 5 and 17 ACRWC[506]. Article 5(3) protects children who have committed crimes from the death penalty, while Article 17 guarantees the right to special treatment considering the dignity of the child, the right to be separated from adults in the place of detention or prison, the right to a timely trial, the right to privacy and the benefit of rehabilitation sentences[507]. Age is relevant when children are victims or witnesses of crime, especially in relation to offences for which it is necessary to establish the

---

[504] *Ibidem*, p. 8.

[505] *Ibidem*, p. 18.

[506] *Ibidem*, p. 11.

[507] *Ibidem*, p. 27.

age of consent to sexual intercourse[508]. Furthermore, registration is an essential prerequisite for issuing birth certificates[509].

The ACERWC expressed awareness that many countries in Africa require the production of birth certificates to enroll children in school or national examinations[510]. In these countries, the right to education is applied in a discriminatory manner, distinguishing between registered and unregistered children[511]. The risk is, therefore, that the right to education provided for in Article 11(1) ACRWC is violated.

The ACERWC stressed that medical care and social assistance, social security and health services are less easily accessible by unregistered children. Essential services such as vaccinations, medical care and subsidies to alleviate extreme poverty could also be endangered by the absence of appropriate identification documentation.

The ACERWC called upon States Parties to ensure that children grow up in a family environment, in an atmosphere of happiness, love and understanding, for the full and harmonious development of their personalities. The ACERWC also recalled the right of every child to parental care and protection and, whenever possible, the right to reside with his or her parents. The ACERWC noted that birth registration is crucial not only in establishing the child's identity and parentage, but also in preserving his or her identity against illegal changes, such as name changes or falsification of family relationships. These occur more easily when the child is not registered and there is no proof of identity[512].

The ACERWC noted that child traffickers take advantage of these gaps when conducting their activities, including illicit interstate adoption. The ACERWC believes that the implementation of the right to registration at birth, through a universal birth registration system, is a valid measure to combat the illegal practice of interstate adoptions[513].

With proof of identity that indicates parental and family relationships, registration at birth is also important in resolving disputes relating to the child's right to inherit parental and family property[514].

Non-discrimination in the context of the rights to a name, registration of birth and acquisition of a nationality means that no child should be deprived of the right to a name and that all children should be registered in a non-discriminatory manner, ensuring their right enshrined in Article 6 ACRWC. This is of greater significance when a child is an orphan, refugee, or displaced, and when a child is born out of wedlock.

---

[508] *Ibidem*, p. 29.

[509] *Ibidem*, p. 31.

[510] *Ibidem*, p. 31.

[511] *Ibidem*, p. 15.

[512] *Ibidem*, p. 33.

[513] *Ibidem*, p. 34.

[514] *Ibidem*, p. 35.

Children with some form of physical, intellectual, or sensory disability must be registered. The ACERWC noted that States Parties are obliged to not discriminate against children born with disabilities. That is, they must take special measures to protect their rights from birth and to ensure that they are duly registered. The registration of children born with disabilities increases their chances of being taken into account for the specific policies and programs designed to ensure that they are treated with dignity and harmoniously integrated into society.

The ACERWC recalled that States Parties are required to respect international obligations deriving from compliance with the Convention on the Rights of Persons with Disabilities (Article 24(3)). In particular, the ACERWC believes that their effective implementation depends on the existence of a universal birth registration system that does not discriminate against children with disabilities[515]. States Parties must take special measures to facilitate the registration of children born to disabled persons. Specific attention should be given to children born to parents with mental and intellectual disabilities. States Parties should contact community leaders for the identification and immediate reporting, to the competent authorities, of any child born to parents with mental or intellectual disabilities. Best practices require that information on birth registration be adapted to people with hearing or visual impairments, to enable them to participate optimally in registration; in addition, registration staff should be trained in sign language and other forms of communication with parents with hearing and visual impairment who register their children.

The ACERWC noted that refugees, children born to the displaced and asylum seekers are vulnerable people, and that their children should benefit from special protection measures contained in the ACRWC. The ACERWC considered that the registration of the birth of refugee children, children born to displaced persons[516], children who have been separated from their parents or guardians during conflicts, and children born to asylum seekers, is a particularly urgent matter. Denying the right of birth registration to children belonging to this category is an act of discrimination and constitutes a violation of their rights not to be discriminated against, enshrined in Article 3 ACRWC and other international instruments. In fact, registration of birth facilitates the return to the country of origin. This proof of identity is also crucial for reunification in situations where family members have been dispersed to various locations. For countries of origin, birth registration facilitates the voluntary return of refugees to their country[517].

For States with large numbers of refugees and displaced persons, it is very important to encourage the provision of civil registration services closer to refugee settlements. This requires the establishment of temporary civil registries offices or the organization of regular mobile registration services for refugees and displaced persons. The ACERWC noted that children without documents are very vulnerable for two reasons. On one hand, their parents or guardians live in fear of being arrested if the administrative authorities discover their status as irregular migrants; on the other, they risk being registered under false identities by parents or guardians[518]. For this reason, the ACERWC

---

[515] *Ibidem*, p. 25.
[516] *Ibidem*, p. 26.
[517] *Ibidem*, p. 26.
[518] *Ibidem*, p. 23.

believes that universal registration at birth as required by Article 6(2) ACRWC means that even undocumented migrant children must be registered at birth, without discrimination.

Evidence of parental identity through non-documentary means should be provided for by the States Parties. Indeed, the problem recurs on an intergenerational level: the new generations are not registered because their parents or ancestors had not been registered[519].

In Ghana, birth registration on a national scale increased from 2 percent[520] in 2002 to 66 percent in 2013, also as a result of the intensification of awareness through the distribution of information material and the modernization of the system for registering births and deaths. The main challenges are the lack of motivation to register births and deaths, the weak coverage of registration, the lack of funding of registry activities, and adherence to traditional and socio-cultural practices in certain regions of the country according to which children tend to not be registered at birth[521].

An important development advocated for by the ACERWC is the decentralization of birth registration services. States Parties should use appropriate alternative mechanisms to ensure that the system of birth registration reaches the remote areas of their respective territories. They should consider mobile registration methods or registration system via mobile phone, where the mobile phone networks cover the territory and their use is reasonably extended among the general population. Another alternative could be to use existing networks. The mobile registration system could also count on local community leaders to collect data on birth records[522].

The ACERWC noted that the States Parties that have set up a birth registration system with modern systems connecting hospitals, clinics, dispensaries (when necessary) and other social services have achieved better results regarding birth registration than those who did not[523]. When digital interconnectivity is not available, the ACERWC has encouraged the establishment of partnerships between the national registry with hospitals, clinics and dispensaries, as well as national statistical offices, to ensure timely exchange of information and maximize exchanges of recovered data.

States Parties must establish a legal framework for the protection of sensitive personal data, including details of birth registration and other vital statistical data. The protection of sensitive personal data entails the additional obligation to ensure the integrity, confidentiality and availability of data. Integrity means that the data must be authentic, complete and protected against improper or accidental modification and destruction. Birth certificates should include security features or

---

[519] *Ibidem*, p. 24.
[520] Ghana Initial Report on the Implementation of the ACWRC, p. 24 (http://acerwc.org/?wpdmdl=8775, accessed on 27 December 2015).
[521] *Ibidem*, p. 27.
[522] *Ibidem*, p. 32.
[523] *Ibidem*, p. 32.

features to detect fraud[524]. Support measures must ensure that data are not lost completely, in case of destruction of the original information because of disruptive events such as natural disasters, wars, accidents, power outages, fire or attacks[525].

National legislation must also address issues such as the responsibilities of internal staff who have access to or process data on a daily basis (civil registrars, archivists, data cleaners or system administrators) and of the external staff to whom the services of the technology may be decentralized (mobile network operators, Internet service providers). The legal framework must also provide for control mechanisms, to ensure that the data are always safe[526].

In addition to legislative measures to guarantee that all conditions are in place to ensure that children are entitled to their right to a name, birth registration and nationality acquisition, States Parties must take all necessary steps to ensure coordination between the central civil registration authority and other civil offices. These coordination measures must ensure cooperation between all governments and private agencies that have access to the civil registry. States Parties should consider establishing a body to coordinate the work of all governments and private agencies (such as UN agencies) involved in these processes[527].

States Parties are also responsible for launching campaigns to raise awareness, among all components of the population, of the benefits of birth registration. Special efforts must be made to reach the most vulnerable populations and communities, whose children are otherwise at risk of becoming stateless or undocumented if they are not identified[528].

For example, in Congo[529], to increase awareness of the importance of birth certificates, the Government partnered with UNICEF to hold an awareness-raising campaign on the issue of birth certificates. In Congo, many factors hinder birth registration. An example are the difficulties faced by the population in reaching the registry office closest to their place of residence, especially in rural and remote areas of the country. In the 2004–2010 registration campaigns, teachers were used in the smallest remote communities. Sixty-four percent of indigenous peoples living in the forest did not have a birth certificate. With the campaign titled "Total and free registration of unregistered children in the civil register" of the Directorate General of Social Affairs and Family and the Directorate General of Territorial Administration, from 2006 to 2009, birth registration increased from 48 306 to 67 149 birth certificates[530].

---

[524] ACERWC. General comment on Article 6 ACRWC. *Op. cit.* (http://acerwc.org/?wpdmdl=8606, accessed on 07 June 2016, p. 76).

[525] *Ibidem*, p. 79.

[526] *Ibidem*, p. 78.

[527] *Ibidem*, p. 104.

[528] *Ibidem*, p. 46.

[529] Congo Initial Report on the Implementation of the ACWRC, p. 37 (http://acerwc.org/?wpdmdl=8796, accessed on 7 June 2016).

[530] *Ibidem*, p. 37.

The ACERWC has expressed concern that many births in remote areas are not registered. The ACERWC recommended that the Government of Sudan take appropriate measures to cover the entire national territory, in terms of structures to collect birth declarations, and to improve the capacity of such facilities, to significantly increase the percentage of birth registration. The ACERWC suggested creating mobile centres, to reach the population more easily and facilitate the registration of births and deaths[531].

Ethiopia set itself the goal of raising public awareness of birth registration, and organized a campaign in which public figures, intellectuals, leaders and members of the administration and NGO representatives participated. In collaboration with UNICEF, regional and federal offices implemented a pilot project on the registration of children in 10 rural and 8 urban areas[532].

Similarly, in Senegal a campaign on birth registration was conducted every year in all areas where illiteracy or semi-illiteracy prevails. With the support of various ministries, a network was set up to facilitate the registration system and the acquisition of birth certificates[533].

According to the General Comment, for the birth registration system to work and to ensure that the right to birth registration is effectively protected, States Parties must design continuing education programs for the various stakeholders, including registry officials, lawmakers, members of the government, agencies, health officials, judicial offices and all those involved in the development of population statistics at all levels.

With regard to the promotion of international cooperation, the ACERWC referred to international organizations and agencies involved in the promotion and protection of children's rights, to extend their collaboration to States Parties in the implementation of laws, policies, programs and strategies aimed at the achievement of the rights to birth registration and to the acquisition of nationality. NGOs, civil society groups (such as youth groups), women's organizations and traditional leaders have an important role to play in promoting awareness of the right to birth registration[534].

In the Concluding Observations on the Mali report, the ACERWC revealed that the country features a very low birth registration rate (48 percent) and identified, as the main obstacles to birth registration, the following factors: the lack of knowledge of the procedures by the staff responsible for the declarations; the illiteracy of the child's parents; the weight of tradition; discriminatory practices against the women who wish to make the registration; and poor reception in health centres. Shortcomings have also been noted regarding the training of civil registry officials; raising public awareness; and developing and implementing projects to support birth registration. The ACERWC recommended that the Government of Mali take steps to overcome these obstacles and

---

[531] Concluding Observations and Recommendations of the ACERWC on the Sudan Report, p. 10, http://www.acerwc.org/?wpdmdl=8757, accessed on 5 February 2016.

[532] Ethiopia Initial Report on the Implementation of the ACWRC, p. 45 (http://acerwc.org/?wpdmdl=8645, accessed on 27 December 2015).

[533] Senegal Initial Report on the Implementation of the ACWRC, p. 48 (http://acerwc.org/?wpdmdl=8788, accessed on 27 December 2015).

[534] General Comment on Article 6 ACRWC, *op. cit.*, p. 114.

make birth registration free for children aged 0 to 6 years. Finally, the ACERWC encouraged the State to continue with its decentralization policy, to bring civil state centres to the population[535].

Regarding the Ethiopia report, the Government should raise awareness among society and make registration accessible in rural areas where poverty and illiteracy prevail. The ACERWC referred to General Comment No. 2 on Article 6 ACRWC, for a better implementation of the right to a name, nationality and birth registration[536].

In the Guinea report, the Concluding Observations of the ACERWC recommended the following measures, to increase the percentage of birth registration: remove all costs associated with birth registration, as well as fees and penalties, to ensure that birth registration is entirely free; promote campaigns to reach all parts of the country; and establish a system of mobile registration units to reach remote areas[537].

As yet, too few States Parties (Senegal, Congo, Ethiopia) have taken the initiative to promote awareness campaigns on the importance of birth registration. Article 6 ACRWC does not expressly provide for such an obligation. However, it falls within the discretion enjoyed by States as established by Article 1, among the obligations of States that may also consist in the provision of further measures for the better welfare and realization of the ACRWC rights.

The ACERWC has suggested that states take action to reach rural areas through mobile means, and to register refugee children. However, state reports do not contain information on the implementation of these indications.

To implement Article 6 ACRWC, the Commission, on one hand, has encouraged States to raise awareness on the importance of birth registration, especially in rural areas. On the other, it helps the recipients by providing states with indications on enhancing the organization of the services offered with adequate and modern means, also in light of the peculiarities of the territory and rural areas in question, with particular attention to the most vulnerable categories such as the disabled and refugees, to avoid discrimination.

The ACERWC has provided very detailed recommendations, including indications of an administrative and technical nature. In fact, according to Article 32 ACRWC, because the ACERWC aims to promote and protect the rights and welfare of the child, it must also address the implementation, by the states, of the rights enshrined in the ACRWC and their effectiveness.

---

[535] Concluding Observations and Recommendations of the ACERWC on the Mali Report, p. 3, http://www. acerwc.org/?wpdmdl=8748, accessed on 7 June 2016.

[536] Ethiopia Initial Report on the Implementation of the ACWRC, p. 5 (http://acerwc.org/?wpdmdl=8744, accessed on 5 February 2016).

[537] Concluding Observations and Recommendations of the ACERWC on the Guinea Report, p. 4, http://www. acerwc.org/?wpdmdl=8745, accessed on 5 February 2016.

III.8 Communications

According to Article 44 ACRWC, "[t]he Committee may receive communication, from any person, group or non- governmental organization recognized by the Organization of African Unity, by a Member State, or the United Nations relating to any matter covered by this Charter."

Communications[538] may be submitted by individuals, including child victims or his or her parents or legal representatives, witnesses, groups of individuals or NGOs recognized by the AU, a Member State or any other institution of the UN system. The author of the communication must specify whether it is the victim of a violation of the right established in the Charter, or whether it acts on behalf of a victim or of other eligible parties. A communication[539] may also be submitted on behalf of victims without their consent, provided that the author is able to prove that this is in the best interest of the child. Child victims who are able to express their opinions must be informed of the communications presented on their behalf.

The ACERWC will decide, by means of a simple majority of members present, on the possible admissibility of a communication in accordance with the provisions of Article 44 ACRWC. In any case, some formal requirements must be respected. The communication[540] must be signed, written and concern a State that has signed the Charter.

The ACERWC[541] may also accept a communication from a State that has not signed the ACRWC, if it is in the best interest of the child. In doing so, the ACERWC must collaborate with other related bodies that implement the conventions and the charters to which the non-signatory is party.

According to Article 44 ACRWC, any relationship or grievance from a State, an individual or an NGO that denounces injurious actions for one or more rights of the child, shall be considered communication.

According to Article 1(1) of the ACERWC's Guidelines for Communications, communications may be submitted by individuals, including child victims or their parents or legal representatives, witnesses, a group of individuals or NGOs recognized by the AU, by a Member State or any other institution of the UN system.

According to Article 1(3), a communication may be filed on behalf of a victim without his or her consent provided that the author of the communication is able to prove that such action has been taken in the best interest of the child. Child victims who are able to express their opinion must be informed of the communications presented on their behalf. Furthermore, Article 3 provides for the participation of minors. The ACERWC must implement measures that ensure the effective and meaningful participation of the child or children involved in the assessment of the validity of

---

[538] *Revised Guidelines for the Consideration of Communications.* Article I.1: http://www.acerwc. org/?wpdmdl=8763, accessed on 29 March 2016.

[539] *Ibidem.* 1.III.

[540] *Ibidem.* II.1.

[541] *Ibidem.* 2.II.

communications and their author(s). If the children are able to express their opinions, they must be heard by a member of the ACERWC.

The substantive conditions that determine the admissibility[542] of a communication are the following:

a) The communication must be compatible with the provisions of the AU's Constitutive Act and with the ACRWC;
b) The communication must not be based exclusively on information that has appeared in the media;
c) The same issue should not be subject of another international investigation, procedure or regulation;
d) The author of the communication must have exhausted all possible remedies at national level and must not be satisfied with the solution provided;
e) The communication must be submitted within a reasonable period with respect to the appeals made at national level;
f) The text of the communication must not be offensive.

According to Article 2 of the ACERWC's Guidelines for Communications, after deciding on the admissibility of a communication, the ACERWC, Working Group or Rapporteur will confidentially bring the communication to the attention of the State involved and request an explanation in writing with its observations, within three months.

Article 4 addresses the monitoring of the ACERWC's decisions. The ACERWC appoint one of its members as being responsible for monitoring its decisions and regularly presenting reports to the ACERWC. The President of the ACERWC will provide in this respect to the President of the AU Commission. The decisions of the ACERWC will be submitted to the Assembly of Heads of State and Government of the AU. The decisions will be made public after the assessment of the Assembly and the States Parties involved; the latter ensure their dissemination in their respective countries.

When the ACERWC[543] decides that a communication is admissible, it may send to the State Party involved a request for the implementation of provisional measures that the ACERWC considers necessary to prevent any other harm to the child or children who would have been the victim of violations. The ACERWC may send one of its members to carry out field checks.

If the State Party does not present a report and does not provide any information on the implementation of the ACERWC's decision, the ACERWC will notify the violation of Article 1(1), Section XXI, and request the report within 90 days of notification. After 90 days, if the State Party has not submitted the report, the ACERWC will notify the matter to the AU Assembly for appropriate intervention.

---

[542] *Ibidem*. II.3.
[543] *Ibidem*. VII.

It should be noted that decisions on the ACERWC's communications are not binding on States, while decisions on the Communications of the African Commission on Human and Peoples' Rights may become binding.

The Commission has not established follow-up mechanisms regarding the recommendations, nor do any systems exist that could somehow oblige States to comply with the recommendations received. In principle, these recommendations are not binding; however, they can become so when they are adopted by the Assembly of Heads of State and Government of the AU.

By analogy, this mechanism could also be applied to the ACERWC's observations.

III.8.1 Decision on the Communication of the Institute for Human Rights and Development in Africa (IHRDA) and the Open Society Justice Initiative (OSJI) against the Government of Kenya

On 20 April 2009, the Secretary of the ACERWC received a Communication from the Institute for Human Rights and Development (based in Gambia) and the Open Society Initiative, based in New York, USA, in the interest of children descended from the Nubian people in Kenya. According to the authors of the Communication, the Kenyan government had violated the right to nationality of Nubian children living within the borders of Kenya, considering that the right to nationality is a requirement for the realization of other rights in the country.

The Nubians in Kenya descend from the Nuba mountains, in Sudan. They were forcibly recruited into the British colonial armed forces in the early 1900s, when Sudan was a British colony. At the time of demobilization, although they had requested to return to Sudan, the colonial government refused and forced them to remain in Kenya[544]. The applicants claimed that the British colonial authorities had allocated land for the Nubians, including a settlement known as Kibera, but had not granted them British citizenship[545]. When Kenya gained independence in 1963, the authors note that the Nubians did not have Kenyan nationality. The greatest difficulty in recognizing the right to effective nationality for Nubian children is the fact that in Kenya, Nubians encounter difficulties in registering the birth of their children, as they themselves often lack valid identity documents[546]. Moreover, birth registration certificates do not constitute proof of citizenship, which leaves even registered children in an ambiguous situation, contrary to Article 6 ACRWC. They can only apply for citizenship at 18 years of age. This limitation is confirmed by the Kenya National Human Rights Commission[547].

---

[544] ACERWC. Decision on the Communication Submitted by the Institute for Human Rights and Development in Africa and the Open Society Justice Initiative (On Behalf of Children of Nubian Descent in Kenya) Against the Government of Kenya. N. Com/002/2009, 22 March 2011, p. 2, para. 2, (http://www.acerwc.org/download/acerwc-decision-on-children-of-nubian-descent-in-kenya/?wpdmdl=8690, accessed on 22 March 2011).

[545] *Ibidem*, p. 2 para. 3.

[546] *Ibidem*, p. 4.

[547] Kenya National Commission Human Rights, "An Identity Crisis? Study on the issuance of national identity cards in Kenya" (2007). p. VI (http://www.knchr.org/Portals/0/EcosocReports/KNCHR%20Final%20IDs%20Report.pdf, accessed on 9 June 2016).

The authors of the Communication argued that the situation infringed mainly Article 6, in connection with Article 2 (the rights to birth registration and to acquire a nationality at birth), Article 3 (the prohibition on discrimination), Article 11(3) (on equal access to education) and Article 14 (equal access to health care) of the ACRWC[548].

The ACERWC considered that there is a strong and direct link between birth registration and nationality. The definition according to which a child is a person up to 18 years of age (Article 2 ACRWC) would run counter to the practice of waiting for children to turn 18 before acquiring Kenyan nationality. Therefore, the Kenyan practice according to which Nubian children cannot acquire a nationality for the long period of 18 years is not in line with the spirit and purpose of Article 6 ACRWC. It does not promote the best interest of the child and constitutes a violation of the ACRWC[549].

Children descended from Nubians in Kenya do not have identity documents, although these are essential to prove their nationality[550]. Therefore, the issue of stateless children is central to the Communication. One of the main purposes of Article 6(4) ACRWC is precisely to prevent or reduce statelessness, or the condition of those persons who, according to the 1954 UN Convention Relating to the Status of Stateless Persons, are "not considered as a national by any State under the operation of its law".

Stateless children often inherit an uncertain future. For example, they cannot benefit from the protections and constitutional rights guaranteed by States. This includes difficulties in travelling freely or in accessing judicial remedies, when necessary. Statelessness is particularly devastating for the realization of children's socio-economic rights, such as access to health care or education. In short, for a child, being stateless child is generally directly opposed to his best interest[551].

Accordingly, in this case, the duty enshrined in Article 6(4) ACRWC to ensure that "a child shall acquire the nationality of the State in the territory of which he has been born" fully applies to the Government of Kenya[552].

This interpretation was strongly endorsed by the ACERWC, which affirmed that States are required to take all appropriate measures, both internally and in cooperation with other States, to ensure that every child has a nationality upon birth[553].

---

[548] ACERWC. Decision on the Communication Submitted by the Institute for Human Rights and Development in Africa and the Open Society Justice Initiative (On Behalf of Children of Nubian Descent in Kenya) Against the Government of Kenya. *Op. cit.*, p. 7.

[549] *Ibidem*, p. 9.

[550] *Ibidem*, p. 43.

[551] *Ibidem*, p. 46.

[552] *Ibidem*, p. 50.

[553] ACERWC. Decision on the Communication Submitted by the Institute for Human Rights and Development in Africa and the Open Society Justice Initiative (On Behalf of Children of Nubian Descent in Kenya) Against the Government of Kenya. *Op. cit.*, p. 51.

Furthermore, for the ACERWC, the Kenyan Government has not undertaken any efforts to ensure that children acquire the nationality of another State, thus violating Article 6(4): "States Parties to the present Charter shall undertake to ensure that their Constitutional legislation recognize the principles according to which a child shall acquire the nationality of the State in the territory of which he has been born if, at the time of the child's birth, he is not granted nationality by any other State in accordance with its laws"[554].

Many African States implement Article 6(4) ACRWC in their legislation. Article 38 of the Constitution of Lesotho[555] provides that persons born in Lesotho have Lesotho citizenship. The Cameroon Family Code[556] recognizes citizenship to every child born of Cameroonian parents, every child adopted by parents of Cameroon and every child born in Cameroon, even if the parents are foreigners. The Senegal report[557] refers to Article 5 of the Nationality Code[558], according to which Senegalese citizenship is granted to "a legitimate child of a Senegalese mother and a father with no nationality or of unknown nationality". The Mozambique report[559] refers to Article 23 of the Constitution, which states that "[t]he following shall be Mozambican nationals, provided they are born in Mozambique: [...] b. Children born of stateless parents or parents of unknown nationality or of unknown parents". The provisions of the Burkina Faso law on the right to nationality[560] certify the belonging, of persons, to the State and consider several scenarios, to prevent children from statelessness. Thus, Burkinabe citizenship is granted to children born in Burkina Faso if their father and mother are from of Burkina Faso, their parents are unknown, they have no other nationality of origin, or their parents are foreigners. The provisions relating to nationality indicate a desire for openness, thus preventing the statelessness of children. This risk is avoided by granting them citizenship.

The ACERWC then found that a violation of the right to non-discrimination had taken place, because in Kenya, Nubian children are treated differently from other children. Ethnic and racial discrimination is prohibited by the ACRWC, which at Article 3 states that "Every child shall be entitled to the enjoyment of the rights and freedoms recognized and guaranteed in this Charter irrespective of the child's or his/her parents' or legal guardians' race, ethnic group, colour, sex,

---

[554] *Ibidem*, p. 52.

[555] Concluding Observations and Recommendations of the ACERWC on the Lesotho Report, p. 27, http://www.acerwc.org/?wpdmdl=8774, accessed on 27 December 2015.

[556] Cameroon Initial Report on the Implementation of the ACRWC, p. 26, http://acerwc.org/?wpdmdl=8781 (accessed on 27 December 2015).

[557] Concluding Observations and Recommendations of the ACERWC on the Lesotho Report, p. 27, http://www.acerwc.org/?wpdmdl=8774, accessed on 27 December 2015.

[558] Law 61-10 of 7 March 1961.

[559] Mozambique Initial Report on the Implementation of the ACRWC, p. 35 (http://acerwc.org/?wpdmdl=8650, accessed on 27 December 2015).

[560] Burkina Faso Initial Report on the Implementation of the ACRWC, p. 36 (http://acerwc.org/?wpdmdl=8780, accessed on 27 December 2015).

language, religion, political or other opinion, national and social origin, fortune, birth or other status"[561].

The ACERWC then found a violation of Article 14(2) ACRWC for the failure to provide health care in fields and slums[562], as well as of Article 14(2)(c), until adequate food and drinking water could be ensured.

The ACERWC noted that the violation also includes an infringement of Article 11(3) ACRWC, which provides for the right to education. States must take all appropriate measures with a view to its full implementation. Article 11(3)(a) requires, in particular, free and compulsory basic education; thus, schools, qualified teachers, equipment are necessary for the fulfillment of this right.

The ACERWC[563] therefore concluded that Kenya committed multiple violations: of Articles 6(2), 6(3) and 6(4), Article 3, Article 14(2)(b), (c) and (g); and Article 11(3). It recommended that the Kenyan Government take all legislative and administrative measures necessary to ensure that otherwise stateless Nubian children could acquire a Kenyan nationality from birth.

With this decision, the ACERWC reiterated the importance of implementing Article 6 ACRWC, in view of the supreme interest of the child.

III.8.2   Decision on the Communication submitted by the Centre for Human Rights (University of Pretoria) and the *Rencontre Africaine pour la Défense des Droits de l'Homme,* against the Government of Senegal

On 27 July 2012, the ACERWC received a Communication from the Centre for Human Rights of the University of Pretoria (South Africa) and of the *Rencontre Africaine pour la Défense des Droits de l'Homme* (RADDHO) of Senegal.

The authors stated that 100 000 children known as *talibés*, aged between 4 and 12 have been sent by their parents to live in Quranic schools, known as *daars*. These schools are located in the urban centres of Senegal and, according to reports, provide a religious education.

The ACERWC has learned from reports that only half of the *talibés* in Senegal are Senegalese. The others are in the country because of child trafficking from neighbouring countries, including Guinea Bissau and Mali, where poor families are promised that their children will receive an Islamic education in the *daars* under the care of figures known as *marabouts*. Once they have reached the *daars*, the children can no longer contact their families. As they do not have any

---

[561] ACERWC. Decision on the Communication Submitted by the Institute for Human Rights and Development in Africa and the Open Society Justice Initiative (On Behalf of Children of Nubian Descent in Kenya) Against the Government of Kenya. *Op. cit.*, p. 12.

[562] *Ibidem*, p. 14.

[563] *Ibidem*, p. 16.

other contacts in Senegal, they depend entirely on the *marabouts* for food, medical care and accommodation.

The authors of the Communication also alleged that the *marabouts* force the children to beg. This practice has existed since 1980, even though the Senegalese Criminal Code prohibit forcing children to beg. This provision is enhanced by the law against human trafficking and related practices adopted in 2005, which punishes forced begging with a term of imprisonment between 5 to 10 years and a fine ranging between 5 million to 20 million francs. In practical terms, Senegal has made little effort to apply the law. As at 2011, only nine *marabouts* have been convicted and the maximum sentence handed down was a term of imprisonment of 1 month[564].

The applicants claimed that the living conditions in the *daars* were deplorable, being unsafe and unhygienic structures. Children are rarely given enough food and are chronically malnourished; they frequently fall sick, and the *marabouts* do not provide medical assistance. The *talibés* must bring back rice, sugar or money; if they fail, they are beaten and punished. The *talibés* usually spend between 6 and 8 hours begging. Therefore, 5 hours remain for the study of the Quran[565]. However, they are often unable to study the Quran as envisaged, because they are focused on reaching their daily quotas they fail to study the Quran as contemplated[566]. The *talibés* are also physically attacked and severely punished if they attempt to leave the *daars*.

According to the appellants, violations had occurred of Article 4 (the best interest of the child); Article 5 (the right to survival and development); Article 11 (right to education); Article 12 (right to leisure, recreation and cultural activities); Article 14 (right to health and health services); Article 15 (prohibition of child labour); Article 16 (protection against child abuse and torture); Article 21 (protection against harmful cultural and social practices); and Article 29 (prohibition of sale, trafficking and kidnapping of children) of the ACRWC.

Senegal, in response to the alleged violations, claimed that various constitutional, political, legislative and administrative measures had been adopted to protect children from forced begging.

In particular, Senegal referred to the establishment, in February 2013, of a committee that adopted recommendations for the withdrawal of all child beggars from the streets and their temporary placement in public institutions, centres and volunteer families, as well as their reintegration into their families or countries of origin. This requires the implementation of measures on educational aspects and economic support to families. Senegal sought to show that positive and lasting change had been taking place towards the effective application of the ACRWC, and that there was a strong will to eradicate child begging.

---

[564] ACERWC. Decision on the Communication Submitted by Centre for Human Rights and RADDHO (on behalf of Senegalese *talibés*) against the Republic of Senegal, n. 003/Com/001/2012 p. 3 (www.acerwc.org/decision-on-the-talibes-children-case/, accessed on 9 June 2016)

[565] *Ibidem*. p.5.

[566] *Ibidem*. p.3.

With reference to the protection of the *talibés* and other street children from psychological abuse, Senegal stated that the Minister of the Interior has created a special police force, the Children's Brigade, whose mission is to protect endangered children, to identify them and ensure their reintegration, in collaboration with other state bodies.

Furthermore, Senegal underscored that it has ratified numerous international treaties, especially the ACRWC and the Convention concerning the Prohibition and Immediate Action for the Elimination of the Worst Forms of Child Labour. In addition, it has adopted legislation that criminalizes child begging[567] and prohibits it in all its forms[568], and provides for the offences of trafficking in vulnerable persons and forced begging[569]. Other provisions of the Criminal Code[570] prohibit physical punishment and abuse in schools and educational centres, and Law no. 6 of 10 May 2005 criminalizes the trafficking of persons, including children, and similar practices, such as forced begging[571].

The decision of the ACERWC found multiple violations of the ACRWC: Article 4 (best interest of the child); and Article 5 (right to survival and development, health care, education, cleanliness and a safe environment and protection). The ACERWC recommended ensuring an adequate standard of living for children, including the right to life and to physical, mental, spiritual, moral, psychological and social development, as well as to protection from all forms of degrading abuse and treatment, including child labour, for the purpose of rendering effective the right to education.

As for Article 11(5) ACRWC, it states that educational institutions are to treat children with humanity and respect for their dignity, in accordance with the ACRWC. In particular, Senegal violated this provision, which also requires taking all appropriate measures to ensure that children subject to discipline in a school or at the hands of their parents are treated with humanity and with respect for their inherent dignity as children, as well as in accordance with the ACRWC. Senegal's violation consists in the failure to provide free and compulsory education for all children and to control and modernize the *daars*.

Furthermore, Senegal has violated Article 14 on the right to health and health services; Article 15 on the prohibition of child labour; and Article 29 which prohibits the sale, trafficking, abduction

---

[567] Article 245 of the Criminal Code of Senegal: "La mendicité est interdite. Le fait de solliciter l'aumône aux jours, dans les lieux et dans les conditions consacrées par les traditions religieuses ne constitue pas un acte de mendicité"

[568] Decree no. 64-088 of 6 February 1964 cited in Decision N° 003/Com/001/2012 on the Communication against the Government of Senegal, *op. cit.*, p. 10 (http://www.acdhrs.org/wp-content/uploads/2015/10/DECISION-CADBE_Version-Fran%C3%A7aise.pdf, accessed on 9 June 2016).

[569] Law 2005-06. *Ibidem*, p. 2.

[570] Decree 79-1165 of 20 December 1975. *Ibidem*, p. 10.

[571] In Senegal, begging places children in a situation of extreme vulnerability and is prohibited by the penal code. Imprisonment of 3 to 6 months is envisaged for the beggar or other persons who allow the child to beg alone. The punishment may range from 2 to 5 years or more when begging is accompanied by violence or weapons or other objects used to commit the offense. The provision is reinforced by Law no. 02-2005 of 29 April 2005. The law imposes imprisonment for 5 to 10 years and a fine of 5 million to 20 million CFA francs. It also allows associations to enter an appearance in the trial. See the Senegal Report, *op. cit.*, p. 17.

of children and begging. Furthermore, the imposition of a "quota" that the children must collect each day suffices to define the activity as begging and child labour for the purpose of economic exploitation, and as conduct threatening to disturb the education of the children. The children's impossibility to communicate with their family means that the crime of abduction is made out.

The beatings meted out by the *marabouts* violate Article 16 ACRWC, which protects children from abuse and mistreatment. The ACERWC has qualified the beatings of the *talibés* as physical punishment that causes pain. Indeed, the *talibés* reported that they would be locked in a room, stripped naked, and beaten with an electric cable or a stick if they failed to meet their begging quota for the daydid not report the altitude[572].

Although there are social and legislative initiatives in Senegal to protect children's rights in general, the government has failed to take specific administrative and judicial measures against *marabouts*. Senegal has not denied that, since 2010, there have been only 9 convictions. The ACERWC noted the absence of sufficient educational and social measures that could lead to a change in the situation of the *talibés*.

Furthermore, the ACERWC found that Article 21 on negative social and cultural practices had been violated. Employing children as beggars is a harmful practice that is clearly prohibited by Article 29 ACRWC; states must take all necessary measures to counteract it. Indeed, such conduct constitutes a denial of the dignity and integrity of the individual and a violation of the human rights and fundamental freedoms established in the CRC and in the ACRWC. Discrimination against children is harmful as it has negative consequences, among which physical, psychological, economic and social harm. It constitutes a form of violence against them and limits their ability to participate fully in society or develop and increase their full potential[573].

The ACERWC recommended that Senegal take the following measures, to meet its obligations under the ACRWC:

a) Ensure that all *talibé* children are removed from the streets and returned to their families;
b) Through cooperation with the neighbouring home countries of the children and national and international organizations, facilitate the reunion of *talibés* with their families;
c) Ensure that children receive social, medical and psychological assistance;
d) Establish norms and standards for all *daars* on health, safety, hygiene, quality, educational content and accommodation;
e) Integrate *daars* into the formal educational system;

---

[572] Human Rights Watch, "Off the backs of children: forced begging and other abuses against talibes in Senegal", Report, 4 April 2010, (https://www.hrw.org/report/2010/04/15/backs-children/forced-begging-and-other-abuses-against-talibes-senegal, accessed on 5 February 2016).
[573] Committee on the Rights of the Child and Committee on the Elimination of Discrimination against women, Joint general recommendation/general comment No. 31 of the Committee on the Rights of the Child on harmful practices, November 2014, UN DOC: /C/GC/31-CRC/C/GC/18, para. 15.
http://jurist.org/paperchase/CEDAW_General_Comment_31.pdf, accessed on 8 February 2016.

f) Inspect *daars* regularly to ensure that the standards they apply comply with the ACRWC and local legislation, and close noncompliant *daars*;

g) Combat impunity and prevent forced begging and the sale, abduction and trafficking of children, to ensure that all perpetrators are brought to justice and held accountable for their actions through criminal measures;

h) Ensure that education contributes to the promotion and development of their personalities, talents and their physical and mental abilities, as well as their greatest potential;

i) Review the national educational policy in light of the aim of promoting respect for human rights and fundamental freedoms, and ensure free and compulsory basic education;

j) Legally training judges, social workers, religious and traditional leaders, and parents;

k) Carry out collective studies with neighbouring States on the situation of the *talibés* in Senegal and in the countries of origin;

l) Fully recognize and implement the rights enshrined in the ACRWC and other international instruments;

m) To draft a report according to Article 43 ACRWC on the implementation of the ACERWC's decision;

n) Cooperate with the AU, national and international organizations, UN agencies, UNICEF, the ILO, and the WHO, to fully implement these recommendations and alleviate the challenges facing the *talibés*[574].

More generally, the right to education according to Article 11 ACRWC should strive to preserve and strengthen the positive moral values, traditions and cultures of Africa, and cannot contrast with the other ACRWC rights, nor with the promotion and development of children and their physical and mental talent and ability. In this case, the education of minors was exploited for lucrative purposes and exploitation.

The ACERWC proceeded on two levels: on one hand, it recommended protecting the right to education pursuant to Article 11 ACRWC, which promotes free education in schools that comply with minimum standards approved by the State to foster the development of the child's personality, talents and physical and mental abilities; on the other, the ACERWC urged the State to remove the obstacles to the full implementation of the content of said article, by means of inspections in schools and bringing to justice those who commit abuses in schools.

With regard to Article 29 and the appropriate measures to prevent the phenomenon of *talibés*, the ACERWC took into account the preventive and care aspects, urging Senegal to re-monopolize education to ensure compulsory and free education in conformity with human rights. It also recommended collaborating with other states and NGOs to investigate the causes of human rights violations against *talibès* and to prosecute those responsible for the practice, to deter with effective justice. As for *talibès* who were forced to beg, the ACERWC urged the provision of social recovery measures.

---

[574] ACERWC. Decision on the Communication Submitted by Centre for Human Rights and RADDHO (on behalf of Senegalese *talibés*) against the Republic of Senegal, n. 003/Com/001/2012 p.2 3 (www.acerwc.org/decision-on-the-talibes-children-case/, accessed on 9 June 2016).

III.8.3 Decision on the situation of children in Northern Uganda

In 2005, the ACERWC received a Communication from Professor Michelo Hunsungule. The case was presented by the students of the Centre for Human Rights of the University of Pretoria, as part of their work in the Master's program in Human Rights and Democratization in Africa. The students prepared the case with Professor Hansungule and the other staff members of the Centre[575]. The case concerns the children of Northern Uganda and the violations committed against them by Uganda.

For twenty years, starting in 1986, a civil war raged in Northern Uganda, causing massive migration and multiple violations of human rights and children's rights. Instability was such that the population was forced to take shelter in refugee camps, where they lived in quasi-subsistence conditions. Health and education services were lacing and people depended on humanitarian aid to survive. Despite the initiatives of the Ugandan government, the rebels were able to enter the camps, kidnap people, destroy property and commit atrocities.

Thousands of children were kidnapped by the Lord's Resistance Army (LRA) to serve in support and combat roles. The authors of the Communication stressed that the ACRWC rights were violated, including the protection of children from involvement in armed forces pursuant to Article 22; the right to education enshrined in Article 11; the right to life, survival and development established in Article 5; the right to enjoy the best state of health, physical, mental and spiritual envisaged by Article 14 and the right to be protected from sexual abuse and violence (Articles 16 and 27).

The ACERWC stated that the ACRWC is the first international instrument to set the minimum age for enlistment to 18 years. Therefore, even voluntary enlistment before the age of 18 constitutes a violation of Article 22 ACRWC. Article 31 ACRWC, which deals with the responsibilities of children towards their family, society and State cannot be used to support the involvement of minors in armed conflicts, as Article 22 absolutely forbids the recruitment and use of minors in various capacities in armed conflicts[576].

The ACERWC thus found numerous violations concerning the right to education. The violations concern the inadequate allocation of financial resources to the educational sector, particularly in areas affected by the conflict; the lack of effective measures to facilitate access to education for demobilized children; and the availability, accessibility and quality of the education for children in refugee camps. Child soldiers who have been involved in armed conflict fall into the category

---

[575] Centre for Human Rights, University of Pretoria, Viljoen, "African children's right Committee finds Uganda conscripted child soldiers in case submitted by Centre for Human Rights students", (www.chr.up.ac.za, accessed on 29 March 2016).

[576] ACERWC. Decision on the Communication Submitted by Michelo Hunsungule and Others (on behalf of Children in Northern Uganda) against the Government of Uganda, no. 1/2005, 15-19 April 2013 (http://www.acerwc.org/?wpdmdl=8687, accessed on 27 December 2015). P. 15.

of children in disadvantaged situations. To guarantee their right to education, special measures are required[577].

The ACERWC recommended making express provision in the Criminal Code for those who enlist children under 18 in armed conflict, in line with Article 22 ACRWC. In addition, recovery programs should be provided for children taken from armed groups, together with the disarmament programs, and reintegration and demobilization efforts, in collaboration with the UN, the AU and other partners are also desirable[578].

In the Congo report[579], it was noted that in 2001, the Government created the High Commission for Reintegration of Ex-Combatants. This body is responsible for the disarmament, demobilization and reintegration of former combatants, as well as for the Committee monitoring the ceasefires, agreements and cessations of hostilities. In addition, the Government, with the support of the international community, financed two programs. The first was the "Emergency Program for Demobilization and Reintegration (PDR)", between 2002 and 2004, to reintegrate 9 000 ex-combatants and 3 222 microfinance projects. The second program was the "National Program for Disarmament, Demobilization and Reintegration (PNDDR)", held from 2006 and 2009.

In addition, the Government of Uganda should provide alternative measures to detention for minors under the age of 18, including the use of restorative measures such as truth depositions, traditional healing ceremonies and reintegration programs, because the primary consideration is the best interest of the child, as well as to promote the reintegration of children into their family, community and society[580].

Article 11(2)(c) ACRWC on the right to education should preserve and encourage, for example, the conservation and strengthening of the positive moral values, traditions and cultures of Africa[581] and foster respect for human rights and fundamental freedoms, with particular regard to those enshrined in the many African instruments on human and peoples' rights and in international human rights declarations and conventions. As a result, it is important to consider and make education an indispensable element in the promotion of tolerance, cessation of conflicts and reconstruction of society[582]. The reading of Article 22(1) ACRWC, which establishes the duty to ensure compliance with the rules of joint international humanitarian law, combined with Article 11 ACRWC, shows how obligations on States Parties are crucial to preserve essential characteristics, such as the availability, access, acceptability and adaptability of the right to education in armed

---

[577] *Ibidem.* p. 16.

[578] *Ibidem.* p. 20.

[579] Congo Initial Report on the Implementation of the ACRWC, p. 103 (http://acerwc.org/?wpdmdl=8796, accessed on 27 December 2015).

[580] *Ibidem*, p. 21.

[581] *Ibidem*, p. 16.

[582] ACERWC. Decision on the Communication Submitted by Michelo Hunsungule and Others (on behalf of Children in Northern Uganda) against the Government of Uganda, *op. cit.*, p. 16.

conflict. In case of armed conflict, adaptability requires – among other things – to set up ad hoc learning centres as an urgent resumption of civic activities[583].

Using school as military targets puts children at risk of attack and violates children's right to education. Appropriate disciplinary measures have not been taken with regard to perpetrators. States Parties should provide for reparations, for those acts or omissions that can be attributed to the State[584].

According to the general principles contained in the Preamble to the ACRWC, the ACERWC considered that children and girls need special care and protection in relation to specific factors linked to socio-economic circumstances, such as armed conflicts. Therefore, in addition to reiterating the ban on the enlistment of children under 18 according to Article 22(1) ACRWC, the ACERWC called for preventive measures and greater protection to be accorded to places where children are kidnapped; therefore, the ACERWC encouraged an extensive interpretation of Article 22, which refers only to protecting children by all possible means in the event of armed conflict.

The ACRWC does not mention psychological rehabilitation for children involved in armed conflicts. However, in the ACERWC's view, measures assuring such treatment can be deduced from Article 39 CRC, according to which States Parties shall take all appropriate measures to facilitate the physical and psychological recovery and social reintegration of all children who are victims of any form of negligence, exploitation or ill treatment; or of torture or any other form of cruel, inhuman or degrading treatment or punishment, armed conflict.

In Algeria, group therapy[585] activities have been organized since 1998, combining therapy and entertainment. In this context, 800 multidisciplinary teams, together with specialized institutions, have been mobilized to provide psychological care to children who have suffered the horrors of violence.

The ACERWC has interpreted Article 22 ACRWC in terms of preventing recruitment through measures such as child registration and, therefore, means to determine children's exact age, as well as the possibility of registering their enlistment and, if applicable, finding. Furthermore, the ACERWC focused on education to stem the phenomenon. This strong call also translates into the continuity of education during armed conflict[586]. Finally, the ACERWC recommended rehabilitation paths, essential to the recovery and reintegration of child soldiers.

---

[583] *Ibidem*, p. 16.

[584] *Ibidem*, p. 13.

[585] Algeria Initial Report on the Implementation of the ACRWC, p. 583 (http://acerwc.org/?wpdmdl=8766, accessed on 27 December 2015).

[586] ACERWC. Decision on the Communication Submitted by Michelo Hunsungule and Others (on behalf of Children in Northern Uganda) against the Government of Uganda, *op. cit.*: "State has a duty to be continually taking measures to build, maintain, improve and when attacked, repair its educational system" (p. 17).

III.9   Publicity of the ACRWC

The last issue worthy of examination in this study is the promotion and circulation of the ACRWC. The primary condition for exercising rights is to be aware of them. Not only: promulgating and promoting norms contributes to the dissemination of a legal culture.

The ACRWC contains provisions on its publicization and on raising awareness of children's rights and related issues. On the other hand, Article 42 CRC expressly affirms that the States Parties undertake to make the principles and provisions of the CRC widely known, by appropriate means, to both adults and children. In any case, the principle of publicity of the ACRWC may be inferred from its Article 1, which requires States Parties to adopt the necessary measures to implement the provisions of the ACRWC. Awareness of the ACRWC remains important to facilitate awareness of its rights and its observation. Indeed, the numerous reports regarding the African States discuss the measures taken to make the ACRWC and the States' reports on its implementation known.

Thus, the Congo[587] has held a wide-reaching advertisement campaign on the ACRWC, through political and administrative authorities and community leaders, in all major cities and districts. In addition, it has established a permanent mechanism for information and education, using also the Children's Parliament.

From the Mozambique report[588] it emerges that a dissemination strategy for the ACRWC has been established. The strategy seeks to informs and encourage children, families, institutions and the general public to respect and strengthen the principles and precepts of the ACRWC, with help from public and private institutions, civil society organizations, NGOs, and UN agencies, through readings, films, radio and television programs, brochures and leaflets on the rights of children. The ACRWC and the CRC have been publicized at national level through the institutions and organizations engaging in such issues: judicial organs (police forces, in addition to judges and lawyers), religious leaders, midwives, traditional healers, journalists, teachers, migration agents, care centres for disadvantaged children, civil society organizations, etc. On the occasion of the International Day of the Child (16 June), for three weeks – the last one of May and the first two of June – readings, debates, marches, cultural and sporting activities are held, and television programs are conducted in sign language. During these weeks, several programs for adults and children on the ACRWC and the CRC are broadcast. Education on children's rights and the ACRWC is included in pedagogy handbooks, pre-school education, and curricula for primary and secondary education.

South Africa[589] has published its initial report and the answers received by the ACERWC. These were transmitted to the country's departments of government and civil society for circulation to

---

[587] Congo Initial Report on the Implementation of the ACRWC, p. 24 (http://acerwc.org/?wpdmdl=8796, accessed on 27 December 2015).

[588] Mozambique Initial Report on the Implementation of the ACRWC, p. 19 (http://acerwc.org/?wpdmdl=8650, accessed on 27 December 2015).

[589] South Africa Initial Report on the Implementation of the ACRWC, p. 21 (http://acerwc.org/?wpdmdl=8787, accessed on 27 December 2015).

the public. In addition, the documents were presented to Parliament and publicized through reports and debates in national and local media. Simplified and children's versions are drafted and disseminated.

In Uganda[590], dissemination takes place through paper or electronic formats, as well as workshops. The report and the ACERWC's comments and recommendations are circulated by means of workshops.

In the Zimbabwe report[591], the Government explained that it had communicated the contents of the ACRWC and the CRC to its Members of Parliament, to ensure that relevant legislation would be adopted. Days to commemorate children's rights have been created and topic-based information is circulated. To make the ACRWC widely known, artistic performances on the various themes of children's rights have been held, attracting people of all ages from all parts of the country.

Publicizing the ACRWC is functional to awareness of the rights it enshrines. In a continent such as Africa, children could learn not only about human rights, but also about the rule of law.

III.9.1   The Day of the African Child (DAC)

While Article 42 CRC provides that States Parties undertake to make the principles and provisions of the present Convention widely known, by active and adequate means to both adults and children, the ACRWC contains no such provision. However, a mechanism to promote the ACRWC and to raise awareness on issues concerning the violation of the rights of the child in Africa does exist.

The Day of the African Child (DAC) was recognized by the AU in 1991. It is celebrated every year on 16 June[592]. The ACERWC establishes the subject of the yearly DAC and communicates it to the States Parties. The DAC is a tool for raising awareness on the status of African children. Celebrating the DAC focuses attention on the public priority that should be given to children's rights in Africa.

The DAC has become a significant annual event that strives to involve States Parties, to reflect and raise awareness on, and identify, strategies regarding issues currently affecting the well-being and development of the African child[593].

---

[590] Uganda Initial Report on the Implementation of the ACRWC, p. 11 (http://acerwc.org/?wpdmdl=8790, accessed on 27 December 2015).

[591] Zimbabwe Initial Report on the Implementation of the ACRWC, p. 201 (http://acerwc.org/?wpdmdl=8778, accessed on 27 December 2015).

[592] On 16 June 1976, in Soweto, thousands of children participated in a protest against the poor quality of their education, claiming the right to express themselves in their own language. More than 100 people were killed and more than 1 000 were wounded. Every year, on 16 June, the International Day of the African Child is celebrated by governments, NGOs, international organizations to discuss challenges and opportunities to realize the rights of African children.

[593] Assim, Wakefield, "Dawn of a new decade? The 16th and 17th sessions of the African Committee of Experts on the Rights and Welfare of the Child", *African Human Rights Law Journal*, 2011, p. 714.

III.10   Conclusions

The ACERWC, within the scope of its duties set forth in Article 42 ACRWC, fulfills its function of interpreting the ACRWC and has elaborated principles and rules to protect the rights and welfare of children in Africa.

The ACERWC has clarified the scope of the provisions of the ACRWC in its General Comments, giving detailed indications of application methods to supplement the normative data.

The ACERWC has clarified how the ACRWC should be applied in specific cases: in the decision on Nubian children in Kenya, it noted that the failure to recognize the nationality of children violated not only Article 6 ACRWC, but also other rights, thus recommending that the Kenyan government take all legislative and administrative measures necessary for the children to acquire Kenyan nationality.

In the decision on the Communication on *talibés*, the ACERWC noted that a violation had occurred not only, obviously, of Article 29 ACRWC on begging, but also of interconnected rights and the duty of States to punish those responsible for forced begging.

In the decision on the children of Northern Uganda, the ACERWC, referring to Article 22(2) ACRWC (according to which the States Parties must ensure the protection and care of minors affected by conflict), described how to develop the post-war arrangements to be implemented, and how to reintegrate former child soldiers in three phases: disarmament, demobilization and reintegration.

In the General Comment on Article 30 ACRWC, the ACERWC has sought to ensure uniformity in its interpretations and applications clarifying key notions of the Charter.

The ACERWC has attempted to foster the effectiveness of the ACRWC in the States Parties. In its recommendations to the States Parties, it urged the creation of special facilities in which to detain mothers, in line with Article 30 ACRWC, the use of alternative measures to prison, and the implementation of laws in line with Article 30 ACRWC. In the General Comment on Article 6 ACRWC, the ACERWC asked States Parties to adopt legislation and appropriate administrative organizations to introduce a civil register, an administrative pre-condition to the effective implementation of Article 6.

CONCLUSIONS

The ACRWC is a fundamental step in the evolution of the human rights system in the African context. The ACRWC increases the standard of protection for African children, establishing norms on specific rights related to the African socio-cultural situation, such as protection against negative social and cultural practices (Article 21), the protection of minors against armed conflicts and their recruitment (in more favourable terms than the CRC), and the protection of child victims of begging (Article 29).

The ACRWC expressly prohibits the negative practice of child marriage by requiring States to take action to this end. The ACRWC also requires the discouragement of HTP, which certainly include FGM, by all necessary means.

However, as emphasized also by the ACERWC, legislative measures are not sufficient to ensure the ACRWC's effective application. Thus, with regard to HTP, States have also taken institutional, administrative and even cultural measures, seeking the support of local and international civil society. The ACRWC, as interpreted and applied by the ACERWC, is also an important tool for national judicial decision-making, as judges are required to discern which local customs are compatible with the rights of the ACRWC and which are illegal because of incompatibility with the ACRWC.

Among the most vulnerable children, the ACRWC protects refugee minors not only from wars but also from civil wars, natural disasters and more. The challenge for States Parties is to fully guarantee the rights enshrined in the ACRWC without discrimination compared to non-refugee minors. Disabled children should also be recalled, regarding whom States Parties have been called upon to eliminate obstacles relating to prejudice and budget constraints. The particular situation of former child soldiers requires particular effort by States, with regard to recruitment prevention and the protection of those children who have been led to participate in armed conflicts as victims, thus accompanying them in disarmament and reintegration into society.

Finally, the decisive role played by the interpreters of the ACRWC, and in particular the ACERWC, should be mentioned. The ACERWC monitors the measures taken by the States in applying the ACRWC, identifies the gaps in protection and proposes new methods and tools for its effective implementation.

The ACERWC has broad powers that enable it to interpret the provisions of the ACRWC. For example, it may draft General Comments, receive direct communications from injured parties and make decisions on alleged violations by African states. Furthermore, the ACERWC has undertaken investigative activities, exercising the powers envisaged by the ACRWC even with regard to two countries that have yet to ratify it, albeit with their prior consent. In the future, the

ACERWC could also exercise its supervisory powers in areas that are not formally provided for in the ACRWC, for example regarding the admissibility of the reservations made by some African States. Currently, the ACERWC's activity remains limited. However, it can be hoped that its contribution will be more incisive with time.

However, above all, the ACRWC is a fundamental step not only on a legal level but also on a more strictly social level in the African context. The ACRWC galvanizes the rule of law and the applicability of valid *erga omnes* norms in highly diverse African states. The objectives yet to be attained, of its wide and extensive circulation and applicability, would contribute to the circulation of the same values within the same national and international community. Naturally, there remains much to do to implement the ACRWC remains long and many issues threaten its effective application. The path indicated by the ACRWC itself is to preserve positive heritage, while also orienting stakeholders towards the rule of law and citizenship. These objectives will be achieved by harmonizing the laws of the States in accordance with the ACRWC and by promoting the ACRWC at all levels and by all means. Only in this way, can the standard of child protection be effectively raised and the ACRWC become "living law".

BIBLIOGRAPHY

ACHILIHU, *Do African Children Have Rights? A Comparative and Legal Analysis of the United Nations Convention on the Rights of the Child*, Universal Publishers, Boca Raton - USA, 2010;

ARMSTRONG, "A Consent and Compensation: The Sexual Abuse of Girls in Zimbabwe", in Ncube (ed.), *Law, Culture, Tradition and Children's Rights in Eastern and Southern Africa*, Dartmouth – England, Ashgate, 1998;

ANSELMI. "Il fenomeno dei bambini soldato quando l'educazione è progettualità di cambiamento". Graduation thesis. Undergraduate degree in "operazioni di pace, gestione e mediazione dei conflitti". Università degli studi di Firenze. 2006-2007, http://gruppocrc.net/IMG/pdf/TESIbambinisoldato.pdf.;

AGBOBLI, SOMDA, AKONUMBO, VOHITO, JOOF-CONTEH, KWEKU APPIAH, CISSÈ, AMADOU, ABOTSI, ODEWALE, WILSON, ATCHADAM, "In the best interest of the child: Harmonising Laws on Children in West and Central Africa", *The African Child Policy forum*, Addis Ababa, 2011;

AHRÈN, "Indigenous peoples culture, customs, and traditions and customary law - The Saami peoplÉs perspective", *Arizona Journal of International & Comparative Law*, 2004;

ALSTON (ed.), *The Best Interests of the Child–Reconciling Culture and Human Rights*, [International Journal of Law, Policy and Family, Oxford, 1994;

ALSTON, "The best interest principle", *International Journal of Law and the Family*, 1994;

ARMSTRONG, "A Consent and Compensation: The Sexual Abuse of Girls in Zimbabwe", in Ncube (ed.), *Law, Culture, Tradition and Children's Rights in Eastern and Southern Africa*, Dartmouth – England, Ashgate, 1998;

ASSIM, WAKEFIELD, "Dawn of a new decade? The 16th and 17th sessions of the African Committee of Experts on the Rights and Welfare of the Child", *African Human Rights Law Journal*, 2011;

BADERIN, "Recent Developments in the African Regional Human Rights Systems", *Human Rights Law Review*, 2005, p. 123-124.

BECCHI, "Il nostro secolo", in J.Becchi (ed.) *Storia dell'infanzia 2. Dal Settecento a oggi*, Bari, Laterza 1996;

BENNETT, "Law as expression of culture", in Steyn & Motshabi (eds), *Cultural Synergy in South Africa*, Knowledge Resources, Johannesburg, 1996;

BENNETT, "Customary Law in South Africa", *Journal of African Law*, 2004;

BOEZAART, "Building bridges: African customary family law and children's rights", *International Journal of Private Law*, 2013;

BOUKONGOU. "Le systéme africain de protection des droits de l'enfant. Exigences universelles et pretentions africaines", *Cahiers de la recherche sur les droits fondamentau*, 2006;

CHIMNI. "International Refugee Law: a Reader". Sage Publications, New Delhi. 2000;

CHIKWA. "The merits and demerits of the African Charter on the Rights and Welfare of the Child" *The International Journal of Children's Rights*, 2002;

Doek. "In the best interests of the child: Harmonising laws in Eastern and Southern Africa" (African Child Policy Forum 2007), p. 17 (http://www.africanchildforum.org/clr/ Harmonisation%20of%20Laws_%20in%20Africa/Publications/supplementary-acpf-harmonisation-es_en.pdf, accessed on 07-06-2016);

De Boeck, Plissart, *Kinshasa. Tales of the invisible city*, Leuven, Leuven University Press, 2004;

Dignelle, Fierens, "Justice et gacaca. L'expérience rwandaise et le genocide". Belgio, Presses Universitaires de Namur, 2003;

Doek, "In the best interests of the child: Harmonising laws in Eastern and Southern Africa" (African Child Policy Forum 2007), p. 17 (http://www.africanchildforum.org/clr/ Harmonisation%20of%20Laws%20in%20Africa/Publications/supplementary-acpf-harmonisation-es_en.pdf, accessed on 07-06-2016).

Gaparayi. "Justice and social reconstruction in the aftermath of genocide in Rwanda: An evaluation of the possible role of the gacaca tribunals". AHRLJ (*African Human Rights Law Journal*) 2001;

Gluckman, *The Ideas in Barotse jurisprudence*, Manchester, Manchester University Press, 1972.

Goodman, "Human Rights Treaties, invalid reservation and State Consent", *American Journal of International Law*, 2002, p. 531.

Goodwin-Gill, Cohn, "Child Soldiers, The Role of Children in Armed Conflict", Clarendon Press, Oxford, 1994.

Gose, "The African Charter on the Rights and Welfare of the Child, Bellville: Community Law Centre". University of the Western Cape, 2002.

Grobbelaar-du Plessis, Van Reenen, *Aspects of disability law in Africa*, Pretoria, Pretoria University Law Press, 2011,

Jourdan, *Generazione Kalashnikov. Un antropologo dentro la guerra in Congo*, Rome, Laterza, 2010, p. 15.

Gates, Reich, *Child Soldiers in the age of fractured States*, Pittsburgh, University of Pittsburgh Press, 2010;

Hamnett. *Chieftainship and Legitimacy: an anthropological study of executive law in Lesotho*, Routledge and Kegan, Londra, 1975;

Heaton, "Some General Remarks on the Concept "Best Interests of the Child", *Tydskrif vir Hedensdaagse Romeins-Hollandse Reg*, 1990;

Himonga, "African Customary Law and Children's Rights: Intersections and Domains in a New Era", in Sloth-Nielsen (ed.), *Children's Rights in Africa. A legal perspective*, Burlington – USA, Ashgate, 2010;

Holleman, *Issues in African Law*, Mouton, The Hague, 1974;

Kaldor, "Transnational civil society", in Dunne, Wheeler, *Human Rights in Global Politics*, Cambridge University Press, Cambridge, 1999;

Kaime, "The protection of Refugee Children Under the African Human Rights System: Finding Durable Solutions in International Law". In *Children's Rights in Africa*. Sloth Nielsen (ed.) Ashgate 2010;

Kadjar-Hamouda. Terre des Homme. "Kids as commodities? Child trafficking and what to do about it". May 2004. http://www.terredeshommes.org/wp-content/uploads/2013/06/commodities.pdf. accessed on 8-02-2016.

KASSAN, "The pyrotection of children from all forms of violence-African Experiences", in Sloth-Nielsen (ed.), *Children's Rights in Africa. A legal perspective*, Burlington Usa, Ashgate, 2010;

KARIN, "The international protection of children's rights in Africa: The 1990 OAU Charter on the Rights and Welfare of the Child", *African Journal of International & Comparative Law*, 1992;

KELLER, ULFSTEIN, *UN Human Rights Treaty Bodies. Law and Legitimacy. Protection of economic and social rights. Studies on human rights convention*, Cambridge, Cambridge University Press, 2012;

KERR, "Customary law, fundamental rights and the Constitution", *South African Law Journal*, 1994;

KERR, *The Bill of Rights in the new Constitution and customary law, South African Law Journal*, 1997;

KOBOYANKWE. "Legal Pluralism and discriminatory application of progressive laws to women subject to customary law in Botswana". Graduation thesis. Loyola University, Chicago School of Law. 2013-2014;

KOYANA, BEKKER, "The indomitable ukuthwala custom", *De Iure*, 2007;

HIMONGA, "The Right of the Child to Participate in Decision Making: A Perspective from Zambia", in Ncube (ed.), *Law, Culture,Tradition and Children's Rights in Eastern and Southern Africa*, Burlington – USA, Ashgate, 1998;

HIMONGA, *Protecting the minor child's inheritance rights. The International Survey of Family Law*, Bristol, Jourdan Publishing, 2001;

HONWANA, "Innocent & Guilty. Child soldiers as Interstitial & Tactical Agents", in Honwana, De Boeck (ed.), *Makers & Breakers. Children and Youth in Postcolonial Africa*, James Currey, Oxford, 2005;

LEHNERT, "Role of the Courts in the Conflict between African Customary Law and Human Rights", *South African Journal on Human Rights*, 2005;

LLOYD. "Report of the second ordinary session of The African Committee of Experts on the Rights and Welfare of the Child". *African human rights law journal*, 2003;

MARIRAKIZA, "L'Afrique et le systeme de justice penale international", *African Journal of Legal Studies*, 2009;

MEZMUR, "African Committee of Experts on the Rights and Welfare of the Child. An Update. The Recent developments", *African Human Rights Law Journal*, 2006;

MOYI. "Access to education for children with disabilities in Uganda: Implications For Education for All". *Journal of International Education and Leadership*. 2012;

MOLO SONGOLOLO, "The trafficking of children for Purposes of Sexual Exploitation: South Africa" Cape Town. 2000, p. 2.(http://www.atria.nl/epublications/2000/trafficking_of_children.pdf, accessed on 29-03-2016);

OKECHUKWU, "The challenges of international criminal prosecution in Africa". *Fordahm International Law Journal*, 2008;

PIVIDORI, *Il principio di complementarietà della corte penale internazionale e il processo di adattamento degli ordinamenti interni*, Editoriale scientifica, Naples, 2016;

MAFFEI. "Sistema africano e meccanismi di controllo", in L.Pineschi (ed.), *La tutela internazionale dei diritti umani*, Giuffrè, Milan, 2004;

MALULEKE, "Culture, tradition, custom, law and gender equality", *Potchefstroom Electronic Law Journal/Potchefstroomse Elektroniese Regsblad*, 2012;

MATUA, "The Banjul Charter and the African Cultural Fingerprint: An Evaluation of the Language of Duties", *Review of the African Commission on Human and Peoples 's Rights*, (1996-7);

MUJUZI, "The protocol to the African Charter on Human and Peoples' Rights on the rights of women in Africa: South Africa's reservation and interpretative declarations", *Law, democracy & development*, 2008;

NAZEEM GOOLAM, "Constitutional Interpretation of the "Best Interests" Principle in South Africa in Relation to Custody", in Eeckelaar and Nhlapo (eds), *The Changing Family: International Perspectives on the Family and Family Law*, Portland, Hart Publishing, 2008;

NDULO, "African Customary Law, Customs, and Women's Rights", *Cornell Law Faculty Publications*, 2011;

NHLAPO, "The African family and women's rights: Friends or foes?", *Acta Juridica*, 1991;

NHLAPO, "South African family law at the crossroads: From Parliamentary supremacy to constitutionalism", *International Survey of Family Law*, 1994;

NJUNGWE. "International protection of children's rights: an analysis of African attributes in the African charter on the rights and welfare of the child", *Cameroon Journal on Democracy and Human Rights*, 2009;

NOMIS, BROWNLEES, Save the Children, "Bambini e armi. L'istruzione per combattere la guerra", ottobre 2008;

(http://images.savethechildren.it/IT/f/img_pubblicazioni/img32_b.pdf., accessed on 28-03-2016).

ODONGO, "The domestication of international standard on the rights of the child: a critical and comparative evaluation of the Kenyan example", *The International Journal of Children's Rights*, 2004;

PARKER, "The Best Interests of the Child–Principles and Problems", *International journal of law policy and the family*, 1994;

PIETERSE, "Culture and Customary Law in a Society Founded on Non- Racialism", *South African Law Journal*, 2001;

POLIDORI, BOCCO, CORVINO, FUCINI, GARAVOGLIA, GIULIANI, LAISO, MISSO, NACCI, PUNZO, Rapporto Centro studi per la difesa e la sicurezza, Conflitti non convenzionali nell'Africa sub-sahariana, 2008;

POLTRONIERI ROSSETTI, "Il diritto alla riparazione per le vittime di crimini internazionali: problemi e prospettive a partire dalle decisioni della CPI nel caso Lubanga", Graduation thesis, School of Law, Università di Trento, 2012-2013;

PRECILLAR. "The relevance of culture and religion to the understanding of children's rights in South Africa", Postgraduate thesis, Faculty of Law, University of Cape Town, 2014;

ROSSI, "La salute mentale attraverso lo spettro dei diritti umani", 22 March 2015 http://www.forumcostituzionale.it/wordpress/wp-content/uploads/2015/03/rossi.pdf;

RWEZAURA, "The Concept of the Child's Best Interests in the Changing Economic and Social Context of Sub-Sahara Africa", *International Journal of Law and the Family*, 1994;

SCARPATI. *I diritti dei bambini*. Modena, Infinito, 2012;

SCHARF, *The other Law: non – State ordering in South Africa*, University of Michigan, Juta, 2001;

SINGER, "Talk is Cheap: Getting Serious about Preventing Child Soldier", *Cornell International Law Journal* 2004;

SLOTH-NIELSEN (a cura di), *Children's Rights in Africa. A Legal Perspective*, Burlington – USA, Ashgate, 2010;

STEINBOCK, "Unaccompanied Refugee Children in Host Country Foster Families", *International Journal on Refugee law*, 1996;

THOMPSON. "Legal and Practical Obstacles to Prosecution of Child Labour Exploitation in Southern Africa", paper presented at the Conference on "Reducing Exploitative Child Labour, Johannesburg, Sud Africa, July 2006 (http://www.queensu.ca/samp/migrationnews/article.php?Mig_News_ID_=3196&Mig_News_Issue=18&Mig_News_Cat=1, accessed on 09-06-2016);

VAN BUEREN, "The African Charter on the Rights and Welfare of the Child: A New Children's Treaty", *International Children's Rights Monitor*, 1991;

VAN DER WATT, OVEN, "Contextualizing the practice of Ukuthvala within South Africa", *South African Journal*, 2012

VAN DER VYVER, "Children's Rights, Family Values, and Federal Constraints", *Journal of Markets and Morality*, 2012;

VARGAS-BARÒN. "National Policies to prevent the recruitment of child soldiers". In Gates, Reich. *Child soldiers in the age of fractured states*. Pittsburgh: University of Pittsburgh Press, 2010,

VILJOEN, *International Human Rights Law in Africa*, Oxford, Oxford University Press, 2012;

VILJOEN, Centre for Human Rights, University of Pretoria, "African children's right Committee finds Uganda conscripted child soldiers in case submitted by centre for human rights students", (www.chr.up.ac.za, accessed on 29-03-2016).

WADESANGO, REMBE AND CHABAYA, "Violation of Women's Rights by Harmful Traditional Practices", *Anthropologist*, 2011;

WALKER, "Why Ending Child Marriage Needs to be An Educational Goal: The Case for Improved Coordination Between Ending Child Marriage and Girls Education Movements in West Africa", Center for Universal Education, 2013;

Printed in the United States
by Baker & Taylor Publisher Services